Modelling the Costs of Environmental Policy

NEW HORIZONS IN ENVIRONMENTAL ECONOMICS

Series Editors: Wallace E. Oates, *Professor of Economics, University of Maryland, USA* and Henk Folmer, *Professor of General Economics, Wageningen University and Professor of Environmental Economics, Tilburg University, The Netherlands*

This important series is designed to make a significant contribution to the development of the principles and practices of environmental economics. It includes both theoretical and empirical work. International in scope, it addresses issues of current and future concern in both East and West and in developed and developing countries.

The main purpose of the series is to create a forum for the publication of high quality work and to show how economic analysis can make a contribution to understanding and resolving the environmental problems confronting the world in the twenty-first century.

Recent titles in the series include:

Environmental Management and the Competitiveness of Nature-Based Tourism Destinations
Twan Huybers and Jeff Bennett

The International Yearbook of Environmental and Resource Economics 2003/2004
A Survey of Current Issues
Edited by Henk Folmer and Tom Tietenberg

The Economics of Hydroelectric Power
Brian K. Edwards

Does Environmental Policy Work?
The Theory and Practice of Outcomes Assessment
Edited by David E. Ervin, James R. Kahn and Marie Leigh Livingston

The International Yearbook of Environmental and Resource Economics 2004/2005
A Survey of Current Issues
Edited by Tom Tietenberg and Henk Folmer

Voluntary Approaches in Climate Policy
Edited by Andrea Baranzini and Philippe Thalmann

Welfare Measurement in Imperfect Markets
A Growth Theoretical Approach
Thomas Aronsson, Karl-Gustaf Löfgren and Kenneth Backlund

Econometrics Informing Natural Resources Management
Selected Empirical Analyses
Phoebe Koundouri

The Theory of Environmental Agreements and Taxes
CO_2 Policy Performance in Comparative Perspective
Martin Enevoldsen

Modelling the Costs of Environmental Policy
A Dynamic Applied General Equilibrium Assessment
Rob B. Dellink

Modelling the Costs of Environmental Policy

A Dynamic Applied General Equilibrium Assessment

Rob B. Dellink

Wageningen University, The Netherlands

NEW HORIZONS IN ENVIRONMENTAL ECONOMICS

Edward Elgar
Cheltenham, UK • Northampton, MA, USA

Published by
Edward Elgar Publishing Limited
Glensanda House
Montpellier Parade
Cheltenham
Glos GL50 1UA
UK

Edward Elgar Publishing, Inc.
136 West Street
Suite 202
Northampton
Massachusetts 01060
USA

A catalogue record for this book
is available from the British Library

Library of Congress Cataloguing in Publication Data

Dellink, Rob B.
    Modelling the costs of environmental policy: a dynamic applied
general equilibrium assessment/Rob B. Dellink.
        p. cm.
    Includes bibliographical references and index.
        1. Environmental policy—Costs. 2. Environmental economics. I. Title.
HC79.E5D4465   2005
333.7'01'1—dc22

2004048851

ISBN 1 84542 109 4

Printed and bound in Great Britain by MPG Books Ltd, Bodmin, Cornwall

Contents

Preface   vii

1. Introduction   1
  1.1   Background   1
  1.2   Objective of the book   3
  1.3   Methodology   4
  1.4   Relation with the SNI-AGE model   6
  1.5   Structure of the book   8

2. Pollution and abatement in economic modelling   11
  2.1   Introduction   11
  2.2   Characteristics of economic models   12
  2.3   Modelling the environment in economic models   24
  2.4   Discussion and conclusions   37
  Appendix 2.I   Conversion factors for environmental themes   41

3. Dynamic analysis of pollution and abatement in an applied general
   equilibrium model   42
  3.1   Introduction   42
  3.2   Different approaches to dynamic AGE models   43
  3.3   A prototype AGE model with pollution and abatement   45
  3.4   A numerical example   54
  3.5   Discussion and conclusions   70

4. Specification of a dynamic applied general equilibrium model with
   pollution and abatement for The Netherlands (DEAN)   73
  4.1   Introduction   73
  4.2   Choice of the prototype model   74
  4.3   Extension of the economic issues   75
  4.4   Extension of the environmental issues   80
  4.5   Full model description   83
  4.6   Discussion and conclusions   88
  Appendix 4.I   Explanation of symbols used   90
  Appendix 4.II   The LES transformation   93

Appendix 4.III   The multi-year period specification   95
Appendix 4.IV   A permit system for stock pollutants   98

5. Calibration of the DEAN model to The Netherlands   101
   5.1   Introduction   101
   5.2   Data for the benchmark accounting matrix   102
   5.3   Abatement cost curves for major environmental themes 110
   5.4   Economic parameter values   124
   5.5   Environmental parameter values   130
   5.6   Discussion and conclusions   136
   Appendix 5.I   Description of the initial equilibrium using a SAM   137
   Appendix 5.II   Environmental input data for The Netherlands, 1990   141
   Appendix 5.III   Realised growth rates for the period 1990-2000   143

6. Dynamic empirical analysis of environmental policy in
The Netherlands using DEAN   146
   6.1   Introduction   146
   6.2   Inputs to the model   147
   6.3   Results for the *NEPP2030* scenario   152
   6.4   Comparing the *Delay* and *NEPP2010* scenarios with *NEPP2030* 169
   6.5   Sensitivity analysis on the model parameters   182
   6.6   Discussion and conclusions   219

7. Alternative specifications of the DEAN model   229
   7.1   Introduction   229
   7.2   Multilateral environmental policy   229
   7.3   Multilateral environmental policy with a fixed exchange rate   236
   7.4   A model with greenhouse gases as flow pollutants   241
   7.5   Alternative recycling of environmental permit revenues 247
   7.6   A model with endogenous environmental innovation   252
   7.7   Discussion and conclusions   264

8. Final discussion and conclusions   269
   8.1   Introduction   269
   8.2   Putting the analysis into perspective   270
   8.3   Conclusions and recommendations   280
   8.4   Final remarks   288

References   289
Index   304

Preface

The first crude ideas for this book come from various projects I carried out at the Institute for Environmental Studies, Vrije Universiteit, Amsterdam and at Wageningen University. Fortunately, whenever there was an obstacle in my path, there were people to help me overcome it. This is the time and place to thank you all.

The first people to thank explicitly are my mentors, Prof. Ekko van Ierland (Wageningen University), Prof. Harmen Verbruggen (Vrije Universiteit) and Dr Marjan Hofkes (Vrije Universiteit). I'm grateful to them for showing me how to be an environmental economist, for reading several unfinished versions of this work and for all our stimulating discussions.

I want to express my appreciation to Prof. Frank den Butter, Dr Reyer Gerlagh, Prof. Leen Hordijk, Prof. Michiel Keyzer and Prof. Cees Withagen for giving valuable comments on the draft version of this book.

A special word of thanks to all the people at Edward Elgar Publishing, who made publishing a book seem easy, to Ivo Mulder for assisting with the final layout and to Elsevier Science for kindly permitting copyright material to be used in Chapter 3 of this book.

Thanks to the students and former students in Wageningen; no one else can give such refreshing insights ('In welfare economics income has to equal outcome'). Thanks also to all my colleagues and former colleagues who have made my job fun, and to all my family, friends and former friends who have made my life fun.

Finally, my deepest gratitude to Ada and Lara, I cannot thank you enough for the seemingly endless stream of love, confidence, patience and support.

Rob Dellink
Wageningen

1. Introduction

1.1 BACKGROUND

Environmental pressure and economic activity have, after several decades of environmental policy, been successfully decoupled for many environmental problems. Well-known examples include the reduction in emissions of CFCs (that contribute to the depletion of the ozone layer) and the reduction of acid rain. Nonetheless, there are important environmental issues that require continued policy attention. For example, in The Netherlands the premature deaths of around 3400 persons in 2000, almost 2.5 per cent of the total number of premature deaths in that year, is attributed to local air pollution (RIVM, 2002a). Moreover, climate change is recognised by scientists, policy makers and the public as a serious threat to society.

The introduction to the fourth National Environmental Policy Plan (NEPP4) in The Netherlands describes it as follows:

> Since numerous countries began implementing environmental policy approximately thirty years ago, much has been accomplished. The burden on the environment has been reduced in many areas. However, there are other areas that national and international policies until now have failed to address sufficiently. (VROM, 2001, p. 4).

To achieve long-term policy targets for these tenacious environmental problems, a substantial reduction of environmental pressure is required. Though emission reductions, often labelled *abatement*, do not necessarily cost money (for example, savings on energy use through 'good housekeeping' will lead to a reduction of costs and hence is profitable in itself), such win-win situations are rare. Moreover, most 'easy' and cheap options have been implemented by now so that more far-reaching and costly adjustments are necessary to reach the policy targets. It is therefore of increasing importance to focus on how to achieve the policy targets in a least-cost manner.

The economic costs of environmental policies have been studied extensively (see van den Bergh, 1999). Most models focus on climate change and restrict themselves to energy-related emission reduction measures (Weyant, 1999; Metz et al., 2001). This restriction simplifies the modelling

1

considerably. Notable exceptions are the EPPA model (Babiker et al., 2001) that does consider non-energy-related greenhouse gas emission reductions, and the RAINS model for acidification (Alcamo et al., 1990). RAINS contains very detailed emissions and abatement modules, but lacks details on the indirect effects of environmental policies.

Some empirical environmental-economic models focus on The Netherlands. Especially the introduction of a European energy tax was extensively analysed (for example, Booij and Velthuijsen, 1992; van Ierland, 1993; Dellink and Jansen, 1995). Moreover, the Netherlands Bureau for Economic Policy Analysis (CPB) and the Netherlands Institute for Public Health and the Environment (RIVM) regularly report on the economic impacts of environmental policy (for example, CPB, 2000; RIVM, 2000). A recent study in this field is CPB/RIVM (2002) which presents two scenarios for economic development in the coming decade and investigates the economic structures and environmental pressure associated with these developments; the environmental module focuses on energy-related emissions. The outcomes are not based on a single model, but rather on a range of different models that both institutes have available. The main conclusion is that additional action will be necessary to reach the policy targets for most substances, even if economic growth is relatively slow.

Despite the availability of these and other empirical environmental-economic models, there are still several issues to be resolved. Firstly, the economic costs of environmental policies are determined by the direct costs of emission reductions and the indirect effects induced by these policies. The direct costs of emission reductions are given by the marginal and total costs of specific pollution abatement technologies; these direct costs can be assessed using a bottom-up methodology. The indirect effects can only be fully represented using a multi-sectoral applied general equilibrium model, which constitutes a top-down approach. Neglect of the characteristics of the direct or indirect costs of environmental policy leads to inaccurate and perhaps biased results from policy analysis. A consistent methodology that covers both direct and indirect effects can contribute to a proper assessment of the interactions between economic activity and multi-pollutant environmental policy.

Secondly, for each individual environmental theme, environmental policy will lead to changes in the behaviour of producers and consumers, and, *ceteris paribus*, will induce costs, either in the form of expenditures on abatement or as foregone profits and utility. These policies, with their economic and environmental effects, will interact within and between the different environmental themes. For example, installing a catalytic converter not only reduces emissions of acidifying substances, but also influences local air quality via emissions of carbon monoxide (CO). Though most technical measures that are available to reduce environmental pressure focus on one environmental problem, changes in economic activity automatically impact pollution[1] for several environmental problems simultaneously. Hence, the isolated analysis of the economic impacts of environmental policy for one individual environmental problem leads to biased results. Therefore, an accurate economic assessment of environmental policy has to be based on the simultaneous specification of multiple pollutants.

Section 1.2 explains how this book can contribute to the literature and formulates the research questions. Then, in Section 1.3, the main elements of the methodology used in this book are discussed. Section 1.4 briefly describes the SNI-AGE study on which the book builds and identifies the main similarities and differences between that study and this. Finally, the set-up of the remainder of the book is presented in Section 1.5.

1.2   OBJECTIVE OF THE BOOK

This book aims at enhancing the understanding of the dynamic mechanisms between economic variables and pollution abatement in the context of environmental policy. The central problem definition can be formulated as follows: How can the direct and indirect costs of environmental policy for multiple pollutants be properly assessed in an applied model?

More specifically, the book focuses on two specific aspects that determine these mechanisms: (i) the integration of a bottom-up model that describes the direct costs of abatement with a top-down model that also covers the indirect costs; and (ii) the simultaneous analysis of environmental policies for several environmental problems. This book is motivated by the lack of a suitable applied model that covers these two innovative aspects.

The first innovative aspect of this book is the development of a new methodology to integrate bottom-up information on pollution abatement technologies into top-down empirical environmental-economic models. Essential information on available abatement options is included in the economic model. This refers to the so-called technical potential, that is the maximum emission reduction that can be achieved if all available measures are implemented, the marginal abatement costs of the different abatement measures and the links of these abatement measures with the rest of the economy (the 'spending effects'). The specific research question concerning the first innovative aspect is:

1. How can the main bottom-up information on abatement options be integrated into a top-down dynamic applied general equilibrium model?

The second innovative aspect of this study is the analysis of simultaneous environmental policies for several environmental problems within a dynamic applied general equilibrium framework with special attention to pollution and abatement. This leads to a better understanding of the economic implications of environmental policies, as the various environmental problems interact. The second innovative aspect is covered by the following research question:

2. How can policies for various environmental problems be simultaneously analysed in a dynamic applied general equilibrium model?

The integrated model that is built using this new methodology leads to an improved empirical analysis of the dynamic reactions of economic agents to pollution control, explicitly taking the direct and indirect effects of abatement on economy and environment into account. Such an approach allows for formulating better answers to the following empirical research questions:

3. What are the impacts of currently proposed environmental policies in The Netherlands on economic growth, sectoral structure, international trade, pollution and abatement in the twenty-first century?
4. What is the optimal mix of technical abatement measures and economic restructuring that achieves the policy targets at least costs?
5. How do the economic impacts of environmental policy in The Netherlands depend on the timing of the policy?

The combination of methodological and empirical research questions illustrates that the purpose of the book is to develop an *applicable* methodology.

1.3   METHODOLOGY

In line with the research questions identified above, the focus of this book lies on a dynamic macro-economic analysis of environmental policy for multiple pollutants within a neo-classical framework. The implications of each element in this focus are discussed in more detail below.

The *dynamic* perspective implies an explicit time dimension for the variables used in the model. The development of production, consumption, investments, pollution and abatement costs over time is a central issue here. A balance is found between intertemporal detail and the other dimensions, such as the specification of production sectors and consumer groups.

The focus on *macro-economic analysis* has several implications. Firstly, the natural science aspects of the environmental problems present are deliberately kept simple. The environmental issues analysed are confined to pollution and abatement; the ecological processes associated with pollution are not studied. Secondly, the literature survey in Chapter 2 mainly focuses on models that can investigate macro-economic impacts of policies. Other model types that may shed light on the interaction between pollution abatement and economic activity, including firm- and sector-specific models and game theoretic models, are not investigated.

Environmental policy is exogenous to the argument presented here. The economic costs of existing policy targets are assessed, without any claim as to whether these costs are justified or not. The main reason why the analysis is confined to cost-effectiveness of exogenous policy targets and no environmental cost-benefit analysis is carried out is the lack of sufficient data to properly assess the environmental benefits of the various environmental problems (see chapters 2 and 3 for more details).

In the model, *environmental policy* is implemented via a system of tradable pollution permits. This policy instrument is chosen because it is a market-based instrument and because it is effective, that is, the targets are met with certainty. It therefore provides a good reference point for policy makers.

The simultaneous analysis of *multiple pollutants* is important, as the reactions of the polluters will differ in a multiple pollutant framework compared to the analysis of a single pollutant. It is desirable yet impossible to model all major environmental problems in the model. Therefore, significant effort is put into modelling most of the major environmental themes that are part of current environmental policy in The Netherlands.

The choice of an economic model based on a *neo-classical framework*, in particular an applied general equilibrium model, will be discussed in detail in Chapter 2. The main advantages of this framework are: (i) it has a strong micro-economic foundation, and (ii) the indirect effects of policies are properly taken into account. The first advantage implies that the behaviour of consumers and producers at a macro-economic level can be traced back to specific behavioural rules for individual households and firms. Therefore, the results of the model are consistent with decision-making in a decentralised market economy and do not depend on a central planner, given the environmental policy targets. The second advantage concerns the assessment of indirect effects induced by the policy. This is essential for a proper analysis of the macro-economic effects of environmental policy and connects directly to the first research question.

Specifying multiple production sectors that all have specific pollution profiles is essential for environmental-economic policy analysis, as a restructuring of the economy from dirty production sectors to cleaner sectors can reduce pollution levels. If technical abatement measures, including end-of-pipe and process-integrated measures, are insufficient or prohibitively expensive, a switch from relatively dirty sectors to cleaner ones or a reduction in dirty economic activity might be necessary to meet the policy targets.

In order to incorporate all these elements, a dynamic applied general equilibrium model with special attention to pollution and abatement is constructed and applied here. The model is labelled DEAN, an acronym for '*D*ynamic applied general *E*quilibrium model with pollution and *A*batement for The *N*etherlands'. The specification of such a model in chapters 2-5 answers the methodological research questions 1 and 2, while the empirical analysis in chapters 6 and 7 shows that the model can answer the empirical research questions 3, 4 and 5.

1.4   RELATION WITH THE SNI-AGE MODEL

This book builds upon previous research, as summarised in Verbruggen (2000), Verbruggen et al. (2001) and Gerlagh et al. (2002). These studies present a comparative-static AGE model for The Netherlands, augmented with pollution and abatement (SNI-AGE). The main purpose of the SNI-AGE model is to calculate a so-called Sustainable National Income (SNI). The concept of SNI was first proposed by Hueting (compare Hueting, 1980) and reflects a welfare indicator related to the maintenance cost approach in the terminology of United Nations (1993). The main difference between the SNI and other indicators of environment-corrected welfare is that economic welfare is not corrected for environmental damages, but rather for the costs of restoring a sustainable level of environmental functions. In the words of Hueting and De Boer (2001, p. 28):

> The supply curve [of environmental functions - RD] is made up of the (rising) costs of the at-source measures required to eliminate the environmental burden, leading to restoration of functions. These are termed the 'elimination costs'. One reason for this choice is that the functions (or services) provided by ecosystems, say, cannot in fact be replaced, or only temporarily so. Restoration of functions by means of elimination is always possible, however, as long as the functions have not been irreversibly damaged of course.

The SNI calculation not only covers the direct restoration costs, but also the indirect economic effects that will arise when sustainability is implemented. These total costs are subtracted from Net National Income (NNI) to calculate the SNI; the difference between NNI and SNI shows the unsustainability of current economic activities. Hueting's approach hinges on the assumption of an absolute preference for the environment: sustainable pollution levels provide a hard constraint on economic activity. One of the main strong points of Hueting's approach is that it does not depend on the valuation of environmental resources.

The sustainable pollution levels in the SNI-AGE study are taken directly from Hueting (as reported in de Boer, 2000a) and are exogenous to the model. The economic module consists of a comparative-static applied general equilibrium model with 27 production sectors and three consumers (private households, government and rest-of-the-world). In the environmental module, nine environmental themes are taken into account: climate change, depletion of the ozone layer, acidification, eutrophication, fine particles (PM10) in air, smog formation through volatile organic compounds (VOC), dispersion of heavy metals and PACs/PCBs to water, desiccation of land (in the report labelled as 'dehydration'), and soil contamination. The main elements of the SNI-AGE model and their interactions are represented in Figure 1.1.

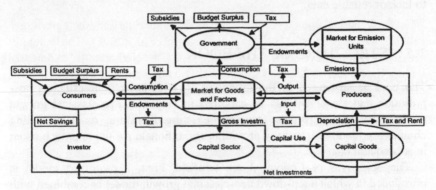

Source: Gerlagh et al. (2002).

Figure 1.1   Overview of the SNI-AGE model

Most of the characteristics of the SNI-AGE model are present in the model described in this book. As will be discussed in chapters 4 and 5, several choices concerning the specification of the model and most of the historical data are directly taken from the SNI-AGE study.

There are, however, also important differences between the SNI-AGE study and this book. Firstly, the book deals with a dynamic analysis, while SNI-AGE is a static model. The transformation to a dynamic model involves not only an extension of the SNI-AGE model (including growth rates of economic activity and emissions), but also some adaptations, especially with respect to the specification of investments (since the static model does not explicitly describe the build-up of a capital stock). Secondly, the model in this book is meant to be used for empirical policy analysis and the modelling assumptions reflect that objective. The SNI-AGE model aims at calculating a welfare indicator, and makes some specific assumptions that make it less suitable for empirical policy analysis. The most important of these is that in SNI-AGE the consumption of the government sector adjusts proportionately to changes in total consumption of private households. In DEAN, the more conventional assumption of 'equal yield', that is, unaffected size of government revenues, is adopted.

Two environmental themes contained in the SNI-AGE model are not analysed here. Depletion of the ozone layer can be neglected, since the success of the Montreal Protocol implies that the use of ozone-depleting CFCs is banned. The only remaining emissions come from existing CFC-containing appliances. Therefore, the policy targets for CFCs will be reached without additional environmental policy (see Chapter 2 for more details). Dispersion of heavy metals to water is also not investigated in this thesis, due to lack of reliable data.

1.5   STRUCTURE OF THE BOOK

The book is structured in the following way. Chapter 2 investigates how pollution and abatement can be captured in empirical neo-classical growth models. By using insights from the existing literature, main modelling choices are identified, thereby providing the rationale for the approach taken in subsequent chapters.

The objectives of Chapter 3 are twofold. First, a prototype model is introduced in which a top-down neo-classical growth model is combined with the main bottom-up information on the available options for pollution abatement. This model is specified in a dynamic applied general equilibrium framework, which is extended with pollution and abatement. It provides the basis for subsequent chapters. This model version is kept as simple as possible to allow for maximum focus on the methodology that describes the main interactions between pollution, abatement and economic activity.

The second objective of Chapter 3 is to compare different approaches to the dynamic issues, while remaining within the neo-classical framework. Three different specifications are analysed: a comparative-static version, a recursive-dynamic version that follows the Solow-Swan methodology and a forward-looking version in the Cass-Koopmans-Ramsey tradition. The mechanisms of the model are illustrated by a numerical example. The prototype model is too simplified to draw firm empirical conclusions; it can, however, illuminate the main mechanisms that drive the behaviour of the agents facing environmental policies.

Chapter 4 extends the forward-looking specification of the prototype model. The extensions make the model suitable for empirical analysis by improving the functioning of the economic and environmental parts of the model. The first economic extension deals with non-unitary income elasticities to capture the difference between basic goods and luxury goods. This difference is especially relevant in the light of the endogenous switch towards cleaner goods. The second economic extension is the specification of international trade. Any empirical model for a small open economy like The Netherlands cannot ignore international trade aspects. Furthermore, some technical aspects are dealt with in this chapter that improve the alignment of the model with national accounts data. In the environmental module, the first extension is the modelling of greenhouse gases as stock pollutants. This gives the opportunity to formulate a climate policy that allows flexibility in the timing of emission reductions. The second environmental extension deals with the dynamic specification of abatement. The development of abatement options over time and their consequences for the model parameters are analysed. Chapter 4 concludes with an equation-by-equation description of the resulting model, labelled DEAN.

The data needed to calibrate the model are presented in Chapter 5. The benchmark accounting matrix for the base year 1990 is presented. Moreover, the calibration of the economic and environmental parameters that govern the reactions of households and firms to the price changes induced by environmental policy is discussed in detail. Specific attention is paid to calibration of abatement data. To this end, abatement cost curves are presented for all environmental themes included in the analysis.

Chapter 6 discusses the results of the simulations with the DEAN model. Current environmental policy objectives are translated into model simulations that illuminate how economic growth, sectoral structure, international trade, pollution and abatement interact. Some alternative environmental policy impulses are compared to investigate the influence of timing of environmental policy on the economy. The results are tested for robustness by performing a range of sensitivity analyses.

Chapter 7 deals with a series of alternative specifications of the model. In this way, the influence of the chosen functional forms of the model equations on the numerical results is investigated. The alternative specifications concern the specification of an internationally coordinated environmental policy, greenhouse gases as flow pollutants, the recycling of environmental permit revenues and a model with endogenous environmental innovation.

Chapter 8 contains the final discussion and conclusions. The chapter puts the model results into perspective by looking at the influence of some of the main assumptions on the methodology and empirical results, and formulates conclusions and recommendations for science and policy.

NOTE

1. The terms 'pollution' and 'emissions' are used interchangeably throughout, though it is recognised that both terms have different definitions in environmental science.

2. Pollution and abatement in economic modelling

2.1 INTRODUCTION

Designing or evaluating environmental policy requires detailed understanding of the relations between economy and environment. Using mathematical models that specify quantitative links between economic activity and environmental pressure can provide insight into the direction and size of the economic implications of environmental policies. Given the increasing importance of implementing costly process-integrated measures and restructuring of the economy to achieve required emission reductions, the need for multi-sectoral economic models with special attention to pollution and abatement is evident.

Many environmental-economic models have been constructed, and many studies have evaluated economic impacts of environmental policy (see van den Bergh, 1999). There are, however, important areas not covered in the existing methodologies that warrant further study. On the one hand, *top-down* models assess macro-economic impacts of environmental policy, but disregard the abatement technologies that have to be implemented to achieve the policy targets. On the other hand, *bottom-up* models focus on specific abatement options, but cannot deal with the indirect effects induced. Integrated models that include the main elements of both types of models for a range of environmental problems are still lacking. Bridging this gap, at least partially, is one of the main objectives of this book.

The current chapter reviews to what extent existing literature can answer the research questions posed in Chapter 1. Different approaches to modelling economic activity, economic growth, pollution and abatement are evaluated on their merits in terms of methodology and empirical applicability. Moreover, the main characteristics of the model type to be developed in this book are discussed. Hence, this chapter provides a framework for the analysis in later chapters.

Due to the large and still rapidly growing number of environmental-economic models that are available, this chapter confines itself to a discussion of different modelling approaches, using some of the most important examples of the literature up to date. In line with the general methodology used in this book (as discussed in Section 1.3), the focus lies on (dynamic) macro-economic empirical models based on neo-classical theory, especially applied general equilibrium (AGE) models and neo-classical growth models.

Section 2.2 deals with different characteristics of environmental-economic models and discusses some basic model types and specification choices that have to be made. Given the special attention to AGE and neo-classical growth models, the basic elements of these types of models are discussed in more detail in sections 2.2.2 and 2.2.3, respectively. In Section 2.3 the modelling of pollution and abatement in economic models is analysed. The section starts with an analysis of the link between pollution and economic activity in Section 2.3.1, while sections 2.3.2 and 2.3.3 deal with the modelling of pollution abatement in an economic context. Section 2.3.4 describes how major environmental problems can be contained in environmental themes. In concluding Section 2.4, the analysis from preceding sections is used to provide the main characteristics of the model to be developed in subsequent chapters of this book.

2.2 CHARACTERISTICS OF ECONOMIC MODELS

2.2.1 Introduction

A large variety of characteristics is found in environmental-economic models. This can be explained partially by the variations in the research questions addressed in the literature. For example, testing the empirical validity of the double dividend hypothesis requires a significantly different focus in the model specification than a model that analyses the impact of climate change on agriculture. Research questions provide guidelines for the choice of model characteristics, without being complete. The choice of model type and other specification issues also reflect the modeller's perspective on the issues involved: different modellers have different opinions (beliefs) on what the most important mechanisms in economic reality are and what type of model best describes these mechanisms.

This section deals with different model types and basic specification choices. These model types and specification choices are used in sections 2.3 and 2.4, which investigate which of these characteristics best suit the model to be developed here.

Different types of models

Well-known types of models used in macro-economic analysis of environmental issues are partial equilibrium models, general equilibrium models, input-output models, neo-classical growth models, endogenous growth models, neo-Keynesian models and overlapping generations models. Several handbooks on macro-economics describe each of these model types, for example, Blanchard and Fischer (1989);[1] many references on modelling approaches in environmental economics can be found in van den Bergh (1999). An introduction to mathematical methods used in most of these model types is given in Chiang (1984). There can be many different classifications of model types, based on different characteristics of the models. For instance, from a theoretic perspective, input-output models are just a special case of general equilibrium models, with all elasticities equal to zero. Similarly, all model types identified above are based on neo-classical assumptions, except the neo-Keynesian models. The classification chosen here is appropriate for applied models as many authors use these labels; moreover, the classification is roughly consistent with historical developments. A complication of this classification is that some models may, in principle, be assigned to different categories, for example, general equilibrium as well as neo-classical growth.

Partial equilibrium models describe those markets in an economy that are relevant for the analysis at hand. For instance, when investigating the impact of a subsidy on the penetration of renewable energy, the model can be restricted to energy markets. In doing so, the impacts of changes in these markets on the rest of the economy are assumed to be negligible (the *ceteris paribus* assumption). This is the major drawback of partial equilibrium models: situations in which the links with the rest of the economy are absent are very rare. The main advantage is that, as partial equilibrium models are often relatively small, emphasis can be put on finding the best functional form and on improving the calibration or estimation of the functional parameters. Partial equilibrium models are based on neo-classical theory for the behaviour of individual agents (households and firms). A practical introduction to partial equilibrium models is given in Tsakok (1990); Mannaerts (2000) uses this model type for material flow modelling.

General equilibrium models are similar to partial equilibrium models, with the main difference that general equilibrium models describe the entire economy. Moreover, they represent the fully closed economic cycle. General equilibrium models are extensively discussed in Ginsburgh and Keyzer (1997) and will be explained in more detail in Section 2.2.2.

Input-output models can be regarded as simplified general equilibrium models, since they assume that substitution possibilities are absent. Inputs are combined in fixed proportions in the production of goods. Such simplifications have major advantages, as these models are much easier to solve and require less data. This comes, however, at the cost of being suitable only for short-term analyses of small policy changes, where the substitution effects can be neglected. The seminal article in this field is Leontief (1970) who applies the input-output technique (that he developed himself) to environmental problems; van Ierland (1993) provides a highly detailed analysis of this modelling type for environmental policy in The Netherlands.

Neo-classical growth models share their micro-economic foundation with general equilibrium models, but look at the development of the economy over time. Dynamic general equilibrium models are effectively neo-classical growth models. Neo-classical growth models can be used to investigate the driving forces behind sustained economic growth. Moreover, they are the appropriate tools to analyse the conditions under which economies of different countries will converge, that is whether poor countries can get rich. Section 2.2.3 discusses these models; a good reference is Barro and Sala-i-Martin (1995).

Endogenous growth models emerged from neo-classical growth models, as many authors were dissatisfied with the fact that exogenously-given technological change is the driving force of economic growth in the neo-classical growth models. Therefore, models were developed that describe technological change endogenously. The main determinants of technological change studied in this literature are investments in research and development, learning effects and knowledge spillovers. For an introduction into this literature, see Barro and Sala-i-Martin (1995) or Aghion and Howitt (1998); Smulders (2000) discusses applications in the field of environmental economics.

Neo-Keynesian models are not based entirely on micro-economic theory, but rather on extrapolation of historic trends. The focus of these models lies on the demand side of the economy. As neo-Keynesian models do not rely on the principle of market equilibrium, they are sometimes labelled 'disequilibrium models'; another commonly encountered name is 'macro-econometric models'. Correlations between certain variables that are derived from the data may be included in the model, even though this relationship cannot be fully supported by economic theory. In most cases, models that are based on historical trends are better capable of short-term projections (given that the economic structure does not change rapidly), while models with a theoretical basis are more suitable for long-term analysis. Neo-Keynesian models are relatively rare in the international literature, but have a long tradition at The Netherlands Bureau for Economic Policy Analysis (for example, van den Berg et al., 1988). Applications in the field of energy-economics are given in Barker et al. (1993) and den Butter et al. (1995).

In recent years, applications of so-called *overlapping generations models* have become increasingly popular. While other dynamic models assume an infinitely lived consumer, overlapping generations (OLG) models specify generations that die after some periods and are replaced by new generations. Normally, several generations coexist at any point in time. Overlapping generations models can contain the most state-of-the-art economic theory, but are notoriously hard to calibrate and solve. OLG models are described in Auerbach and Kotlikoff (1987) and in most handbooks on economic growth (for example, Barro and Sala-i-Martin, 1995); applications in the field of environmental economics include Howarth and Norgaard (1992) and Gerlagh and Keyzer (2001).

Different specifications of models
Within each modelling structure, there is room for variation in the specification of the model. Basic characteristics that have to be considered include:

- Theoretical versus applied (empirical): does the model describe a hypothetical economy, allowing maximum focus on the mechanisms of the model (theoretical approach), or does it provide statements on the size of policy effects in a real economy (empirical approach)? The neo-Keynesian models do not lend themselves easily to methodological analysis, as these models are based on extrapolating historical trends.
- Static versus dynamic: the number of periods in a model can be one (static model), multiple but finite (most dynamic models) or infinite (some dynamic models); another distinction often encountered in the literature is between models describing the past, the present, the near future or the far future.
- For dynamic models, myopic versus forward-looking: agents can base their behaviour purely on the current allocation of resources (myopic behaviour) or can take a long-term view for their decisions (forward-looking behaviour). The knowledge about future prices can be perfect (perfect foresight) or incomplete. If all agents are myopic, the model can be solved in a recursive-dynamic procedure, solving for one period at a time, while forward-looking models are solved for all periods simultaneously.
- Deterministic versus stochastic: the model may or may not contain uncertainty with respect to the expectations of agents, the model structure and the data. The stochastics may concern individual agents or the whole economy.
- Calibrated versus estimated: the parameters of the model may be chosen by the modeller based on existing literature and expert

judgement, or they may be econometrically estimated, using historical time series data. Most neo-classical models are calibrated, while most neo-Keynesian models are econometrically estimated.

- Geographical scale: there are models that describe one individual firm or household (micro-economic models), while others describe the whole world; other commonly used aggregation levels are sectoral, regional and national.
- Different parts of the model can be fully integrated or specified in separate sub-models, which can have different characteristics; feedbacks between the modules can be one-way (for example, the economic module can affect the environmental module but not *vice versa*) or both ways.
- The specification of technological progress can be absent, exogenous or endogenous.

These characteristics are used at the end of this chapter and in subsequent chapters to characterise the model developed in this book and are implicitly used in the description of the models discussed below.

2.2.2   General Description of Applied General Equilibrium Models

Applied general equilibrium models (AGEs)[2] are based on neo-classical theory on individual firms and households and describe the entire economy. A general equilibrium model consists of a set of 'economic agents' (consumers and producers), each of which demands and supplies commodities or 'goods'. Agents are assumed to behave rationally. Each agent solves its own optimisation problem. The agents take prices, which provide information about the decision environment (such as the behaviour of other agents and government policies), as given.

This section does not aim at providing a formal introduction into general equilibrium theory, but rather sketches the basic building blocks commonly encountered in standard AGEs.[3] An introduction to applied general equilibrium models is given in Shoven and Whalley (1992); a more recent book that extensively discusses generalisations of these basic building blocks is that by Ginsburgh and Keyzer (1997). For an overview of the use of AGE models in the field of environmental economics, see Destais (1996), Conrad (1999, 2001) and Harrison et al. (2000).

The AGE model describes the relationships between the economic agents. These economic agents can be households (consumers), firms (producers), other countries and sometimes the government. Firms are grouped together into production sectors. Producers operate under full competition and maximise profits, subject to their production technology, for given prices.

Under constant returns to scale, this leads to the first of the three basic conditions: the *zero profit condition*. Households are grouped into household groups. If the model assumes all households to behave identically, they can be aggregated into one representative consumer. Households maximise their utility subject to a budget constraint, for given prices and given initial endowments. This is the second basic condition: the *income condition*. The economy is said to be in equilibrium if every agent can satisfy his/her demand or supply for each good given a set of (relative) market prices that is common to all agents. In other words, total demand must equal total supply on all markets. This is referred to as *market clearance*, the third of the basic AGE conditions. Equilibrium is attained through adjusting the relative prices. The resulting prices are called equilibrium prices.

The three basic conditions of AGEs

The *zero profit condition* means that under constant returns to scale the value of output has to equal the value of all inputs.[4] This condition is called the zero profit condition because firms that have a constant returns to scale production function and that operate under full competition will never be able to reap any excess profits. Note that this does not imply that there is no return to capital: capital is one of the inputs to production and receives a payment like all other inputs.[5] The intuition behind this condition is that if any firm is capable of reaping any profits, this will induce a new firm to compete on this market (in the absence of entry barriers). Then total supply of the produced good will increase, which leads to a reduction in the price. This lower price will then decrease the profit for both the old and the new firm. This process continues until the excess profits equal zero. If profits are negative, the rational firm will cease production. Note that under constant returns to scale, a firm that can make a profit will increase its scale to infinity and hence reap infinite profits; this is clearly in contradiction to reality.

Households cannot increase their expenditures above their income. This is known as the *income condition*. Total income may stem from payments for the supply of labour and capital to the firms and from tax revenues. As households always prefer more to less (by assumption), the full income will always be used for consumption and savings and nothing will be left unused. Dynamic models may assume that intertemporal borrowing is possible, which allows a temporary budget deficit.

For each good, the *market clearance condition* has to be satisfied, that is, total demand equals total supply. For the primary production factors, labour and capital, this means that total demand for these goods must be equal to the total amount available (endowments). For produced goods, total supply is equal to the total amount produced plus imports of that good. Total demand is made up of demand by other firms (intermediate deliveries) and demand by households plus exports (final demand).

If at a certain price the demand for a good is larger than the supply, there is excess demand. If supply exceeds demand, there is excess supply. The supply of a good will increase if the price increases, while the demand for a good decreases with increasing prices. Hence, if excess demand exists, the price of the good can be increased: this leads to an increase in supply and decrease in demand. Eventually, an equilibrium price will emerge in which the supply equals demand. Similarly, if excess supply exists, lowering the price of the good can bring supply and demand into equilibrium. In order to get equilibrium on several markets simultaneously, a more elaborate procedure is needed, due to the interactions between markets.

Applied general equilibrium models are generalised input-output models, where substitution is allowed and prices are determined within the model. They can be seen as a system of non-linear equations, which can be solved simultaneously. The essence of AGEs is that prices of all goods are determined within the model such that all the conditions stated above are satisfied simultaneously.

The economy can be described in the AGE model as a set of balances: for every demand there is a supply. This implies that all financial flows in the model are closed. In an open economy, the flow of physical goods is not closed, due to international trade, but the condition that the trade deficit is exactly matched by the budget deficit of domestic consumers implies that financial flows are also closed in an open economy specification. This feature of closed (financial) flows is often referred to as a fully closed economy cycle and is a major distinction between AGE models and partial equilibrium models, where such closure is not necessarily imposed.

In the AGE model, not only the direct effects of a policy on the firms and households are taken into account, but also the indirect effects. These indirect effects are caused by changes in behaviour of firms and households and imply that a policy that influences one market will also have an impact on other markets.

Empirical specification of AGEs

What distinguishes *applied* general equilibrium models from theoretical general equilibrium models is that functional forms and parameters are chosen to represent a specific situation with real data and that these are used to calculate a numerical solution of the model. Specifying the parameter values of the AGE equations to represent the real data is called calibration. As Shoven and Whalley (1992, p. 103) phrase it: 'Numerical, empirically based general equilibrium models can be used to evaluate concrete policy options by specifying production and demand parameters and incorporating data reflective of real economies' and 'Calibration is most easily understood as the requirement that the entire model specification be capable of generating a base-year equilibrium observation as a model solution'. This implies that the model should be able to calculate the initial situation, using data for the base year and the calibrated parameter values. If this replication check fails, there must be an error in the model specification.

For the calibration of a comparative-static[6] AGE, two types of data are needed: (i) data describing the initial allocation of resources; and (ii) data describing the reaction of agents to changes in circumstances. To carry out actual policy simulations, additional information is needed to describe the policy impulse. Furthermore, dynamic models need data on growth rates of variables.

The first type of data needed in AGEs is the data describing the *initial allocation of resources*. These data are usually taken from the National Accounts and describe a historical year. They include expenditures by production sectors and households on the various goods and the division of production factors over producers.

Secondly, data are needed that describe the *reactions of the agents* to the impulse given. These reactions are usually specified in terms of elasticities. For the households, price and income elasticities govern the change in the demand for a good if a price changes or if the income changes. Note that the demand for one good may not only change due to changes in the price of the same good, but also due to changes in the prices of other goods. For the production sectors, only price elasticities have to be specified.

The data describing the *policy impulse* is the quantitative equivalent of some new policy, for example, the change in a tax rate. Alternatively, an impulse can describe a change in availability of one or more endowments, for example, an increase in total labour supply.

For the calibration of a dynamic AGE, additional information is needed on growth rates of all variables in the *benchmark projection*, that is, the development of all variables without additional policies needs to be specified. Moreover, an intertemporal elasticity of substitution has to be specified for households (which may be zero to reflect a situation that households are myopic).

Advantages and disadvantages of the AGE approach
One of the main advantages of the AGE model is that it gives a complete description of the economy (in contrast to partial equilibrium models, which describe one or a few markets). All economic agents are taken into account, albeit sometimes at a very aggregated level.

Another major advantage of the AGE model is that it has a sound micro-economic foundation in neo-classical theory. Using well-known theories on firm and household behaviour at the level of individual agents, a model for the whole economy can be derived. This is a property of AGEs that neo-Keynesian models and input-output models lack. The questions answered with AGEs may be about interactions between taxation, economic development, welfare distribution, allocation of goods and trade issues.

A third advantage of AGEs is that, as compared to input-output models, the functions that describe the behaviour of firms and households are endogenous: agents respond to price changes by changing their production or consumption patterns. Moreover, AGE models use resource constraints in their description of markets. The extension to environmental resources is therefore relatively straightforward.

Until recently, the main disadvantage of AGEs was that they could not be solved numerically (and the models are too complex to solve analytically). Powerful computers are needed to calculate the model results, as the AGE models are quite large systems of interdependent equations. However, with the development of capable solvers and the increase in computational power of personal computers, numerically solving AGEs is nowadays not much of a problem.

Another aspect of AGEs is that they require a lot of data: not only are data needed for the initial situation, but also for the reactions of firms and households to the policy changes. These data are often hard to find.

2.2.3 General Description of Neo-classical Growth Models

As in AGE models, the basis of neo-classical growth models is formed by neo-classical economic theory for individual households and firms, while describing the entire economy. As the name suggests, neo-classical growth models deal with the development of the economy over time. If a neo-classical growth model is empirically calibrated and encompasses several production sectors, it is effectively a dynamic AGE model.

The main question that neo-classical growth models attempt to answer is under which circumstances sustained (that is, everlasting) economic growth is possible. These models focus on the driving forces behind the growth of per capita consumption. A good entry into the literature on neo-classical growth models is Barro and Sala-i-Martin (1995); most macro-economic textbooks also give an introduction to these growth models, for example, Blanchard and Fischer (1989).

The neo-classical growth model with a fixed savings rate
It is useful to start the discussion of neo-classical growth models with the simplest model possible. Imagine a closed economy with one representative consumer that lives forever (think of this representative consumer not as an

individual but rather as a family dynasty). One good is produced in each period, using labour and capital as inputs. There is no uncertainty, perfect competition on all markets, agents behave rationally and the state of technology is given (no technological progress). The consumer saves a fixed proportion of its income and consumes the rest. Under these circumstances, the allocation of resources by a central planner who maximises the utility of the representative consumer is identical to the allocation of resources in a decentralised market economy.

The labour supply is exogenously given and determined by the size of the population. More specifically, it is assumed that the growth rate of labour supply equals the growth rate of the population. For capital, the development over time is influenced by depreciation due to 'wear and tear', which is assumed to be a constant fraction of the existing capital stock, and by investments, which equal savings. The increase in the per capita stock of capital then positively depends on the rate of savings (due to more investments) and negatively on the growth rate of labour and depreciation. This is known as the fundamental differential equation of the Solow-Swan model, named after the two most important contributors to this line of theory: Solow (1956) and Swan (1956).

Neo-classical growth models assume that capital accumulation is subject to diminishing returns, that is, the marginal productivity of new units of capital decreases when the capital stock grows. In the absence of technological progress, the growth rate of output is determined solely by the growth rate of labour supply and capital accumulation. Moreover, the growth rate of output per capita is only determined by the growth rate of capital per capita. For a given savings rate, the growth rate of capital is known, as savings equal investments. If the growth rate of capital is larger than the growth rate of labour supply, the per capita capital stock will increase over time, thereby inducing a reduction in the returns to capital. Similarly, if the growth rate of capital is too small, capital accumulation can be increased, given the high returns to capital.

The outcome will be a situation in which the per capita stock of capital will be constant; investments exactly cover population growth and depreciation. This implies that per capita production will be constant, as per capita labour supply is also constant, and hence also per capita consumption is constant. Welfare, measured as the net present value of current and future per capita consumption, is therefore also constant. This is known as the *steady state*. The conclusion for this simple model must be that while the economy can grow in absolute size with the growth rate of the population, economic growth in per capita terms cannot be sustained. Perhaps even more importantly, changes in choice of production technology, savings rate and depreciation rate do not affect the steady state growth rates of the economy; they only influence the level of the various quantities.

For each savings rate, there is a unique steady state per capita capital stock, given the production function, the growth rate of labour and depreciation. As per capita consumption in the steady state depends on the savings rate, one can calculate which savings rate maximises per capita consumption. This savings rate is known as the *golden rule* savings rate. The steady state per capita consumption is maximised when the marginal product of capital equals the growth rate of labour plus the depreciation rate. This is known as the *golden rule of capital accumulation*, as it defines the capital stock that maximises the steady state per capita consumption level. In the Solow-Swan model, the golden rule capital stock is only attained if the savings rate coincides with the golden rule savings rate; the savings rate is, however, not determined within the model.

In this simple model, each economy will grow towards its own steady state level. If all countries have the same technologies, population growth, savings and depreciation rates, then poor countries will grow faster than richer countries, since they are further from their steady state levels. This is known as *convergence*. If the characteristics of the countries differ, then each country will grow towards its own steady state, and there will be conditional convergence: countries that are further from their steady state will grow faster.

Clearly, the model prediction that per capita consumption is constant over time is inconsistent with empirical observations. To overcome this, the simple Solow-Swan model described above can be augmented with technological progress. Assume that the efficiency of workers improves over time such that a worker can produce more output with the same input of capital. This is known as *labour-augmenting technological progress*, as it raises production in the same way as an increase in the population. Then, effective labour can be used as the amount of production the labour force can produce. In the absence of technological progress, this depends only on the amount of workers and hence on the population growth rate, but with technological progress, this effective labour supply increases also with the growth in technology. This means that in the steady state, per capita production can have a positive growth rate, if capital growth can keep up with the growth rate of effective labour. In this situation, investments do not only cover population growth and depreciation, but also technological progress. The result is that capital, production and consumption in per capita terms all grow at the speed of technological progress. This is known as a balanced growth path.

The neo-classical growth model with a flexible savings rate

The description above assumed that consumers choose a fixed savings rate. To make the model more realistic, one can assume that the savings of consumers are determined endogenously within the model. In this case, the consumer chooses the savings rate such that the net present value of the stream of per capita consumption is maximised. Consumers know the future state of the economy, and hence can consistently plan a consumption path for the current and all future periods. This set-up of the neo-classical growth model is based on the early writings of Ramsey (1928), which are further elaborated by Cass (1965) and Koopmans (1965).

In principle, the consumer chooses the savings rate such that the rate of return on savings, given by the interest rate, equals the rate of return on consumption, which is determined by the rate of time preference and the rate of decrease of marginal utility of consumption. There are two reasons why consumers prefer consumption today over consumption tomorrow. Firstly, they discount future utility at the rate of time preference; the current members of the family dynasty prefer consumption for themselves over consumption by future family members. Secondly, marginal utility is assumed to decrease with increasing utility levels and therefore consumers have a desire to smooth the consumption patterns over time.

The endogenous savings rate does not influence the steady state growth: the per capita growth rates of the economy are still only determined by the rate of technological progress. The resulting levels of the economic variables may differ from the Solow-Swan model, since there is impatience in the form of a positive time preference in the Ramsey model.

As the savings rate is endogenous, it is possible to attain the golden rule capital stock and hence maximise the steady state per capita consumption. This is indeed optimal if the discount rate is zero (that is, no time preference). If the discount rate is positive, the optimal per capita capital stock is smaller than the golden rule level and can be determined by the so-called *modified golden rule*.

Note that in these neo-classical growth models, all welfare improvements are explained by technological progress, but technological progress itself is not explained in the model. Mankiw et al. (1992) showed that neo-classical growth models are capable of mimicking empirical developments. Several authors have developed theories that focus on explaining technological progress within the model; these theories are grouped under the umbrella term 'endogenous growth theory', also called 'new growth theory'. Analysis of endogenous growth models is beyond the scope of this book; an introduction into the literature is given in Barro and Sala-i-Martin (1995) and Aghion and Howitt (1998); Löschel (2002) provides a survey of technological change in environmental economic models and

Smulders (2000) investigates the relation between economic growth and the environment.

2.3   MODELLING THE ENVIRONMENT IN ECONOMIC MODELS

In order to model the economic costs of environmental policy, environmental issues have to be specified. Firstly, the link between economic activity and environmental pressure needs to be assessed; Section 2.3.1 discusses how this is done in the literature. Secondly, the specification of abatement in environmental-economic models is analysed in general terms in Section 2.3.2, while Section 2.3.3 focuses on abatement in neo-classical growth models, with an emphasis on empirical models. Finally, Section 2.3.4 deals with the specification of multiple pollutants.

2.3.1   Linking the Environment and Economic Activity

Most environmental-economic models take emissions as the starting point for their environmental modelling (see Van den Bergh, 1999). This makes sense, as emissions are naturally linked to economic processes. Linking emissions and economic activity is, however, not as straightforward as most models suggest. The problem is that the appropriate way to model emissions is to aggregate economic activity by homogeneous processes; for example, the production of wooden chairs and tables versus the production of metal chairs and tables. For economic modelling the appropriate aggregation is based on homogeneous products, for example, chairs (wooden or metal) versus tables (wooden or metal). At higher levels of aggregation, a classification based on homogeneous products will automatically imply heterogeneity in processes. Thereby, the variety in emission coefficients within the aggregated sector is overlooked. Some attempts have been made to create macro-economic models based on homogeneous processes (for example, Mannaerts, 2000; Elzenga et al., 2001), but these have not been very successful so far. Moreover, widespread adoption of process-oriented economic data would require a major change in economic accounting practices. For more information on the links between economic and material flows, see Kandelaars (1998) and Ayres (1999).

Emissions as undesirable output or necessary input
There are two different ways in which emissions from production activity can be covered in economic models. Firstly, one can regard emissions as undesirable outputs from production. The production function then follows a

joint-production approach, where a certain combination of inputs produces a certain combination of desirable outputs ('goods') and undesirable outputs ('bads'). This approach is used, for example, in Färe et al. (1996) and Pasurka (2001). Applying this methodology within a general equilibrium framework, Komen and Peerlings (2001) distinguish three alternative technologies which represent different possible combinations of good and bad outputs within the dairy farming sector. All available technologies are explicitly formulated and hence no functional form for the production function is required. This so-called activity analysis has the advantage that no parameters for a production function have to be calibrated[7], but the requirement of explicit formulation of all alternatives makes it impractical for wide-ranged environmental-economic modelling. Aiken and Pasurka (2002) use a (parametric) continuous production function for joint production of goods and bads and argue that it provides the best specification of process-integrated abatement options.

The majority of models, however, use a second approach. This involves treating the environment as a necessary input to production. An intuitive way of looking at this is to think of environmental services as inputs for production for which emission permits are required. These environmental services can be regarded as the allowance to emit polluting substances to the environment. The costs associated with this input concern the payments for the emission permits that are required to use the environmental resource, that is, a transaction between the polluter and the government. This approach is used in AGE modelling by, amongst others, Bergman (1990, 1991), Conrad and Schröder (1991, 1993), Robinson et al. (1994) and Welsch (1996), and is discussed in more detail in the next chapter.

In some cases, modelling the environment as an input to production allows for a direct link between emissions and certain inputs in the production function. For example, CO_2 emissions can be linked to energy use (for example, Manne and Richels, 1992). Similarly, consumption emissions can be linked to the consumption of specific goods. Note, however, that such a link between emissions and specific goods cannot be made for all pollutants. The reason for this is that heterogeneous processes underlie the homogeneous goods categorisation. Therefore, linking emissions to certain inputs is almost solely applied in the existing literature to energy-related emissions and in detailed sector-specific models (for example, Komen, 2000).

Feedback links between economy and environment
Integrated environmental-economic models should ideally not only specify the effect of economic activity on the environment but also the feedback from the environment to the economy. To be able to do this, an environmental module has to be specified, in which the environmental effects of emissions are captured. Then these environmental effects may have an impact on

production and/or utility (see Smulders, 1994). Hofkes (1996) specifies an integrated model in which the environment provides extractive as well as non-extractive services to the production process. Smulders and Gradus (1996) go even further and model the environment as a life-support system, where life is impossible below some critical level of environmental quality. A famous example of a feedback link on production is the specification of environmental damages from global warming in integrated climate-energy-economy models such as DICE (Nordhaus, 1991, 1994), MERGE (Manne and Richels, 1992; Manne et al., 1995) and more recently EPPA (Babiker et al., 2001); for an overview of this type of model see Weyant (1999) and Metz et al. (2001). Such a link also appears in some models for acidification (for example, Alcamo et al., 1990). Nonetheless, feedback links from the environment to production are more common in theoretical models (see Smulders, 1994) than in applied models.

Another way to model a feedback from the environment to the economy is by specifying the amenity value of environmental quality: the utility of private households is higher if environmental quality is higher (for example, Smulders, 1994). Hofkes (2001) also includes environmental quality in the utility function and stresses that short-term effects of environmental policy may be significantly different from long-term effects. Alternatively, one can model a disutility stemming from emissions (for example, Hettich, 2000). Espinosa and Smith (1995) do this in an indirect manner by estimating mortality effects of emissions and including these in the utility function.

A major advantage of having a two-sided interaction between the economy and the environment is that it allows for the calculation of an optimal environmental policy, that is, that level of pollution control at which marginal benefits of pollution abatement equal marginal costs of pollution abatement. These feedback loops are, however, very difficult to specify at an empirical level. Models that only cover the link from the economy to the environment but not the feedback link, have to restrict themselves to cost-effectiveness analysis where the economic costs of a given level of environmental policy are investigated.

Wolfgang (1999) stresses that the optimal level of emission reduction may not always be positive. In specific circumstances, emissions may be public goods rather than public bads and in such cases emissions should be stimulated, not reduced. This could happen if the only way to reduce emissions that were highly damaging in one environmental area was to increase emissions that were damaging in a less crucial area. An example of such interlinkage between environmental problems is the increase in tropospheric ozone concentrations that may be induced by lower nitrous oxide emissions (to reduce acidification). The circumstances under which it is optimal to increase emissions are, however, rare, and in most instances marginal reduction costs and reduction rates can be assumed positive.

Non-emission-related environmental problems

The treatment of non-emission-related environmental problems is a separate field of study. Specialised models exist to analyse the economic impacts of environmental problems such as waste (for example, Bartelings et al., 2004), biodiversity and nature conservation (van Kooten and Bulte, 2000) or land use (for example, Fischer et al., 1996). There are hardly any empirical studies trying to integrate these different problems. In fact, this holds for emission-related environmental problems as well. Many models exist that focus purely on one environmental problem, while others combine different problems that are related, for example, all emissions caused by energy use or models for local or regional air quality (for example, Alcamo et al., 1990; Brink et al., 2001; Schmieman, 2001; see also Section 2.3.2).

2.3.2 Modelling Pollution Abatement

The reduction of pollution is labelled 'abatement'. Pollution abatement can take the form of (i) prevention of pollution, including, for example, conservation of energy through good housekeeping; (ii) end-of-pipe measures, for example, installing a catalytic converter; (iii) process-integrated measures, mostly in the form of input substitution in production; and (iv) reduction of economic activity. The first three forms of abatement affect pollution via the environmental intensity of economic activity, that is, how much pollution is generated per unit of production or consumption. In a narrow definition, pollution abatement only covers technical measures to reduce pollution, and prevention and activity reduction are not included. For clarity, this narrow definition of abatement will be labelled 'technical abatement', to emphasise that it deals with technical measures that polluters can implement to reduce their pollution.

Top-down versus bottom-up modelling

The abatement information that is most important for calculation of the economic costs of environmental policies is the information included in marginal abatement cost functions. Nonetheless, most applied general equilibrium models contain this information only implicitly. These top-down models treat abatement costs purely as the profits or utility foregone as a result of forced changes in behaviour induced by environmental policy. By comparing profits and utility that can be realised in the absence of the abatement effort with the profits or utility remaining under the emission restriction, the net abatement costs can be calculated. This calculated reduction in profits or utility thus implicitly covers all direct and indirect costs of environmental policy. The accuracy of these total or net abatement costs depends crucially on the proper specification of all available options to reduce emissions. Pure top-down models cover these only through the available changes in production inputs. Though the notion of abatement costs as foregone profits or utility is not incorrect, it disregards the micro-economic information on the available abatement technologies, which should constitute the direct costs of abatement. If the estimation of the direct costs is inaccurate, the estimate of total costs will also be inaccurate.

At the other end of the spectrum are the bottom-up models that contain detailed empirical information on the technical characteristics of specific abatement options. Nowadays, most of these models do estimate the associated direct costs of the measure. Bottom-up models aim either at an analysis of the costs of a specific abatement measure, for example, the evolution of the costs of wind power over time, or compare different substitute abatement measures, for example, minimising the costs of a given energy demand by choosing the optimal mix of fossil fuels and renewable energy sources. A well-known example is the MARKAL model (Seebregts et al., 2001) for the energy markets. Another detailed example is Sunman (1991). Grubler and Messner (1998) use a bottom-up model to show that early abatement efforts should be encouraged as these stimulate technological development. Anderson (2001) augments a bottom-up model with some elements of technological progress and analyses the relation between abatement and per capita income. Isoard and Soria (2001) focus on learning effects and returns to scale to explain innovation and diffusion of clean technology in an empirical setting. They find that learning effects are an important source of productivity growth and that for newly invented technologies, there may be substantial diseconomies of scale (due to barriers to diffusion and high uncertainty), while the longer run may be characterised by constant returns to scale (when diffusion barriers are overcome).

For a proper assessment of the total costs of environmental policies, that is, the direct *and* indirect costs, the bottom-up approach can be integrated with a top-down model. In this manner, the bottom-up module can be used to determine the direct costs, the top-down module to assess the indirect costs. By combining both approaches, the economic costs of environmental policies can be evaluated in a fully consistent manner, using the best available information on both the direct and indirect costs.

The easiest way to integrate the bottom-up model with a more top-down oriented economic model is via so-called soft-linking. In this approach, two separate models are specified, and the outcomes of one model are entered as exogenous inputs into the other model and vice versa. The converging outcome is then achieved via an iterative procedure. Examples of this approach are given in Jacobsen (1998) and Klaassen et al. (1999).

Other studies aim more at integrating the bottom-up and top-down modules into one model (so-called hard-linking). This allows for more elaborate endogenous feedbacks between both modules. Noteworthy examples of such integrated models are the NEMO model (Koopmans et al., 1999; Koopmans and te Velde, 2001) and the model by Böhringer (1998). The disadvantage of hard-linked models is that they provide less flexibility in the modelling of individual modules. Moreover, Böhringer uses a discrete specification of all available technologies, that is, an activity analysis. While this may be suitable for energy models, where the number of alternative technologies is limited, this approach is practically impossible in more general cases where the number of alternatives may be much greater.

Full-scale estimation of abatement costs is not common in top-down environmental-economic models. The detailed description of the abatement processes in terms of economic inputs as used in Nestor and Pasurka (1995a) is an exception; Nestor and Pasurka (1995b) show that a proper specification of abatement costs is vital for quantitative estimates of the economic costs of environmental policy. Given the different ways in which emissions can be reduced, the marginal costs of reductions cannot be directly inferred. Nonetheless, applied general equilibrium models can be used to calculate the implicit marginal abatement costs at different levels of emission reductions. This approach is taken in Ellerman and Decaux (1998) and in Eyckmans et al. (2001). Though these studies have the advantage that total direct and indirect costs of emission reductions are properly taken into account, they contain only indirect information on the costs of alternative options for emission reduction and the cost estimates are only as good as the quality of the abatement cost information that is used as input to the model.

Neo-classical models covering several environmental problems simultaneously are not common. Komen (2000) uses the NAMEA accounting framework (Haan and Keuning, 1996) as the basis for his AGE model for The Netherlands. He focuses on the agricultural sector and links emissions to specific economic activities; end-of-pipe abatement is not included. Xie (1996) and Xie and Saltzman (2000) distinguish between pollution abatement activities for air quality, water quality and soil quality. Xie (1996) also reports that empirical abatement cost data at a disaggregated level are not available and employs some ad hoc assumptions to calibrate the abatement costs.

A separate strand of micro-economic literature focuses on the incentives of firms to adopt, or not to adopt, cleaner technologies. This literature builds on Magat (1978) and Milliman and Prince (1989); recent entries into this literature include Baudry (2000) and Phaneuf and Requate (2002). Most of this literature is theoretical and centres on the strategic behaviour of individual firms in interaction with an environmental regulator. Insights from this literature are therefore not readily implementable in (dynamic) applied general equilibrium models.

Empirical aspects of pollution abatement

One can also look at pollution abatement from a more empirical point of view. The relevant questions then become where, when and how much to abate and how much this will cost. The where question relates to the geographical, as well as to the sectoral location of abatement activities. Regarding the how much question, the optimal level of abatement can be calculated only if the benefits of abatement are known. Pasurka (2001) stresses that the costs of abatement have become more difficult to measure in recent years, as the emphasis has shifted from end-of-pipe measures to process-integrated abatement.

The when question touches upon the issue of intergenerational distribution of the costs of environmental policy. To answer this question, a dynamic model is required, in which current and future consumption can be compared. Rutherford (2000) shows that the intertemporal incidence of environmental policy can best be analysed in an overlapping generations framework. Gerlagh (1998) and Bovenberg and Heijdra (2002) also use this type of model to investigate intergenerational issues. Wendner (2001) uses a similar type of model to analyse whether the revenues from CO_2 taxation can be used to finance the pension system. If intergenerational incidence analysis is not the main aim of the study, a Ramsey type model is also suitable.

Side-effects of pollution abatement

Abatement can be characterised by the pollutants that are reduced. Apart from the primary environmental target at which the abatement measure is aimed, impacts on other pollutants can be taken into account. These environmental secondary or side-effects are very common and can be either harmful or beneficial (Metz et al., 2001). One commonly ignored side-effect is that of abatement on the economy. This includes the so-called spending effects of abatement: implementing a technical abatement measure is in itself an economic activity that is linked to the rest of the economy. Therefore it affects economic activity in other sectors of the economy (in turn affecting pollution).

Another side-effect is in the field of technological development: abatement can be regarded as diffusion of a pollution reduction technology. The literature on technological development provides strong arguments for a positive impact of diffusion on innovation of other technologies, amongst others via learning-by-doing and research and development (R&D), though it is not conclusive (Aghion and Howitt, 1998). For example, Goulder and Schneider (1999) show how implementation of cleaner technologies as a result of a carbon tax may induce R&D in the field of renewable energy, but at the same time reduce R&D in other sectors via crowding-out effects. Otto et al. (2002) investigate the empirical relation between diffusion and innovation using an econometric approach. Gradus and Smulders (1993) analyse how different specifications of technological development influence the growth rate of the economy if preferences for environmental quality change. A recent contribution to this technology literature is Jaffe et al. (2002); Jacobsen (2001) presents an overview of existing approaches.

2.3.3 Pollution Abatement Modelling in Neo-classical Growth Models

In dynamic models, not only the currently available abatement technologies are of interest, but also the estimation of future abatement costs. This means that trajectories of emissions and abatement, and their associated costs, have to be specified. This section investigates how existing neo-classical growth models deal with the specification of abatement.

When the analysis is restricted to energy-related greenhouse gases, the modelling of abatement can be hugely simplified. Most of these energy-economic models assume that end-of-pipe measures are prohibitively costly compared to fuel switches, and therefore can be neglected in the model. All major integrated climate-energy-economy models developed in the 1980s and 1990s share this assumption (Whalley and Wigle, 1991; Burniaux et al., 1992a, b; Manne and Richels, 1992; Peck and Teisberg, 1992; Alcamo, 1994; Nordhaus, 1994; Nordhaus and Yang, 1996; Capros et al., 1998; Naqvi, 1998), as do more recent models (for example, Böhringer and Rutherford, 2002). Recently, attempts have been made to include other sources of greenhouse gases for which end-of-pipe measures are relevant (Babiker et al., 2001; Hyman et al., 2002). Since the aim of this study does not extend to the multi-regional modelling of climate change, detailed analysis of these models is beyond the scope of this chapter.

Blitzer et al. (1994) specify a dynamic AGE model with special attention to energy to analyse carbon emission restrictions for an individual country (Egypt). One of the most distinctive features of this model is that it has a discrete modelling of production technologies (that is, an activity analysis). Carbon emissions are coupled to production and consumption activities via fixed coefficients, much as in the global energy-economy models. They show that the impact of carbon emission restrictions on GDP is highly non-linear and that sector-specific reduction targets have higher economic costs than global targets and may even be infeasible. Smajgl (2002) extends the energy

AGE analysis by including fossil fuel extraction and shows how fossil fuel scarcity interacts with carbon emission restrictions.

In the early 1990s, Jorgenson and Wilcoxen (1990, 1993a, b) used econometric estimation to construct an intertemporal applied general equilibrium model. A similar study was carried out by Hazilla and Kopp (1990). These models have a much larger basis in empirical data for the specification of model parameters than calibrated models. Since long-lasting panel data are not widely available, econometric AGEs have not become popular. For practical reasons most modellers prefer to calibrate their parameter values using existing literature. Moreover, the econometric approach can only be applied to those environmental problems that are 'well established' in the sense that time series data are available on emissions and abatement costs. Since some environmental problems (such as dispersion of fine dust) have only recently gained policy attention, such time series data on abatement costs are not available for all major environmental problems.

Vennemo (1997) pays detailed attention to the feedbacks from the environment to the economy based on several air pollutants. These feedbacks go via the impact of environmental quality on utility, via reduced labour productivity and via increased capital depreciation. Using a dynamic AGE model of the Ramsey type, he analyses what happens in the economy if these feedbacks are introduced and finds substantial reductions in consumption and GDP in the second half of the twenty-first century.

Rasmussen (2001) extends the Ramsey model with learning-by-doing in the renewable energy sector to capture endogenous technological progress. He finds that the presence of endogenous interactions between carbon abatement and technological progress leads to substantially lower abatement costs and a lower optimal level of short-term emission reductions due to rapidly declining abatement costs over time. Van der Zwaan et al. (2002) and Gerlagh and van der Zwaan (2003) use a similar approach, while specifying multiple technologies. They find that including endogenous innovation will lead to earlier and cheaper emission-reductions than models with exogenous technological change predict, especially through the development of carbon-free technologies.

Bye (2000) analyses an environmental tax reform and the possibilities of a double dividend in a Ramsey-type dynamic AGE model for Norway. She finds that a small welfare gain from the environmental tax reform is possible, partially because a shift from leisure to labour boosts employment. Moreover, existing tax inefficiencies are reduced. In countries where the marginal costs of public funds are high, such as Norway, the welfare gains from reducing distortionary taxes can be substantial. This issue is also emphasised by Goulder (1995), though he concludes that a double dividend cannot be reaped. Babiker et al. (2003) show in a large-scale empirical model that redistributing the proceeds of environmental taxes via a reduction of existing distortionary taxes may not always have superior welfare effects to redistributing the proceeds as lump sums. For more detailed analyses of the welfare implications of an environmental tax reform in an analytical framework, see Bovenberg and de Mooij (1994), Bovenberg and Goulder (1996), Ligthart and van der Ploeg (1999) and de Mooij (1999).

Jensen (2000) also uses a Ramsey-type model in an analysis of carbon taxes in Denmark. He shows that delaying abatement activities while keeping the accumulated emission reductions within the model horizon constant can substantially reduce the economic costs of environmental policy. Given the significant structural differences between a large economy such as the USA and relatively small open economies such as Norway, Denmark or The Netherlands, comparisons of the numerical results are complicated. Perhaps even more importantly, though all these models share their micro-economic foundation as they are based on a Ramsey-type model with perfect foresight and intertemporal optimisation of utility, there are specific differences between the models, for instance with respect to functional forms of the production functions or assumed mobility of capital across sectors.

A recent contribution to the literature of dynamic environmental AGE models is from Dissou et al. (2002). They introduce monopolistic competition in a Ramsey-type model for Canada with carbon emissions. The numerical results on the costs of compliance with the Kyoto Protocol suggest that the competition setting may have only a minor impact on the estimated GDP losses, while the estimated welfare costs are substantially higher in the monopolistic competition setting than in the more common perfect competition framework.

2.3.4 Representing Environmental Problems in Environmental Themes[8]

In this study, environmental problems are aggregated into so-called environmental themes. In the words of VROM (1998b, p. 211): 'An environmental theme is a label used to refer to closely interrelated environmental problems. Classifying by theme makes "passing the buck" from one environmental medium (soil, water or air) to another visible'. The main rationale for using environmental themes in this book is that they form the basis for environmental policy in The Netherlands. Moreover, combining different related polluting substances in an environmental theme ensures that the interactions between the substances involved are properly taken into account. The emissions of different substances that contribute to a certain environmental theme are converted to theme-equivalents to be able to add them up. The conversion matrix from polluting substances to environmental themes is given in Appendix 2.I. The environmental themes used in this book, and the basis for the theme-equivalents, are discussed below. For more details on these environmental problems see Adriaanse (1993), European Environmental Agency (1998) and RIVM (2002a).

Climate change

Climate change encompasses both the enhanced greenhouse effect and the depletion of the (stratospheric) ozone layer (VROM, 1998b). The increase in temperature induced by so-called greenhouse gases is known as the greenhouse effect. This is a natural phenomenon that is vital for life. Emissions of greenhouse gases mix uniformly in the earth's atmosphere and remain there for a long time. Major gases that contribute to the enhanced greenhouse effect are carbon dioxide (CO_2), methane (CH_4), nitrous oxide (N_2O), chlorofluorocarbons (CFCs), hydrochlorofluorocarbons (HCFCs), hydrofluorocarbons (HFCs) and halons. Increased concentrations of these greenhouse gases in the atmosphere lead to among other things, an increase in global atmospheric temperature, more extreme weather events (for example, tropical storms), a rise in sea levels and, hence, more floods. For more information see Houghton et al. (1992) and Metz et al. (2001).

Many human economic activities cause the emissions of greenhouse gases. The most important are combustion and transformation of energy, industrial processes, agriculture, extraction and distribution of fossil fuels, waste treatment and disposal, solvent use and transport.

The different greenhouse gases can all be expressed in CO_2-equivalents, based on their long-term global warming potentials. The global warming potential of a greenhouse gas is derived from the relative contribution to radiative forcing compared to the contribution of CO_2 (see IPCC, 1996, for more details).

The depletion of the ozone layer is primarily caused by CFCs. International environmental policy agreements targeted at the reduction of CFCs emissions, mainly the Montreal Protocol, were very successful in the early 1990s. The use of CFCs in new appliances is banned. Hence, the only remaining emissions stem from existing appliances. Over time, these will phase out and consequently CFC policy targets will be reached without additional policies. Therefore, there is no need to include the depletion of the ozone layer as a separate environmental theme in this study. Consequently, the theme Climate change only concerns the enhanced greenhouse effect.

Acidification

The most important acidifying substances emitted as a consequence of human activities are sulphur dioxide (SO_2), nitrogen oxides (NO and NO_2) and ammonia (NH_3). Their reaction products are acids (H_2SO_4, HNO_2 and HNO_3)

and aerosols that may be converted into acids. The deposition of these acids in the form of acid rain causes damage to flora and fauna, especially to trees, and to buildings in cities. Moreover, in agriculture crop yields diminish due to the acidic environment.

Acidifying substances are emitted mostly via combustion and transformation of energy, industrial processes, transport and agriculture. The various acidifying substances are aggregated into acid-equivalents, using their content expressed in moles of potentially available acid (H^+).

Eutrophication

Nutrients, including phosphates (P) and nitrogens (N) are essential for all organisms. An excess of nutrients, however, benefits more opportunistic, quickly growing species at the expense of less opportunistic, slower growing species. This causes changes in the ecosystem. The greater the added nutrient flows, the larger the concentrations of nutrients in water and soil are and the fewer species will remain. Eutrophication is caused to a large extent by agriculture via the extensive use of fertiliser, but also by households and industrial processes.

The equivalent nutrient emission is the weighted sum of N and P emissions, using the 'natural occurrence' weights 0.1 and 1, respectively (RIVM, 2002b).

Smog formation

'Summer smog' or 'photochemical smog' is a type of air pollution in which oxidants are formed that have negative effects on life. This smog type often occurs on sunny summer days with low wind velocities in regions where volatile organic compounds (VOCs), carbon monoxide (CO) and nitrogen oxides (NO_x) are emitted. The presence of sunlight and these gases in the lower 12 km of the atmosphere (that is, the troposphere) enables a complex and highly non-linear set of chemical reactions to occur, in which ozone is formed; therefore, this environmental theme is sometimes labelled 'Tropospheric ozone'. The emissions of VOCs are the critical factor in the formation of ozone, which affects human health and flora and fauna. Continuously increased ozone concentrations damage natural and agricultural vegetation. The peak levels occurring at summer smog conditions have a negative influence on the respiratory organs, irritate the mucous membranes of the eyes, nose and throat of humans and probably of many animals, and cause visible damage to plants.

The main sources of VOC emissions are the use of solvents (for example, in paint), road transport and agriculture; households are another major emitter of VOCs. Both Smog formation and Dispersion of fine dust concern local air quality and have a relatively short life span.

Dispersion of fine dust

The effects of particulate matter in the air depend on their size and composition. Fine particles, smaller than 10 micrometers (PM_{10}), are inhaled and affect human health. Irritation of mucous membranes may occur at high dosages. Dust from sources such as road traffic has carcinogenic components, including polycyclic aromatic carbohydrates (PAC) and asbestos. The smaller the particles are, the more easily they are inhaled into the lungs. Road transport is the main source of fine particles, especially via wear and tear of tyres.

Desiccation

Desiccation is a collective term for all effects of the lowering of the groundwater table on forests, nature and the landscape, both as a result of water shortage and changes in the effects of seepage and precipitation. Major causes are drainage of agricultural area and groundwater extraction for drinking and industrial use. This process has been going on in The Netherlands for a long time, and intensified in the latter half of the last century. The main effects are the impoverishment of natural vegetation and its sequential effects, particularly on fauna.

Soil contamination

Soil contamination refers to situations where pollutants are present in the soil, preventing some or all soil functions and threatening human health or ecosystems. Contaminated soils are categorised as severely or non-severely contaminated, urgent or not urgent and investigated or not investigated. One of the problems involved with the theme Soil contamination is that the inventory of all contaminated sites is not yet completed, let alone that all suspected sites have been investigated. As a consequence, it is extremely difficult to model this environmental theme properly. Therefore, only a rough estimate of the total costs of cleaning up polluted soils are taken into account in this book, without attempting to assign these costs to different actors.

Desiccation and Soil contamination are treated in this book in a different way than the other environmental themes. The assumption is made that these two themes are not related to emissions by the production sectors or private households, but rather that they constitute a necessary expense for the government. This is in line with the historical observation that the majority of the costs involved for these two themes are borne by the government.

Other environmental themes

Several other environmental themes exist, some of which have already been discussed in Section 2.3. These include dispersion to water, biodiversity, waste management, disturbance (including noise and odour nuisance and major external hazards) and resource dissipation, that is, the efficient and sustainable use of natural resources. Though these environmental themes are by no means unimportant, they are excluded from the analysis, as major data (including abatement cost curves) and/or conceptual problems have to be resolved before they can be included.

2.4 DISCUSSION AND CONCLUSIONS

This chapter shows that there are many alternative specifications of environmental-economic models, each of which serves its own purpose. Nonetheless, a methodology that can properly assess both the direct and indirect costs of environmental policies (research question 1 in Chapter 1), and that covers pollution and abatement of major environmental problems simultaneously in a dynamic applied economic model (research question 2 in Chapter 1), does not exist. Given the research questions laid down in Chapter 1 and based on the analysis of existing literature, the model to be specified in this book should contain the following characteristics (see Section 2.2.1).

- An *applied general equilibrium* (AGE) approach is suitable because, among other things, it allows for a detailed sectoral specification and covers all the indirect economic effects of environmental policy. Consequently, the indirect costs of environmental policies can be properly assessed (research question 1 in Chapter 1). The neo-classical framework of the AGE approach also gives the model a firm foundation in micro-economic theory. If intergenerational incidence of environmental policy costs is a major aim of the analysis, an overlapping generations (OLG) approach may provide superior results. Nonetheless, for calculating the economic and welfare costs of environmental policy a dynamic AGE approach using Ramsey's framework has the advantage that it is easier to calibrate and hence allows for more empirical detail.
- The choice of an *applied* model instead of a theoretical analysis follows directly from the empirical research questions 3-5 and needs no further explanation.
- The model should be *dynamic*, as the underlying processes are essentially dynamic in nature. For example, the abatement costs of existing measures are often decreasing significantly over time and climate change is caused by concentrations, that is, accumulated emissions, of greenhouse gases. Furthermore, comparative-static models can lead to biased results if the underlying mechanisms are dynamic; this issue will be investigated in more detail in Chapter 3.

Finally, a dynamic model allows for an analysis of the impact of timing of environmental policies as the transition path towards the new equilibrium is explicitly portrayed (research question 5 in Chapter 1).

- The decision whether the model should specify *myopic or forward-looking behaviour* for the households is postponed to the next chapter, where this choice is analysed in detail.

- The model should be *deterministic*. A stochastic approach would have the advantage that the uncertainties inherent in the environmental-economic anaysis are explicitly represented in the model. Leaving the deterministic approach implies, however, a substantial complication of the model and is beyond the scope of this book.

- Long-term time series data are not available for all economic and environmental variables. Therefore, the model parameters will have to be *calibrated*, not estimated. Calibration has the advantage that currently emerging environmental problems, for which by definition no time series are available, can also be covered in the model.

- The research here focuses on environmental policy in The Netherlands from a macro-economic perspective, and therefore the geographical scale of the model should be *national*.

- The environmental and economic submodules should be *integrated as far as possible*. The specific links are described below.

- Environmental problems should be captured in so-called *environmental themes*. The aggregation of several interacting pollutants in one environmental theme ensures that the interactions between related pollutants are properly taken into account. Moreover, environmental policy in The Netherlands is specified in terms of environmental themes and hence using the same set-up here is helpful in answering empirical research questions 3-5 in Chapter 1.

- Emissions should be specified as a *necessary input* in the production and utility functions. While the alternative approach of modelling emissions as an 'undesirable', joint output of production may provide the most accurate modelling of process-integrated abatement measures, the input approach has major advantages as it allows a natural way of modelling emission permits and allows a link of emissions to specific inputs. Moreover, the explicit modelling of all available technologies, as commonly done in the joint-output approach, is not pragmatic for wide-ranged analysis with potentially large numbers of alternative technologies.

- *Abatement* is itself an economic activity and should be modelled as such. Many models ignore the interactions between abatement activities and the rest of the economy, even though these interactions may be significant. There is no readily available methodology to include the empirical direct costs of abatement measures in a top-down economic model; such a methodology will be discussed in Chapter 3. Consistent modelling of the direct costs of abatement measures improves the assessment of economic costs of environmental policy and therefore contributes to research questions 1, 3 and 4 in Chapter 1.

- Given the lack of empirical data, no *feedback mechanism* from the environment to the economy, for instance via production damages, is specified. This implies that the optimal level of pollution abatement cannot be calculated and no evaluation can be made whether or not the costs of environmental policy are justified. The analysis has to be confined to a cost-effectiveness analysis of an exogenously given policy target.
- *Endogenous specification of technological progress* is desirable from a theoretical perspective, but may not be feasible for empirical analyses. The methodology developed in the next chapter exhibits endogenous diffusion of technology, while environmental innovation is exogenously captured.

Summarising, this book focuses on the development of a multi-sectoral dynamic AGE model in which several environmental themes are covered simultaneously. A methodology is developed that allows for explicit attention for available abatement options, including non-energy-related environmental problems, and the detailed specification of abatement costs. The integration of such bottom-up information into a top-down model for multiple environmental themes is new. In this way, both the direct and indirect costs of multi-pollutant environmental policies can be properly assessed and the research questions can be answered.

NOTES

1. They label neo-Keynesian models 'new Keynesian models'; this is just one example of the lack of a common terminology encountered in the literature.
2. Some authors prefer the name *computable* general equilibrium model (CGE). There seems to be no consensus in the literature on the differences between CGEs and AGEs.
3. Advanced AGE models can have more general restrictions; for example, temporary profits may be implemented if a producer can exert some monopoly power.
4. This condition does not have to hold when decreasing or increasing returns to scale are assumed. In those cases, the condition can be formulated more generally as profit maximisation subject to technology constraints.
5. The rate of return on capital includes dividend to stockholders and interest payments to creditors.
6. The term 'comparative' is used to indicate that two distinct equilibria are compared.
7. For more information on this non-parametric approach to production analysis, see Varian (1984).

8.   The description of the natural science behind the environmental themes is based on de Boer
     (2000a) and Ignaciuk et al. (2002).

APPENDIX 2.I   CONVERSION FACTORS FOR ENVIRONMENTAL THEMES

Table A2.1   Environmental theme equivalents

		Climate change (CO_2-equiv.)	Acidifica-tion (acid-equivalent)	Eutrophica-tion (P-equiv.)	Smog formation (kilogram)	Dispersion of fine dust (kilogram)
CO_2	(kg.)	1.000	0	0	0	0
CH_4	(kg.)	36.699	0	0	0	0
N_2O	(kg.)	142.131	0	0	0	0
CFC_{11}	(kg.)	1480.742	0	0	0	0
CFC_{12}	(kg.)	4286.496	0	0	0	0
CFC_{113}	(kg.)	2075.424	0	0	0	0
CFC_{114}	(kg.)	5763.356	0	0	0	0
CFC_{115}	(kg.)	10370.177	0	0	0	0
$Halon_{121}$	(kg.)	650.629	0	0	0	0
$Halon_{1301}$	(kg.)	2862.767	0	0	0	0
NO_x	(kg.)	0	0.022	0	0	0
SO_2	(kg.)	0	0.031	0	0	0
NH_3	(kg.)	0	0.059	0	0	0
P	(kg.)	0	0	1.000	0	0
N	(kg.)	0	0	0.100	0	0
VOC[*]	(kg.)	0	0	0	1.000	0
PM_{10}	(kg.)	0	0	0	0	1.000

Note: [*] Volatile Organic Compounds, excluding methane.

Source: Statistics Netherlands (2000).

3. Dynamic analysis of pollution and abatement in an applied general equilibrium model[*]

3.1 INTRODUCTION

In order to make a good assessment of the economic costs of environmental policy, it is important how the abatement costs, and the characteristics of the underlying abatement techniques, are specified. The main objective of this chapter is to develop a methodology to integrate bottom-up information on the abatement techniques into a top-down multi-sectoral applied general equilibrium (AGE) framework. To this end, a dynamic AGE model is constructed including pollution and abatement. Special emphasis is placed on the inclusion of the abatement options in the economic model. Key abatement information to be included is (i) the potential emission reduction that can be achieved when all available abatement measures are fully implemented, (ii) the curvature of the abatement cost curves, and (iii) the cost components of the abatement measures.

The dynamic setting is essential, as most of the major interactions between economy and environment are dynamic in nature (see Chapter 2). The impacts of the dynamic issues are analysed using (i) a comparative-static specification, (ii) a recursive-dynamic specification, and (iii) a forward-looking specification.

This chapter describes a methodology that combines the advantages of the top-down approach with the main information of the bottom-up approach. Standard AGE models do not pay explicit attention to the characteristics of the technologies involved, but use smooth, continuous production and utility functions (see Chapter 2). This is a common criticism from technically-oriented scientists of these top-down economic models. However, the large number of technological options available for pollution reduction complicates the use of discrete technology modelling in broad empirical environmental-economic analysis. Models that do consider the technical aspects of changing economic structures usually do not model the indirect economic effects of these technologies (Seebregts et al., 2001). In the long run the economic impacts of environmental policy are likely to be significant and hence such a partial approach is not suitable. The model presented here combines the detailed information on the direct costs of pollution abatement with a proper assessment of the indirect costs.

Section 3.2 compares different approaches to a dynamic specification of the AGE model. Section 3.3 comprises an outline of the main economic and environmental modelling issues. Section 3.4 presents a numerical example that illustrates the working of the model. Finally, Section 3.5 contains the discussion and conclusions of this chapter.

3.2   DIFFERENT APPROACHES TO DYNAMIC AGE MODELS

Three prototype AGE models are discussed, each reflecting a different approach to the modelling issues: a comparative-static model, a recursive-dynamic model and a forward-looking dynamic model.

The *comparative-static model* is the simplest AGE model. Essentially, the comparative-static model is a static model, where an equilibrium at one point in time is compared to an equilibrium that would emerge when some policy impulse is given. The comparative-static model is useful in illustrating the equilibrium that may emerge in the long run and can be used to analyse the steady state properties of the equilibrium. This type of model, however, cannot be used to analyse the transition paths from the current equilibrium to a new equilibrium. Two authors who have persistently analysed pollution using static AGE models are Bergman (see for example Bergman, 1988 and 1991) and Conrad (see Conrad and Schroeder, 1991, 1993; Conrad, 1992; and Böhringer et al., 2000). These models focus on national economies. For the Dutch economy, static AGE models with pollution include Mot et al. (1989), Dellink and Jansen (1995), Komen (2000) and Gerlagh et al. (2002). Recent additions to the international literature include Felder and Schleiniger (2002) and Nugent and Sarma (2002); an overview of environmental-economic AGEs is given in Conrad (1999, 2001).

The *recursive-dynamic model* is characterised by a series of individual one-period AGE model simulations and is based on the assumption that agents in the economy have no forward-looking behaviour. Hence, the model can be solved recursively, for each period separately, where the periods are linked through the changes in endowments, including the capital stock. In comparison to the comparative-static model, the recursive-dynamic approach has major advantages: it enables the calculation of the transition path from the initial steady state to a new steady state. The inclusion of the transition path may have significant impacts on any policy recommendation to be drawn from the analysis. A well-known example of a large-scale environmental-economic model using a recursive-dynamic framework is the EPPA model (Babiker et al., 2001).

The *forward-looking model* is a standard Ramsey-type AGE model with perfect foresight. This type has the advantage over recursive-dynamic models that consumers maximise their utility not only based on the current state of the economy, but also on future welfare (discounted to present values). Recursive-dynamic models lack this intertemporal aspect. Empirical estimates suggest that, in reality, consumers look ahead to some extent, but do not maximise their utility till infinity (see Srinivasan, 1982; and Ballard and Goulder, 1985). Consequently, the forward-looking and recursive-dynamic models provide extreme cases between which decision-making in reality resides. The perfect foresight assumption has been used in many empirical environmental-economic general equilibrium models. Jorgenson has carried out several dynamic analyses of environmental policy questions within an AGE context (see for example Jorgenson and Wilcoxen, 1990, 1993a, b). He uses econometric estimation of the relevant parameters, based on long-term US economic data. Other empirical studies using dynamic AGE models with emissions are Manne and Richels's MERGE model (Manne and Richels, 1995, 1999), Böhringer (1998), Böhringer et al. (1999), Rutherford (2000) and Rasmussen (2001). To an increasing extent, aspects from endogenous growth theory are used in these models; see Jaffe et al. (2002) and Löschel (2002) for an overview.

Both the recursive-dynamic and forward-looking specifications are based on neo-classical growth theory. As discussed in Chapter 2, there are two basic types of neo-classical growth models: (i) the Solow-Swan models with a fixed savings rate, and (ii) the Cass-Koopmans-Ramsey models where the optimal savings rate is determined within a forward-looking framework. For an overview of neo-classical growth theory, see for example Chaudhuri (1989) and Barro and Sala-i-Martin (1995).

The model types discussed above are based on approximation of the infinite-horizon assumption with a finite number of periods. A model is set up for T periods, and all periods after that horizon are irrelevant to the model (though so-called 'transversality conditions' concerning capital stock and utility are used to avoid erratic results for the last period). Consequently, the total number of markets (both current and future) and thus the number of decision variables is finite. Alternatively, one could specify an infinite-horizon model. These include two sub-types: Overlapping Generations (OLG) models and dynastic models. In OLG models, consumers live for a finite time (longer than one period but shorter than the model horizon), so that in each period, two or more generations co exist; the number of generations is infinite. In this way, the OLG framework deviates from the dynastic model, which assumes a finite number of consumers that live infinitely long (see Ginsburgh and Keyzer, 1997). Good examples of environmental-economic OLG-models are presented in Gerlagh (1998), Wendner (2001) and Bovenberg and Heijdra (2002).

3.3   A PROTOTYPE AGE MODEL WITH POLLUTION AND ABATEMENT

This section outlines the prototype AGE model with pollution and abatement. As discussed above, there are several ways in which the economic dynamics can be specified. Therefore, in Section 3.3.1, three alternative settings ('model specifications') are distinguished: (i) a comparative-static specification, (ii) a recursive-dynamic specification, and (iii) a forward-looking specification. Section 3.3.2 deals with the inclusion of environmental issues into the economic model specifications and Section 3.3.3 describes in detail how the technical information on pollution abatement techniques can be handled in the model. The source codes for these three model specifications are downloadable from the website of Wageningen University: http://www.socialsciences.wur.nl/enr/gams.

3.3.1   Modelling Economic Issues

The model specifications outlined in this chapter are of the *applied general equilibrium* (AGE) type. A general equilibrium model consists of a set of 'economic agents' (households and firms), each of which demands and supplies commodities or services, hereafter denoted in brief as 'goods'. Agents are assumed to behave rationally. Each agent solves its own optimisation problem. The agents take prices, which provide information about the decision environment (such as the behaviour of other agents and government policies), as given. Equilibrium is defined as the allocation of resources such that the actions of all agents are mutually consistent and can be executed simultaneously. In other words, demand equals supply on all markets, and equilibrium is attained through adjusting relative prices (see Shoven and Whalley, 1992; or Ginsburgh and Keyzer, 1997).

All three model specifications use a common accounting matrix for the base year of the benchmark projection. The assumption is made that this base year is consistent with a balanced growth path. This implies that investments are sufficient to (i) replace depreciated capital, and (ii) augment the capital stock, so that capital grows at the same speed as labour supply. The benchmark projection for the recursive-dynamic and forward-looking model specifications consists of the balanced growth path that is determined by the base year accounting matrix and the balanced growth rate. For the comparative-static model, the balanced growth path is not specified, as there is only one period modelled. To make this specification as comparable as possible to the other specifications, the balanced growth condition on investments is also imposed in the comparative-static specification.

There are two categories of agents: consumers and producers. For reasons of simplicity, international trade is not modelled in this chapter. Consumers maximise their utility under a budget constraint, for given prices and given initial endowments. Producers maximise profits under the restriction of their production technology, for given prices. Demand and supply, which result from the agents' optimisation problems, meet each other on the markets. The model is specified in a complementarity format in the software package GAMS/MPSGE.

The *private households* are included as the single representative consumer. They own the production factors labour and capital (the endowments) and consume produced goods. A nested CES-type[1] utility function is used to determine how much of each good is consumed.

In the comparative-static and recursive-dynamic model, the households optimise current, or instantaneous, utility subject to the current budget constraint. In the recursive-dynamic model, this current budget constraint is applied to all periods separately. In the forward-looking model, the households maximise the present value of current and future utility. In this case, the private households' budget constraint is only applied to the present value of all periods, that is, there are in principal unrestricted opportunities for borrowing and saving for the private households. However, in this closed economy such an intertemporal transfer of funds cannot occur, as all other agents obey a per period budget constraint.

Labour supply is fixed, but the wage rate is fully flexible; an exogenous growth of labour supply is assumed. Growth in labour supply reflects increases in the population as well as a more efficient use of labour due to increases in technological efficiency, that is, labour productivity increases. This labour-augmenting growth drives the growth of the economy. In the comparative-static model there is no increase in labour supply as there are no periods distinguished; the growth rate is, however, used in this specification to calculate the investment and capital stock for the base year accounting matrix.

In all three specifications, the *capital stock* is determined endogenously, but the way in which capital and investment are modelled differs between the alternative specifications. In the comparative-static model, the capital stock is determined by steady state requirements, where the rental price of capital is constrained so that the price of new capital equals the price of existing capital (that is, the value of Tobin's Q equals unity; see Hayashi, 1982). This guarantees that capital grows at the same speed as labour supply. These conditions also determine the optimal savings and investment level in the comparative-static model.

In the recursive-dynamic model, total capital stock and investment level are determined for each period after solving the model for that period, assuming a constant proportion of household income for savings.[2] The endogenous rental price of capital adjusts such that demand for capital equals supply, which is determined by the savings decision of the households. Then, using the new investment level and capital stock, the model is solved for the next period. The recursive-dynamic specification is hence essentially a model in the Solow-Swan tradition.

In the forward-looking model, the rate of return on investments is determined on the domestic market.[3] The capital stock and investment levels are fully endogenised; households choose to save part of their income until the rate of return on investments equals the exogenously given interest rate. In turn, producers use these savings as capital investments. The consumers are endowed with a certain capital stock in the first period. They demand capital in the last period, to ensure that the transversality condition is satisfied. The transversality condition states that the capital stock in the last period should equal capital stock in the period before times one plus the balanced growth rate of the economy.[4] The forward-looking behaviour of the agents and the endogenous savings rate make this a model of the Cass-Koopmans-Ramsey type.

The *government sector* collects taxes on all traded goods and factors and uses the proceeds to finance public consumption of the produced goods and pay for a lump-sum transfer to the private household. For government behaviour the assumption is made that government utility is unaffected by the model simulations, that is, it follows the balanced growth path as determined in the benchmark projection (the common 'equal yield' assumption). This is achieved by proportionately changing the existing tax rates to compensate changes in income and/or expenditures of the government. This implies that the government budget surplus/deficit remains constant over all periods.

Producers (firms) have a limited choice of technologies with which to produce and maximise their profits under given prices. The potential substitution between the different production technologies is captured via a nested-CES production function. Inputs in this production function are labour and capital and intermediate deliveries from the other producing sectors. Each producer produces one unique output from the inputs. As full competition and constant returns to scale are assumed, no excess profits can be reaped and the maximum-profit-condition diminishes to a least-cost condition.

3.3.2   Modelling Environmental Issues

In the model both production and consumption processes lead to *pollution*. As argued in Chapter 2, there are several ways to link pollution to economic activity. The approach used here follows Bergman (1991) and others; pollution is linked to total production and consumption values of each polluter on the input side of the production and utility functions.

Environmental policy is implemented by means of tradable pollution permits. Practical considerations may lead to a different choice of policy instrument in reality. Nonetheless, the approach taken here can serve as a reference point for evaluating other policy instruments. Tradable permits are also a natural extension of the AGE approach as they can be regarded as traded commodities for which demand cannot exceed supply and market clearance is reached via a set of equilibrium prices.

Polluters have to buy the pollution permits in order to produce and consume. In the model, the pollution permits are regarded as a necessary input for the production and utility functions. To account for the fact that different pollutants contribute to the same environmental problem, pollution is aggregated into environmental themes using equivalence factors for different pollutants. All major greenhouse gases are aggregated into the environmental theme Climate change using the global warming potentials of the different pollutants. Similarly, acidifying emissions are aggregated into the theme Acidification.

In the benchmark projection, the government distributes exactly the number of permits that allows the producers and consumers to maintain their original behaviour. In the policy scenarios, pollution is controlled by the government by means of annual tradable pollution permits that the producers and consumers can buy from the government. The government uses the proceeds from the permit sales to reduce existing taxes. In this way, a market for pollution permits is created, where prices are determined endogenously by equating demand and supply. Polluters have the choice between paying for their pollution permits and investing in pollution abatement. This choice is endogenous in the model, and the polluters will always choose the cheaper of the two. A third possibility for producers and consumers is reducing production and consumption of the pollution intensive good, respectively. This reduction of economic activity becomes a sensible option when both the marginal abatement cost and the price of the permits are higher than the value added foregone in reducing production or utility foregone in reducing consumption.

Environmental quality is not directly included in the utility function. Instead, it is assumed that the government sets the environmental targets by issuing a restricted number of pollution permits. Consumers' environmental expenditures on pollution permits and abatement do have an impact on the maximum achievable consumption and utility level, but environmental stocks and damages are not taken into account. In policy terms, the model is not used for Pigouvian analyses (Pigou, 1938), where the optimal tax rate is determined by the trade-off between abatement costs and damage costs, but rather for Baumollian exercises, where the cost-effective way to reach a predetermined policy target is analysed (Baumol, 1977).

The calibration of the possibilities and costs of *abatement* options is important to get a good estimate of the economic costs of environmental policy. In most of the literature, the abatement costs are only implicitly modelled, as profit or utility losses, or modelled through a quadratic abatement cost curve (for example, Nordhaus and Yang, 1996). Key exceptions are the detailed energy-economic models (for example, Manne et al., 1995) that specify alternative ways to produce energy (a form of emission abatement), but these do not include end-of-pipe measures. More general specifications of abatement are used by Nestor and Pasurka (1995a), Böhringer (1998) and Hyman et al. (2002). A key feature of the methodology presented below is that the expenditures on abatement are specified to cover as much information as possible on the technical measures underlying the abatement options. The use of marginal abatement cost curves as an input into an AGE model is opposite to the approach used in, for example, Ellerman and Decaux (1998) and Eyckmans et al. (2001), where marginal abatement cost curves are derived as output from an AGE analysis.

3.3.3   Including Bottom-up Abatement Information

The inclusion of bottom-up information on abatement techniques involves several steps. Firstly, abatement cost curves are constructed for each environmental theme. Secondly, per environmental theme a so-called 'Pollution – Abatement Substitution' (PAS) curve is estimated that best describes the abatement cost curve. Thirdly, key information from these PAS curves, containing the theme-specific potential for emission reduction via abatement techniques and the elasticities that describe the curvature of the abatement cost curves, is integrated into the economic model. Fourthly, the supply of abatement techniques and the associated cost components are included in the model using a fictitious 'Abatement production sector'. Each step will be elaborated upon below.

As the *first* step in including technical abatement information in the model, abatement cost curves are constructed for each environmental theme from the raw technical data for the base year. This step involves making an inventory of all available options to reduce pollution, either end-of-pipe or process integrated. Every option is characterised as a reduction measure that states how much pollution can be reduced with this option and what the costs of implementing the option are. These raw technical data come from existing inventories; for Climate change, the ICARUS database is used (Blok et al., 1991). The inventories for other environmental themes are described in Dellink and van der Woerd (1997).

The pollution reduction realised by each measure is given as a fixed amount in physical units. Therefore, the measures have to be interpreted as additive. In this way, cumulative pollution reductions and the corresponding cumulative abatement costs can be calculated. In the abatement cost curve, all measures are ranked by cost-effectiveness. This involves solving some methodological and practical issues such as how to deal with measures that exclude each other and measures that have to be taken in a fixed order. For details on this first step see Dellink and van der Woerd (1997). Note that this ranking implies that the abatement cost curves are convex.

Note also that the abatement cost curves contain all known available technical options to reduce pollution, both end-of-pipe as well as process-integrated options, including substitution between different inputs (for example, fuel-switch). Taking process-integrated measures into account is very important as they account for a substantial and increasing part of all reduction potential. However, reliable cost estimates for this type of measure may be more difficult to gather (Pasurka, 2001). The abatement cost curve does not contain economic restructuring, that is, changing production quantities of the different sectors. Output changes and associated changes in consumption are covered endogenously in the economic model through the markets for produced goods.

In the construction of the abatement cost curves, all costs are transformed into annual costs, including capital costs (annuity interest and depreciation payments) of investments. In the model, these capital costs of abatement investments are treated similarly to 'conventional' man-made capital, that is, the firms pay the capital costs while the households provide the means necessary for investments (in the form of savings).[5] This means that the order in which the measures are represented in the abatement cost curve is appropriate to the way rational firms decide upon the adoption of a measure. The additional assumption is made that the measures will be renewed at the end of their lifetime; this implies that the annual costs are constant throughout the model horizon. Potential liquidity problems due to high investments in a single year are ignored, which resembles a situation where the polluters are always able to negotiate a loan at the market interest rate.

In the *second* step of the procedure, the abatement cost curves are translated for each environmental theme into the PAS curve. This means that the abatement costs are presented as a function of pollution (a downward sloping curve). Then, for each theme a CES function (the PAS curve) is calibrated to best fit the abatement cost curve. This function states that different combinations of pollution and abatement can deliver the same 'environmental services', that is, they allow the same level of production for firms or the same level of consumption for the households. A constant elasticity of substitution governs how much additional abatement is needed to reduce pollution by one additional unit. The sum of the squared vertical distances between the empirical abatement cost curve and the modelled PAS curve is minimised (a standard OLS estimation). The difference between estimated and actual abatement expenditures is weighed with the pollution reduction achieved by the technical measure to ensure that measures that reduce a lot of pollution are given sufficient weight in the procedure. The CES elasticity thus estimated describes the environmental theme-specific possibilities to substitute between pollution and abatement (hence the name 'Pollution – Abatement Substitution' curve) and reflects the marginal abatement costs.

The potential to reduce pollution through technical abatement activities, that is, without economic restructuring, provides an absolute upper bound on abatement in the model. This is a clear difference from the traditional quadratic abatement cost curves, where no true upper bound on abatement activities exists (the abatement costs will always be finite, no matter how much pollution is abated). The empirical importance of an absolute limit on environmental technology has been emphasised by Hueting (1996) and Hueting and de Boer (2001). The upper bound on abatement is implemented by assuming that part of the pollution ('technically abatable' emissions) can be reduced as a result of abatement activities, and the remaining part of pollution is directly coupled with the production quantity of the producers, and with total consumption of the private households. This remaining, 'technically unabatable', pollution can only be reduced via reduction in economic activity of these polluting sectors, sometimes labelled 'volume measures' (Hueting and de Boer, 2001).

Figure 3.1 illustrates the concept of the abatement cost curve and associated PAS curve. Note that the x-axis gives emissions instead of emission reductions. In the case of Climate change, emissions in The Netherlands might have been reduced from 254 megatons of CO_2-equivalents to 164 megatons of CO_2-equivalents in 1990, through implementing technical measures, without restructuring the economy and given the current state of technology. The graph and underlying data are based on analysis for 1990 as described in Dellink et al. (2001). Each mark on the abatement cost curve gives an individual technical measure; the line without markers shows the estimated PAS curve.

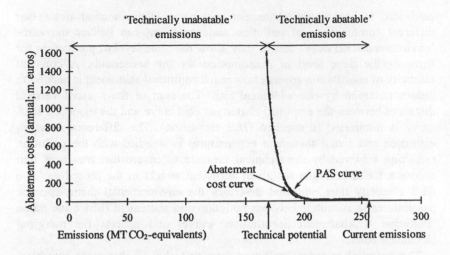

Figure 3.1   A Pollution – Abatement Substitution (PAS) curve for climate change

As the *third* step, the trade-off between pollution and abatement is modelled as a nested CES function that delivers 'environmental services'.[6] These environmental services are added to the production function via a Leontief function, indicating that some combination of emissions and abatement is necessary to be able to produce. The only way to reduce the level of environmental services is by reducing the production level. For consumers, the environmental services are coupled to total consumption in a Leontief manner.

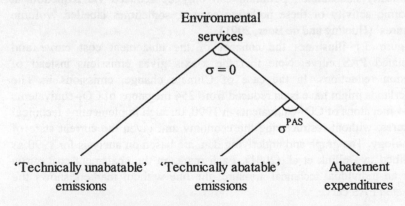

Figure 3.2   The CES nesting structure for emissions and abatement

The lower level of the function for environmental services brings together the 'technically abatable' emissions and expenditures on abatement with a substitution elasticity based on the PAS curve discussed above (σ^{PAS}). On the highest level, 'technically unabatable' emissions are combined with the aggregate of technically abatable emissions and the abatement expenditures, with a substitution elasticity of zero. This structure is shown graphically in Figure 3.2.

The *benchmark* division between technically abatable and technically unabatable emissions is based on the technical potential. This technical potential represents the share of total emissions that can be reduced via technical abatement measures, without economic restructuring. However, both technically abatable and technically unabatable emissions are endogenous in the model as they are related to abatement expenditures and economic activity, respectively. Hence this division will change with the policy simulations, as the model finds the optimal allocation under the restriction of environmental policy.

The *fourth* and final step concerns the abatement sector, which is modelled as a separate production sector. This fictitious sector produces 'abatement services' using both produced goods and primary production factors as inputs. This is roughly in line with Nestor and Pasurka (1995a), but in their study the abatement sector is an implicit part of the government sector and hence does not have a specific structure. In the model presented here, an abatement sector production function is calibrated on data that are derived from abatement cost curves. The inputs in this CES production function represent the cost components of the underlying technical measures, including capital costs and operational costs such as energy and labour costs. These so-called 'spending effects' are based on the average division between different cost components for all technical measures and hence are assumed to be constant over the complete abatement cost curve and do not differ between environmental themes.[7] Consequently, there is only one abatement sector, even though there is a separate PAS curve for each environmental theme. This assumption also implies that the cost-effectiveness of the different measures does not change over time; the order of the measures in the abatement cost curves will therefore also not change.

The output of the abatement sector is demanded by the other producers and by consumers, so each producer and consumer in principle has the same set of abatement technologies available. The costs of abatement will differ between the producers, as they have different initial combinations of abatement costs and pollution levels and hence demand different amounts of abatement services. The marginal abatement costs, however, will be equalised in the model, because the resulting equilibrium is characterised by cost-effectiveness. The marginal abatement costs in the new equilibrium will also equal the price of the pollution permits. Hence, all polluters are indifferent at the margin between polluting and investing in abatement.

3.4   A NUMERICAL EXAMPLE

The model specifications described above are illustrated with a numerical example, based on data for The Netherlands, with 1990 as the base year. This section shows the main mechanisms that are at work in the model and how these mechanisms are influenced by the basic modelling assumptions.

3.4.1   Parameter Values for the Numerical Example

Most data for the initial calibration year and parameter values are based on an aggregation of the data in the static version of the model as reported in Gerlagh et al. (2002). GDP is calibrated to 231 billion euros and abatement expenditures amount to 163 million euros. In interpreting the results one should keep in mind that the description of the economy is kept simple, with only three production sectors (Agriculture, Industry and Services) and no international trade. Moreover, the only environmental problems included are Climate change and Acidification.

The environmental data refer to emissions. Emissions for various substances are combined into environmental theme aggregates (see Chapter 2). For climate change, the emissions of CO_2, N_2O, CH_4 and various CFCs and halons are combined using their global warming potential;[8] total emissions in 1990 equal 254.53 billion CO_2-equivalents. For Acidification, the emissions of NO_x, SO_2 and NH_3 are aggregated using their acidifying potential;[9] total emissions for Acidification in 1990 amount to 40.18 million acid-equivalents.

The policy simulations with the recursive-dynamic and forward-looking model specifications will be compared to the common benchmark projection. In the benchmark it is assumed that the economy is in a steady state in the first year of the simulations (1990), and will continue to move along the balanced growth path. The benchmark projection is constructed through simulation of the model without the environmental policy impulse, but including a system of environmental permits, where the number of permits equals the pollution levels on the balanced growth path. The benchmark price of pollution permits is based on the slope of the PAS curve, that is, it is the shadow price of abatement at the initial combination of abatement and pollution. Moreover, there are positive abatement expenditures in the benchmark.

For the comparative-static model specification, the balanced growth path is not specified. The accounting matrix for the base year 1990 is identical to that for the recursive-dynamic and forward-looking model specifications.

The balanced growth path of the economy is fuelled by an autonomous increase in effective labour supply of 2 per cent per year. An autonomous pollution efficiency improvement of 1 per cent per year for acidifying emissions and 1.5 per cent for greenhouse gas emissions is assumed, resulting in a growth of emissions of 1 per cent and 0.5 per cent per year, respectively.[10] The resulting benchmark projections for emissions for greenhouse gases and acidifying emissions and for GDP (Gross Domestic Product) are represented in Figure 3.3.

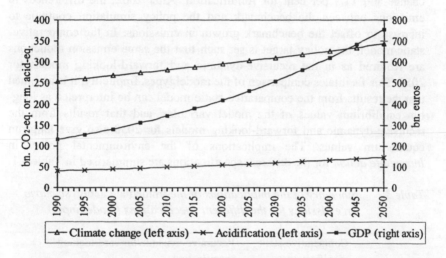

Figure 3.3 Benchmark projections for emissions and GDP

The substitution elasticity between abatement and technically abatable pollution is set to 1.26 for climate and 1.4 for acid related emissions (based on Verbruggen et al., 2001). The high autonomous efficiency improvement, high initial price, low substitution elasticity and low technical potential for Climate change abatement reflects an abatement curve with a relatively long initial part of very low costs, combined with a steep increase in marginal abatement costs further in the curve. For Acidification, the marginal abatement costs increase more gradually.

3.4.2   The Policy Scenarios

To analyse the influence of the choice of the policy scenario, three alternative scenarios are designed: an *Immediate action* scenario, a *Late action* scenario and an *Allow growth* scenario. These alternative policy simulations are chosen to clarify the mechanisms in the model and are not meant for policy recommendations.

The environmental policy impulse analysed in the *Immediate action* scenario is a stabilisation of emissions at the level of 1990 from 2002 onwards. As emissions have grown between 1990 and 2002, this implies a sudden reduction in the number of permits issued of 5.8 per cent for Climate change and 11.3 per cent for Acidification. After 2002, the differences in emissions between the benchmark and the policy simulation continue to increase to offset the benchmark growth in emissions. In the comparative-static model, the policy target is set such that the same emission reductions are required as in the recursive-dynamic and forward-looking models for 2050. This facilitates comparison of the model types. Implicitly, it is assumed that the results from the comparative-static model can be interpreted as long-run equilibrium values of the model variables, and that results from the recursive-dynamic and forward-looking models for 2050 also give long-run equilibrium values. The implications of the environmental policy in *Immediate action* for the different specifications are summarised in Table 3.1.

Table 3.1   Summary of the implications of the Immediate action *scenario on emissions for the different specifications (model input)*

	Comparative-static specification	Recursive-dynamic/forward-looking specification
Climate ch. emissions	-25.9% compared to benchmark	-5.8% compared to benchmark in 2002; stabilisation thereafter (in 2050: -25.9%)
Acidification emissions	-45.0% compared to benchmark	-11.3% compared to benchmark in 2002; stabilisation thereafter (in 2050: -45.0%)

The recursive-dynamic and forward-looking model specifications are highly suited to investigating the consequences of speeding up or deferring environmental policy targets. Therefore, an alternative policy simulation is investigated, labelled *Late action*. In this simulation, the policy target is stabilisation at the level of emissions in 1990, but implemented 10 years later than in the *Immediate action* scenario. Note that this delay in environmental policy will cause lasting differences in environmental quality for stock pollutants.

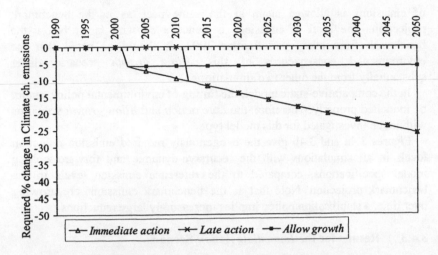

Figure 3.4a   The policy impulse for Climate change: exogenously required emission reductions in the simulations for the recursive-dynamic and forward-looking specifications

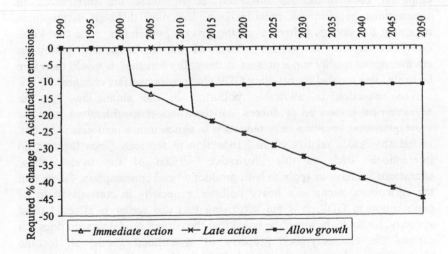

Figure 3.4b   The policy impulse for Acidification: exogenously required emission reductions in the simulations for the recursive-dynamic and forward-looking specifications

In the *Allow growth* scenario, the number of permits is reduced in 2002 to the level of emissions in 1990, as in *Immediate action*. But after 2002, growth of emissions is allowed again at the same pace as in the benchmark projection. The level of emissions is hence a constant factor below the benchmark from every period after 2002. It should be noted that the environmental consequences of this *Allow growth* scenario differ substantially from the other two simulations.

In the comparative-static model, the timing of environmental policy cannot be modelled properly. Therefore, the *Late action* and *Allow growth* scenarios will not be investigated for this model type.

Figures 3.4a and 3.4b give the exogenously required emission reduction levels in all simulations with the recursive-dynamic and forward-looking model specifications, compared to the reference emission levels in the benchmark projection. Note that as the benchmark emissions are growing over time, a stabilisation policy implies increasingly large reductions.

3.4.3   Results for the *Immediate Action* Scenario

In the simulations for *Immediate action*, GDP drops in the long run by 1.4 to 2.4 per cent below the benchmark projection, depending on the specification of the model (see Table 3.2). The models are too stylised to draw hard empirical conclusions. As discussed above, there are differences in assumptions between the specifications, including different assumptions regarding the savings behaviour of the private households. Note that GDP does not capture all welfare effects of the environmental policy as environmental quality is not present in the utility function. It would therefore be misleading to label the resulting GDP changes as 'welfare changes'.

The reduction in allowable pollution in the simulations has an asymmetrical impact on producers. All three model specifications give the same qualitative results: a large reduction in agriculture, a moderate reduction in industry and a relatively small reduction in services. Since there is no international trade in this illustrative version of the model, these characteristics have to apply to both production and consumption. Given that the agricultural sector is a heavy polluter, especially in comparison to its contribution to GDP, it is not surprising that this sector is affected most severely. It should, however, be noted that the current model version does not capture the necessary-good property of agricultural goods; all income elasticities equal unity in the model. This can be ameliorated by using the theory on linear expenditure systems (as will be done in Chapter 4).

The sectoral impacts on production for the recursive-dynamic and forward-looking model specifications are graphically depicted in Figure 3.5. The figure shows that for the agricultural sector, the production losses are higher in the recursive-dynamic model, while the production losses for industry and services are mostly higher in the forward-looking model.

Table 3.2   *Percentage changes in volumes of main variables in the*
Immediate action scenario, *compared to benchmark projection,*
for the different specifications and years

	Comp.-static	Recursive-dynamic		Forward-looking	
		2010	2050	2010	2050
Gross Domestic Product	-2.4	-0.1	-1.4	-0.2	-2.1
Private consumption Agricult.	-8.8	-1.1	-8.6	-1.0	-10.0
Private consumption Industry	-4.4	-0.4	-3.4	-0.2	-4.1
Private consumption Services	-1.9	0.0	-0.4	0.2	-0.8
Sectoral production Agricult.	-5.2	-1.1	-9.0	-0.7	-5.5
Sectoral production Industry	-3.4	-0.4	-3.4	-0.6	-3.3
Sectoral production Services	-1.5	0.0	-0.6	0.0	-0.9
Investments	-4.3	-0.3	-2.9	-0.9	-4.6
Abatement services	653.6	106.0	755.4	106.4	818.3
Emissions Climate change	-25.9	-9.5	-25.9	-9.5	-25.9
Emissions Acidification	-45.0	-18.0	-45.0	-18.1	-45.0

This effect can be explained by the composition of investments: the investment sector comprises a relatively large part of total demand for industrial goods and, to a lesser extent, also services. The decrease in investments in the forward-looking model will therefore negatively impact industry and services, more than agriculture. The figure does not show the big 'winner' of the environmental policy: the abatement sector. In an applied general equilibrium framework as used here, environmental policy is likely to create both winning and losing sectors, not only 'losers'. It makes more sense to talk about shifts (of resources) between sectors than about losses in individual sectors. At the high aggregation level used in this chapter, only the abatement sector gains from implementation of the stricter environmental policy. In Chapter 6, a more disaggregated specification will be used, which more easily lends itself for analysing this issue.

If the number of pollution permits distributed by the government is reduced compared to the benchmark, the prices of the permits increase, and it becomes cost-effective to invest more in abatement. The increases in the production of this sector are indeed huge. Abatement expenditures are not evenly spread across both sectors, even though in this prototype model the abatement cost curves are assumed to be identical for all producers. The reason is that the initial levels of abatement differ between the sectors, as do the initial ratios of abatement to emissions (see Section 3.3.2 above). The marginal costs of abatement increase with increasing investments in abatement and the final resulting equilibrium is characterised by the point where marginal abatement costs equal the price of pollution permits for each sector. At this (cost-effective) point, the polluters are indifferent between investing in abatement and paying for the pollution permits.

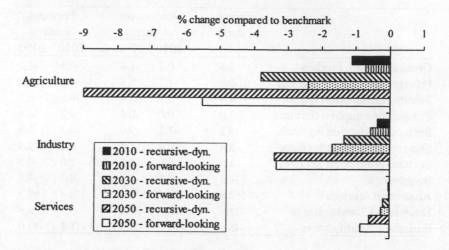

Figure 3.5   Results for the Immediate action *scenario on sectoral production for recursive-dynamic and forward-looking specifications*

In Figure 3.6, the decrease in GDP for the comparative-static model is presented as a function of the strictness of environmental policy. The left side of the curve (0 per cent) represents the benchmark. Going further to the right on the x-axis, the number of permits decreases linearly towards the new policy level for both environmental themes simultaneously.

Figure 3.6 shows that GDP decreases more than proportionately with increasingly strict environmental policy. This is in line with the general set-up of the model with (nested) CES functions: the possibilities of adapting to changing circumstances are limited and the economic costs of stricter environmental policies increase with the strictness of the policy. In economic terms, the possibilities of small, low-cost changes in the production process to substitute from environmentally-intensive to less environmentally-intensive technologies are limited. Moreover, for small decreases in pollution, the costs of abatement are relatively low, but the marginal abatement costs for further pollution reductions are higher. Hence, it can be expected that the economic costs of more stringent environmental policies will be substantially higher.

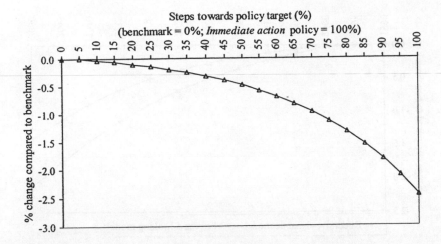

Figure 3.6   Results of the Immediate action *scenario on GDP for comparative-static specification*

Three mechanisms influence the development of GDP in the recursive-dynamic and forward-looking models. Firstly, the benchmark emissions are increasing and hence the required emission reductions are also increasing over time. This implies higher payments for pollution permits and for abatement and consequently less consumption and savings. Secondly, the lower savings slow down economic growth, so that future GDP will be lower. Thirdly, as labour productivity increases over time, abatement techniques become cheaper every period. *Ceteris paribus*, this leads to a smaller drop in consumer income from the environmental policy over time and hence partially counters the first two effects. Figure 3.7 shows that the first effect (the direct policy effect) and the second effect (the indirect slowdown effect) are dominant for both specifications.

The assumption of savings as a fixed part of household income in the recursive-dynamic specification has a big impact on the results. In the forward-looking model, savings and investment levels decrease more than in the recursive-dynamic model. This leads to lower GDP levels, as investments are part of GDP, and to lower economic growth in the long run. But it also leads to higher consumption levels in the short run in the forward-looking model. And since the objective of the households is to maximise the net present value of utility from consumption, not GDP, this is preferred.

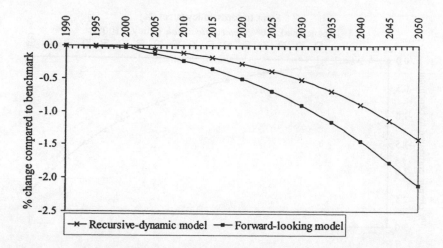

Figure 3.7   Results of Immediate action *scenario on the development of GDP for recursive-dynamic and forward-looking specifications*

Figure 3.8 shows the impact of environmental policy on total consumption of private households. In the forward-looking model, the consumers react to the environmental policy by increasing consumption levels in the short run, at the expense of future consumption. In the recursive-dynamic model, these intertemporal shifts are not possible because the savings rate is fixed. For most periods, total consumption is higher in the forward-looking model, which also implies higher utility. In fact in the forward-looking model, total consumption is above the benchmark projection for more than two decades, whereas it is never above the benchmark in the recursive-dynamic model.

Though the impacts of environmental policy on the economy are significant in terms of percentage reductions from the benchmark projection, one should bear in mind that the benchmark is characterised by a sustained growth of the economy. Consequently, absolute consumption levels are still increasing over time, but to a somewhat lesser extent in the policy simulations than in the benchmark. The absolute levels of total consumption by private households and government are represented in Figure 3.9, which shows clearly that the economic growth in the benchmark dominates the impact of environmental policy.

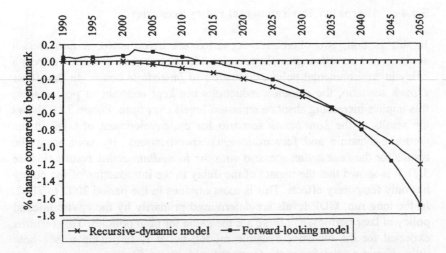

Figure 3.8   Results of the Immediate action *scenario on the development of consumption of private households for recursive-dynamic and forward-looking specifications*

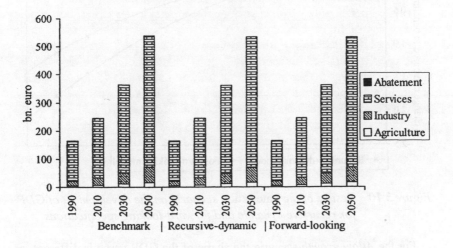

Figure 3.9   Undiscounted levels of total consumption in billion euros by consumption good for the benchmark, the recursive-dynamic model and the forward-looking model

3.4.4 Alternative Environmental Policy Scenarios

In this section, two alternative scenarios are investigated, a *Late action* scenario and an *Allow growth* scenario. The *Late action* scenario reflects a delay in environmental policy, compared to *Immediate action*. In the *Allow growth* scenario, the emission reductions are kept constant in percentages; this implies increasing absolute emission levels over time. Figure 3.10 shows the results of the *Late action* scenario for the development of GDP in the recursive-dynamic and forward-looking specifications. By comparing the results for the *Late action* scenario with the *Immediate action* results (Figure 3.7), it is shown that the impact of the delay in the introduction of the policy has only temporary effects. This is most obvious in the period 2002 to 2012. In the long run, GDP levels are determined primarily by the environmental policy in later periods, and these are the same for both policies. This result is expected for the recursive-dynamic model, but it is surprising to see how little effect the delay has in the forward-looking specification.

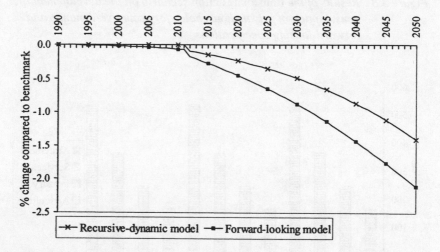

Figure 3.10   Results of the Late action *scenario on the development of GDP for recursive-dynamic and forward-looking specifications*

For the *Allow growth* scenario the shape of the GDP curve is different, as shown in Figure 3.11. Though the long-term environmental policy targets are a constant percentage below the benchmark projection, GDP over time falls more and more behind the benchmark projection (though this effect is minor). This is caused by the slower economic growth induced by reduced savings and investments. This effect is slightly smaller in the recursive-dynamic model, where savings are a fixed share of income. As explained above, this leads to higher GDP levels but lower consumption and utility in the first decades.

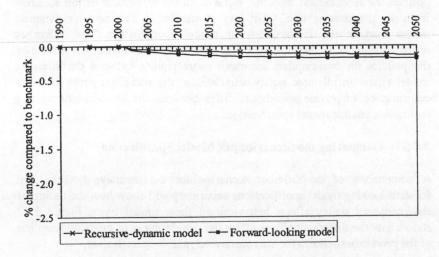

Figure 3.11 Results of the Allow growth *scenario on the development of GDP for recursive-dynamic and forward-looking specifications*

Table 3.3 Percentage changes in volumes of main variables for 2050 for alternative policies compared to benchmark projection for the recursive-dynamic and forward-looking specifications

	Recursive-dynamic			Forward-looking		
	Immed. action	Late action	Allow growth	Immed. action	Late action	Allow growth
Gross Domestic Product	-1.4	-1.4	-0.1	-2.1	-2.1	-0.2
Private cons. Agriculture	-8.6	-8.6	-0.7	-10.0	-10.0	-0.7
Private cons. Industry	-3.4	-3.4	-0.3	-4.1	-4.1	-0.3
Private cons. Services	-0.4	-0.4	-0.1	-0.8	-0.7	-0.1
Sectoral production Agricult.	-9.0	-9.0	-0.7	-5.5	-5.5	-0.4
Sectoral production Industry	-3.4	-3.4	-0.3	-3.3	-3.3	-0.3
Sectoral production Services	-0.6	-0.6	-0.1	-0.9	-0.8	-0.1
Investments	-2.9	-2.9	-0.2	-4.6	-4.6	-0.3
Abatement services	755.4	756.7	51.7	818.3	818.9	52.3
Emissions Climate change	-25.9	-25.9	-5.8	-25.9	-25.9	-5.8
Emissions Acidification	-45.0	-45.0	-11.3	-45.0	-45.0	-11.3

The long-term effects of the alternative policies on the main economic and environmental variables are represented in Table 3.3. For both alternative policies the mechanisms work the same as in the *Immediate action* scenario from the previous section. GDP loss is smaller in the recursive-dynamic model than in the forward-looking model specification. This effect is primarily caused by the differences in effects on investments; the effects of the policies on consumption are much more similar between the different model types. In all three policy simulations, the transition paths for total consumption of private households differ between the forward-looking and recursive-dynamic model specification.

3.4.5   Comparing the Scenarios per Model Specification

A comparison of the different scenarios for the recursive-dynamic and forward-looking model specifications separately will show how the timing of environmental policy affects behaviour in these model types. Figure 3.12 shows how the different policies affect the development of total consumption of the private households for the recursive-dynamic specification.

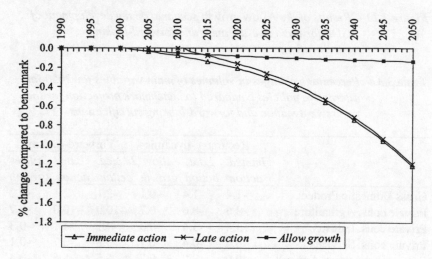

Figure 3.12   Results of different policies on the development of total consumption of private households for recursive-dynamic specification

The most striking observation is that the curves closely reflect the level of environmental policy (compare Figure 3.4), at least in qualitative terms. Given the absence of anticipating behaviour of the households, combined with a fixed savings rate, any shock in the level of environmental policy immediately results in a shock in consumption in the same direction. Only in the long run is there a significant indirect effect as lower consumption and lower savings result in a lower growth rate of the economy and therefore increasingly large differences between the benchmark and the policy simulations.

The three policy scenarios can also be compared for the forward-looking model specification. The results for the development of total consumption of the private households are reproduced in Figure 3.13.

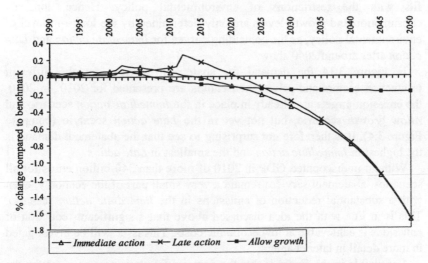

Figure 3.13   Results of different policies on the development of total consumption of private households for forward-looking specification

All three policies lead to an intertemporal shift in total consumption: a relatively higher consumption level in the earlier periods is preferred at the expense of some consumption in the later periods. This leads to the counterintuitive situation that private household consumption increases compared to the benchmark in the year of the introduction of the stricter environmental policy. This is most obvious for the *Late action* scenario, but also holds for the other two policies. The sudden consumption increase is primarily caused by a decrease in savings. As producers are faced with higher costs due to the environmental policy, the demand for capital investment decreases[11] and hence the return on savings decreases. Households respond to this by reducing their savings until the rate of return on their savings is again equal to the exogenously given interest rate.

The differences between the policy scenarios are very similar to the differences in the levels of environmental policy (compare Figure 3.4). The highest total consumption levels for the first periods are observed in the *Immediate action* scenario, the lowest in the *Allow growth* scenario. In other words, the sooner environmental policies are introduced and the stricter they are, the larger the intertemporal shift in consumption. This intertemporal shift is the result of a balancing of the net present value of consumption levels for all periods within the model horizon. By saving less in early periods, the households induce a change in the economic growth rate that, in the long run, fits with the restrictions of environmental policy. Hence, long-run consumption and growth levels are only determined by the long-run level of environmental policy, as the coinciding curves for *Immediate action* and *Late action* after around 2040 show.

In Figure 3.14 the demand for abatement services for the different production sectors and private households are presented for 2010. In 2010, the emission targets are already in place in the *Immediate action* scenario and *Allow growth* scenario, but not yet in the *Late action* scenario (compare Figure 3.4). It is therefore not surprising to see that the abatement demand is the highest in *Immediate action* and the smallest in *Late action*.

With an undiscounted GDP in 2010 of more than 340 billion euros for all scenarios, abatement services remain a very small part of the economy, even with a substantial reduction of emissions in the *Immediate action* scenario. This is in line with the idea discussed above that a significant reduction of emissions is achievable at low economic costs. This issue will be investigated in more detail in later chapters.

Not visible in the figure is that the demand for abatement services for the *Late action* scenario is exactly on the benchmark projection for the recursive-dynamic specification, but slightly different in the forward-looking specification. The knowledge of future environmental policy apparently does not influence the abatement decision itself, even though it does have macro-economic impacts.

The sectoral build-up of the demand for abatement services is very similar across all simulations. Moreover, total demand for abatement services does not differ much between the recursive-dynamic and forward-looking model specifications. This indicates that it is neither the assumption on forward-looking behaviour nor the timing of environmental policy that determines the sectoral structure of abatement demand, but rather the size and growth rates of the sectors themselves.

Figure 3.15 shows that in 2050 the differences in total abatement services across the different policies are quite different from 2010. In the long run, the *Immediate action* scenario and *Late action* scenario are almost identical, both in the recursive-dynamic and forward-looking specifications. The *Allow growth* scenario gives a much smaller demand for abatement services. This is in line with the levels of environmental policy in the scenarios (compare Figure 3.4). As in 2010, the sectoral build-up of abatement demand hardly differs between the simulations.

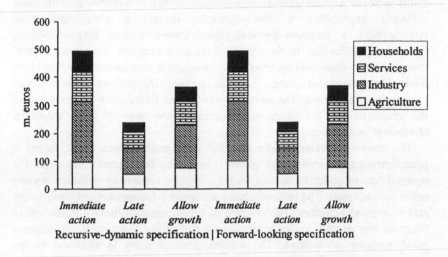

Figure 3.14   Sectoral demand for abatement services in 2010 for the recursive-dynamic and forward-looking specifications

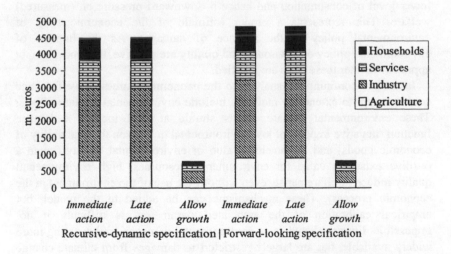

Figure 3.15   Sectoral demand for abatement services in 2050 for the recursive-dynamic and forward-looking specifications

3.5   DISCUSSION AND CONCLUSIONS

In this chapter, the dynamic relations between production, consumption, pollution and abatement are investigated using three prototype models. A multi-sectoral applied general equilibrium model is presented, with three different approaches to the dynamic issues: a comparative-static specification, a recursive-dynamic specification and a forward-looking dynamic specification. In the model, there is a separate 'abatement sector' that provides abatement techniques to producers and consumers. Polluters have the endogenous choice between paying for pollution permits and investing in abatement. The extent to which this substitution is possible and the characteristics of producing abatement are derived from empirical abatement cost curves.

The model provides insight into the least cost options of achieving a predetermined environmental policy objective, but cannot calculate the optimal rate of pollution control, as the damages caused by pollution are not taken into account. The environmental sub-model focuses on pollution levels and abatement activities. The absence of environmental quality in the utility function has another major consequence: the utility function is no longer a good measure of welfare. The welfare measurement is confined to the economic source of welfare: consumption. In reality, however, welfare also depends on other issues, such as environmental quality and leisure. According to the AGE analysis above, environmental policy will lead to a lower level of consumption and hence a downward pressure on (measured) welfare. This represents a proper estimate of the economic costs of environmental policy in the absence of damages. As the impacts of environmental policy on environmental quality are positive, the model cannot appraise whether these costs are justified.

Instead of confining the analysis to the economic sources of welfare, one could attempt to extend the model to include environmental welfare effects. These environmental welfare effects should at least include a damage function (negative impacts of low environmental quality on the availability of economic goods) and the amenity value of environmental quality (given a positive existence value for environmental resources, high environmental quality induces welfare per se, even without the use of the environment in the economic process). These mechanisms can be added to the model, but empirical calibration of the associated parameters is difficult, if not impossible. Empirical studies on environmental damages are becoming more widely available, but are largely restricted to damages from climate change (for example, Tol, 2002a, b). In an empirical study focussing not only on climate change, it seems therefore too ambitious to include environmental damages and the amenity value of environmental quality (see Chapter 2).

The analysis clearly shows that the specification of the dynamic issues in the model is highly relevant. Not only are the numerical results significantly influenced by the model specification, the main interactions between economy and ecology can also be better specified in a dynamic context. Even with a simple specification of the abatement sector, there are dynamic interactions that influence the costs of abatement for the polluters, the price of the pollution permits and the economic impacts of the environmental policy.

Though the models are too stylised to draw hard empirical conclusions, the numerical example shows that a policy of stabilisation of emissions in a growing economy may lead to significant economic costs in the long run. The agricultural sector is most severely affected by the simulated policy, due to its relatively unfavourable ratio between emissions and value added. This ratio is much smaller for the services sector, and hence this sector will observe only small production losses. The size of the abatement sector increases substantially, but compared to the other sectors it remains small throughout all simulations. The share of the polluting sectors in the demand for abatement services is very similar across all simulations, indicating that the main determinants of the sectoral abatement expenditures are the size and growth of the sector itself, and that the assumptions on perfect foresight and the timing of environmental policy play only a minor role.

The comparative-static model simulation shows that the economic costs of environmental policy increase more than proportionately with increasing strictness of the policy targets. This reflects the increasing marginal abatement costs and is in line with the general set-up of the model with nested CES functions, which have the property that the possibilities for adapting to changes in circumstances are limited.

The dominant mechanism that influences the development of GDP in the recursive-dynamic and forward-looking model specifications is that the required emission reduction percentages are increasing over time. This direct policy effect is coupled with the indirect slowdown effect that lower savings will reduce the growth rate of the economy. The decreasing marginal abatement costs and increasing labour productivity over time cannot fully mitigate these effects and hence the difference in GDP levels between the policy simulations and the benchmark projection grows over time.

The main differences between the recursive-dynamic and forward-looking specifications are that in the forward-looking model (i) the savings level can be adjusted to partially mitigate the negative impact of the environmental policy on total consumption in the short run; and (ii) consumers have foresight on future environmental policy. Consequently, the forward-looking model specification gives consumption levels that are higher in the first few decades, but in the long run persistently lower than in the recursive-dynamic specification. Given the low present value of future consumption as a result of the positive discount rate, this is optimal.

Delaying environmental policy has only a temporary impact on economic costs. In the long run, the economic costs are determined by the environmental policy in later periods. To a large extent, this also holds in the forward-looking model specification. The delay does impact the intertemporal shift in total consumption in the forward-looking specification: the sooner environmental policies are introduced and the stricter they are, the larger the shift from future to current consumption. By saving less in early periods, the households induce a change in the economic growth rate that matches the restrictions imposed by future environmental policy.

NOTES

*   A revised version of this chapter is published as Dellink et al. (2004).

1.   A CES function is a function that assumes constant elasticities of substitution between different inputs in the function. A *nested* CES function has different levels ('branches'), each of which can have a different elasticity of substitution. For instance, inputs x_1 and x_2 can be mutually substituted with substitution elasticity σ_L and the composite of these inputs can be substituted by x_3 with substitution elasticity σ_H.

2.   This proportion is constant in *value* terms (fixed budget share). The alternative is to keep the proportion fixed in *volumes*. The difference between the two approaches only arises in a multi-sectoral specification. As there is only one produced good in the original Solow model, the price of investment goods equals the price of consumption goods.

3.   As international trade is not included in this simplified model, there is no international capital market that dictates an interest rate.

4.   This condition assures that investments will not fall to zero near the end of the model horizon. Similar conditions are proposed by Manne and Richels (1992) and Lau et al. (2002). These conditions have the advantage over traditional transversality conditions that restrict the absolute size of the capital stock, that they allow more flexibility in the savings decision of consumers. This issue will be investigated in a sensitivity analysis in Section 0.

5.   As capital is assumed mobile across sectors, this means that capital expenditures for abatement purposes are in full competition with capital expenditures in other sectors.

6.   This use of the term 'environmental services' should not be confused with the notion of 'services provided by the environment' as is sometimes used in theoretical models. The environment is captured in this book purely via pollution and abatement, and the combination of these constitutes 'environmental services'.

7.   Though this denies the variety of technical measures that make up the abatement cost curves, the empirical data do not allow for a more detailed description of the cost components.

8.   The global warming potential of a greenhouse gas is derived from the relative contribution to radiative forcing, compared to CO_2; hence the name CO_2-equivalents. See IPCC (1996) for more details.

9.   This procedure is explained in Adriaanse (1993).

10. One can think of these autonomous pollution efficiency improvements as a result of abatement activities that are present in the benchmark projection.

11. Note that in the model new capital is not necessarily more environmentally friendly than existing capital.

4. Specification of a dynamic applied general equilibrium model with pollution and abatement for The Netherlands (DEAN)

4.1 INTRODUCTION

The main aim of this chapter is to present the full specification of the DEAN model. DEAN stands for *d*ynamic applied general *e*quilibrium model with pollution and *a*batement for The Netherlands. The model builds on the forward-looking prototype model presented in the last chapter; the reasons for choosing this specification as basis for the DEAN model are discussed in Section 4.2.

Some major extensions of the model are needed for the empirical analysis of the subsequent chapters. First, in Section 4.3.1, the Linear Expenditure System (LES) will be explained. The LES specification allows non-unitary income elasticities for the private households. This extension is important to represent the basic good property of agricultural goods. As reported in Chapter 3, the unitary income elasticities lead to an unexpectedly large decrease in consumption of agricultural goods. This section draws heavily on Gerlagh et al. (2002).

The second extension concerns international trade and is discussed in Section 4.3.2. The prototype models are specified for a closed economy, whereas The Netherlands is clearly an open economy. On the one hand, substitution from domestic production of 'dirty goods' to imports is, at least to some extent, a likely effect of unilateral environmental policy. On the other hand, environmental policy may lead to a deterioration of the competitive position of domestic producers in comparison to their international competitors. Hence, the connections between the domestic economy and the rest of the world have to be specified in the model to obtain realistic outcomes. Following Gerlagh et al. (2002) again, an Armington approach is followed.

Section 4.3.3 deals with some more technical extensions of the model that are likely to have only a minor impact on the results. These include trade margins, accounting for work in progress and end-of-year stocks and the recalibration of the model with 5-year periods.

The environmental extensions concern the modelling of greenhouse gases as stock pollutants (Section 4.4.1), public environmental expenditures (Section 4.4.2) and the dynamic specification of abatement (Section 4.4.3). First, modelling the stock pollutant property of greenhouse gases allows for a formulation of environmental policy in terms of additions to the stock of greenhouse gases, which is more logical as damages are related to concentrations of greenhouse gases. The second extension, public environmental expenditures, is relevant as not all environmental problems can be related to emissions: the themes Desiccation and Soil contamination have public goods properties. Third, the intertemporal aspects of the abatement specification are of course highly important as these refer directly to the aim of the DEAN model: the dynamic interaction between pollution, abatement and economic growth.

Section 4.5 gives a full, equation-by-equation description of the DEAN model and Section 4.6 contains the discussion and conclusions. The symbols used are explained in Appendix 4.I, while Appendix 4.II deals with the transformation function for non-unitary income elasticities, Appendix 4.III with the technical details of the multi-year period specification and Appendix 4.IV with the specification of a permit system for stock pollutants.

4.2 CHOICE OF THE PROTOTYPE MODEL

The DEAN model is based on the forward-looking prototype model as described in Chapter 3. This model type has the advantage that the specification is fully dynamic: the agents take not only the current state of the economy, but also future situations into account when making decisions that affect current and future welfare. This intertemporal aspect is lacking in recursive-dynamic models. Empirical estimates suggest that consumers do look ahead to some extent in reality, but do not maximise their utility till infinity (Srinivasan, 1982; Ballard and Goulder, 1985). Intuitively, it is hard to imagine that none of the economic agents in the model takes a long-term view for his or her decisions (Solow, 1974).

A second advantage of the forward-looking prototype model over the recursive-dynamic prototype model is the inclusion of an endogenous savings rate.[1] It seems more realistic to assume that consumers do adjust their savings rate according to changes in their decision environment. Hence, the transition path from the original balanced growth path to a new growth path is more flexible and realistic (Barro and Sala-i-Martin, 1995).

Note that in the dynamic AGE with perfect foresight and endogenous savings under certainty the optimal path of economic growth is equivalent to the equilibrium path of a decentralised economy (Blanchard and Fischer, 1989). This implies that the model can be solved for the macro-economy, while keeping the micro-economic assumptions on the optimising behaviour of individual agents intact.

The numerical example presented in Chapter 3 shows that the main differences between a recursive-dynamic and a forward-looking specification are of a quantitative nature. The qualitative conclusions are to a large extent comparable between both model types.

4.3 EXTENSION OF THE ECONOMIC ISSUES

4.3.1 Non-unitary Income Elasticities

The use of (nested) CES utility functions implies that relative preferences (the preference for one good with respect to other consumption goods) do not depend on the level of income. In other words, the indirect utility function is homogeneous of degree one in income and the income elasticities equal one for all consumption goods. This means that if income increases, *ceteris paribus* there will be no changes in the composition of the consumption bundle. In reality some goods can be characterised as basic goods, that is, goods that have a relatively large share in consumption when income is low, but which declines with rising income. On the other hand, luxury goods exist that will have an increasing share in total consumption as income rises. Basic goods have an income elasticity of less than one, while luxury goods have income elasticities above unity.

One way to introduce non-unitary income elasticities into the model is to use the Linear Expenditure System approach (Stone, 1954). The representative consumer is split into two parts: a 'subsistence consumer' and a 'surplus consumer'. The subsistence consumer represents the basic demand by the consumer. It is specified with a Leontief function, that is, no substitution possibilities between different consumption goods, and has an exogenously given size. The surplus consumer reflects how additional income is spent, and has positive substitution elasticities between the different consumption goods. Though the surplus (sometimes called 'supernumerary') part of consumption has unitary income elasticities, total consumption does not. This is the case because for every good, the division between 'subsistence' and 'surplus' is different. For basic goods, the major part of consumption is attributed to the subsistence consumer, while for luxury goods a relatively large part is attributed to the surplus consumer.

Intuitively, one can think of the introduction of the subsistence consumer as changing the origin for the utility function of private households.

Keller (1980) suggests choosing the base quantities

$$C_{j,t}^{subs.} = \left(1 - \eta_j\right) \cdot C_{j,t} \tag{4.1}$$

where η_j is the income elasticity for good j and $C_{j,t}$ is total consumption of good j in period t. This leads, however, to the unwanted situation that the base quantities are negative for goods with an income elasticity larger than unity. Therefore, the alternative

$$C_{j,t}^{subs.} = \left(1 - \frac{\eta_j}{Max_k\{\eta_k\}}\right) \cdot C_{j,t} \tag{4.2}$$

is chosen. This transformation results in a base quantity equal to zero for the good with the highest income elasticity and positive base quantities for all other goods. If inferior goods are excluded from the model (which can be done without problems given the level of aggregation), all surplus quantities are also positive. Both alternatives give the correct implicit income elasticities; it is shown in Appendix 4.II that any scheme

$$C_{j,t}^{subs.} = \left(1 - \frac{\eta_j}{cst}\right) \cdot C_{j,t} \quad \text{and} \quad C_{j,t}^{priv.} = \left(\frac{\eta_j}{cst}\right) \cdot C_{j,t} \tag{4.3}$$

with cst a strictly positive constant can be chosen. The intuition behind the transformation function is that the constant cst only determines how much of total consumption is assigned to the surplus part of consumption, but does not influence the elasticities.

Figure 4.1 illustrates how the linear expenditure system changes income elasticities. Point A in the figure represents the current consumption bundle, while point B gives the consumption bundle attributed to the subsistence consumer. If income decreases, the subsistence consumption remains constant, so that surplus consumption shifts linearly from A to B, instead from shifting linearly from A to the origin O. In this way, a decrease in the consumption of the private households will lead to a more than proportionate decrease of total consumption of luxury goods, and a less than proportionate decrease in total consumption of basic goods. The transformation constant cst determines where point B is on the line through A and B, without affecting the slope of this line.

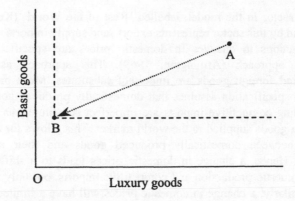

Source: Gerlagh et al. (2001).

Figure 4.1 The linear expenditure system

In effect, the (intertemporal) utility function is of the Stone-Geary type:

$$u(c_i) = \frac{\left(c_i - c_i^{subs}\right)^{(1-\theta_i)} - 1}{(1-\theta_i)} \qquad (4.4)$$

where θ_i refers to the inverse of the intertemporal elasticity of consumption (see for example Phlips, 1974; or Barro and Sala-i-Martin, 1995, for more details).

Consumer income from the sale of endowments is fully attributed to the surplus part of consumption; for the subsistence part, a fixed part of income is transferred from the surplus consumer (modelled as a lump-sum transfer). This ensures that the subsistence part of consumption does not react to the policy impulse. In the presentation of the results, the subsistence and surplus parts have to be grouped together, as they represent only one consumer.

4.3.2 International Trade

For the modelling of international trade the standard 'small open economy' assumption is made. This means that changes on the domestic market, both in prices and volumes, do not influence the world market prices. World market prices are exogenously given (in the foreign currency), and the international market is big enough to satisfy the demand for imports and absorb the supply of exports at these international prices. Under these conditions, all international trade links with other countries can be aggregated into one additional sector in the model, labelled 'Rest of the World' (Keller, 1980). The demand by this sector represents exports and supply imports.

The reactions to changes in domestic prices are specified using the Armington approach (Armington, 1969). This approach assumes that domestic and foreign goods are imperfect substitutes. More precisely, the Armington specification assumes that domestically produced goods and the corresponding competitive imports are imperfect substitutes, as are exports and foreign goods supplied to the world market. This allows for a difference in prices between domestically produced goods and their international substitutes. Hence, a change in domestic prices leads to a shift in demand between domestic production and competitive imports, but only to a limited extent. Similarly, a change in domestic prices will have a limited impact on export.[2] There will be a demand for export goods even if the domestic price is above the world market price (De Melo and Robinson, 1989).

The Armington approach is modelled by adding imports and domestic production per good into an 'Armington aggregate', also labelled 'total supply' per good. This supply is then split up into domestic demand and exports (foreign demand). This implies that imports are disaggregated by imported good, not by importing sector.

All types of goods can be described by the general procedure above, but if imports, exports or domestic production are zero, the specification can be simplified. This applies to non-competitive imports and local goods (goods that are not internationally traded, mainly services). Note that international trade in The Netherlands is characterised by large flows of transit goods (goods that are imported and then exported again). These transit goods cannot be separated from imports that are destined for the domestic market. This implies that the volume of exports can for some goods be larger than domestic production.

In each period, the total trade deficit, that is, the value of imports minus the value of exports, is compensated by a budget deficit of domestic consumers, as otherwise the monetary flows in the model would not close. The exchange rate[3] is endogenous in the model and adjusts such that the trade deficit is constant over time. This implies that the exchange rate should not be regarded as a monetary variable that ensures equilibrium on the money market, but rather as the variable that rations the trade deficit. This closure rule[4] reflects the ad hoc assumption that international trade flows are constrained; this assumption is made to avoid scenario results that contain unrealistically large fluctuations in imports or exports. The consequences of the restriction on the trade balance will be explored in Chapters 6 and 7.

Emissions are assumed to be associated only with domestic production and domestic consumption. There are no emissions from international trade or from international transport. An alternative approach would be to take account of the emissions *caused* by domestic activity, so as to include emissions from imports and subtract emissions from production for export. This alternative is rejected as it does not fit with the way in which domestic emissions are attributed to sectors.

4.3.3 Other Extensions of the Economic Issues

Trade margins

Trade margins are payments made by producers for the distribution and transport of goods. They are normally assumed to be a fixed 'mark-up' over other costs of production and do not represent a physical produced good themselves. Trade margins apply to virtually all economic transactions, both domestic and international. They are given as a separate row and column in the accounting matrix. Their size is too substantial for them to be ignored, and hence they have to be explicitly specified in the model.

For the producers, trade margins are given as a separate input for production, entering the production structure at the highest level in a Leontief structure. In this way, they are fixed in proportion to the other costs of production. This separate input, 'trade margins', is produced by an auxiliary producer, who converts produced goods in Leontief manner into the fictitious good 'trade margins'. In other words, it is purely a transfer of money between production sectors. The production function of this auxiliary producer is hence much simpler than that of the normal production sectors as it does not involve taxes, demand for primary factors, pollution or abatement.

Stock mutations and work-in-progress

In the accounting matrix a separate column shows the mutations in end-of-year stocks and work-in-progress. The entries in this column represent several different things, including unfinished goods (work-in-progress), finished goods at the site of the producer, and delivered but unpaid goods to clients. It is practically impossible to model this in full detail. There are no indications on how end-of-year stocks and work-in-progress will change over time; stock changes for individual years are likely to be volatile over time. Therefore, the values for the base year as reported in the input-output table are not very suitable to take as reference point.

In the model, the stock mutations are aggregated with investments. The rationale for this is that they represent resources that are used this period but that will only be productive, that is, generate income, in the next. In the National Accounts, stock mutations and expansion investments together form the net investments. Given the assumption that investments are recalibrated using the steady state assumption, as described in the previous chapter, this effectively means that stock changes are removed from the model.

Five-year periods
The full model is specified into periods of five years, rather than the annual periods used in the previous chapter. This change is not necessary from an economic point of view; the main advantage is, however, that the number of variables and hence the calculation time of the model are substantially reduced.

The interpretation of the variables in the model is not changed by the introduction of multi-year periods. The values that are specified in the model still reflect annual numbers. The only change is in the transfer between periods. This transfer has to be specified such that the benchmark projection still reflects the balanced growth path. The simple assumption that investments in this period increase capital stock in the next period is then no longer possible. Rather, one has to calibrate what share of investments in this period will lead to an increase in capital stock in the same period and what share will only be productive in the next period. This procedure is described in Rutherford (2001) and explained in Appendix 4.III.

4.4   EXTENSION OF THE ENVIRONMENTAL ISSUES

4.4.1   Greenhouse Gases as Stock Pollutants

Climate change is caused by the stock of greenhouse gases (GHGs) in the atmosphere. Emissions play a role via their contribution to the stock of GHGs. Therefore, it makes sense to model emissions as well as the stock of GHGs. As GHGs mix uniformly in the atmosphere, the relevant stock to be modelled is the global stock. However, emissions in The Netherlands only comprise a small fraction of global emissions (less than 1 per cent; RIVM, 2002a). Moreover, national environmental policy can only influence domestic emissions. Therefore, it is not the stock of GHGs that is modelled and controlled in the DEAN model, but rather the contribution of The Netherlands to the stock over the model horizon (the 'GHG stock addition').

The climate module that is needed to calibrate the GHG stock addition of The Netherlands is kept very simple. Based on the DICE model (Nordhaus, 1994), first an annual decay factor for the existing stock of GHGs is specified (δ_{EM}). This decay factor is assumed to apply to all contributions of The Netherlands to the stock of greenhouse gases and is used to calculate how much of the GHG stock addition in one period remains in the next period.

Secondly, a marginal retention rate (ε_{EM}) determines the share of emissions that contribute to the stock addition. Since not all emitted GHGs remain in the atmosphere, this retention rate is smaller than unity.

Let EM_t denote the GHG stock addition of The Netherlands from the base year of the model, 1990, up to and including year t, and $E_{'climate',jh,t}$ denote greenhouse gas emissions of polluter jh in period t. Then the development of the GHG stock addition can be calculated as

$$EM_t = (1 - \delta_{EM}) \cdot EM_{t-1} + \varepsilon_{EM} \cdot \sum_{jh=1}^{J+H} E_{'climate',jh,t} \qquad (4.5)$$

At the start of the base year of the model, the stock addition equals zero: $EM_{1989} = 0$.

Clearly, environmental policy for Climate change should reflect the stock pollutant property of greenhouse gases. Therefore, the government does not auction emission permits for Climate change, but 'GHG stock addition permits'. The government sets a policy target on the total stock addition of The Netherlands, that is, it restricts the number of permits to be auctioned, and polluters have to buy the 'GHG stock addition permits' to be able to emit GHGs. Hence polluters have annual expenses on Climate change permits, even if the target for the total stock addition is not yet met. This procedure is explained in more detail in Appendix 4.IV.

4.4.2 Public Environmental Expenditures

The use of abatement cost curves is not really appropriate for the environmental themes of Desiccation and Soil contamination, which are best represented by a fixed governmental expenditure, rather than by their inclusion in the behaviour of producers and private households. The activities involved for these themes can be characterised as cleaning up past pollution, rather than mitigating current emissions.

For practical reasons, the expenditures on these 'public environmental themes' are assumed to grow at the same pace as other government expenditures in the benchmark projection. Total costs for Soil contamination are translated into annual costs using an everlasting annuity method and hence they last throughout the model horizon. For Desiccation, the annual costs are assumed to be compulsory throughout the model horizon. The public environmental expenditures are captured in the model as a fixed expenditure of the government on abatement.[5]

4.4.3 Development of Abatement Costs over Time

The model as presented in the previous chapter does not explicitly look at the intertemporal aspects of the abatement costs curves. Implicitly, it is assumed that both the technical potential for emission reduction techniques and the curvature of the substitution curve remain constant over time. However, there are several reasons why these environmental parameters may change over time.

The first effect that takes place when moving from period t to period $t+1$ is that the polluters adopt some abatement measures, that is, diffusion of abatement technology.[6] At first glance, this would lead to a reduction of the technical potential and an increase in average abatement costs, as these are the least-cost options that will be implemented first. However, the substitution curve describes the *annual* abatement costs. A polluter has to pay the costs of the same measure every year. This means that adopting a measure in year t does not imply adoption of the same measure in year $t+1$: the decision is reversible. Consequently, the adopted measures should stay in the substitution curve, which does not change due to this effect. Neither the technical potential for pollution reduction,[7] $\mu_{e,jh,t}$, nor the PAS elasticity, $\sigma^A_{e,jh}$, are influenced by this effect.

The second effect is that new abatement measures will emerge through innovation. Though these new measures are presumably more efficient than existing measures, they are likely to be far from the adoption phase. The impact of the emergence of new measures is partially counteracted by the removal from the curve of old techniques that are obsolete and have never been implemented. On average, the substitution curve will be extending to the above and to the left, thereby increasing the technical potential, $\mu_{e,jh,t}$. The increase in the technical potential is modelled through an exponential growth function, that is, in every period the technical potential grows with an exogenous constant rate g_μ:

$$\mu_{e,jh,t+1} = \mu_{e,jh,t} \cdot (1 + g_\mu) \tag{4.6}$$

The effect of these new measures on the PAS elasticity cannot be predicted beforehand, but is likely to be very small, and hence a constant PAS elasticity may be assumed.

The third effect is a reduction of the marginal costs of all existing measures. Labour-augmenting technological change and other technological progress, such as learning effects and path-dependent small innovations, will induce a reduction in abatement costs that go beyond labour productivity developments. This reduction in abatement costs compared to other goods can be explicitly modelled as an efficiency improvement in the abatement production process, combined with a reduction in the price of abatement, P_A, such that the total value of abatement grows in the benchmark projection with the balanced growth rate. The exogenous efficiency improvements in the abatement sector are covered in the model via a new parameter, φ_A:

$$Y_{A,t+1} = (1 + g_L + \varphi_A) \cdot Y_{A,t} \tag{4.7}$$

Finally, it should be recalled that the model in the previous chapter already contains exogenous technological progress in environmental efficiency, governed by an autonomous pollution efficiency improvements (φ_e).

4.5 FULL MODEL DESCRIPTION

The full model is represented in Table 4.1. The equations of the model will be discussed successively in the sections below.

Table 4.1 Complete listing of model equations

Consumers

$$W_{h,t} = CES(C_{1,h,t}, ..., C_{J,h,t}, ES_{1,h,t}, ..., ES_{E,h,t}; \sigma_h^1, ..., \sigma_h^V) \quad \forall(h,t)^* \tag{DEAN-1}$$

$$U_h = CES(W_{h,1}, ..., W_{h,T}; \sigma_h^{Util}) \quad \forall h \tag{DEAN-2}$$

$$p_{h,t}^W \cdot W_{h,t} = \sum_{j=1}^{J}(1 + \tau_{j,h} \cdot \alpha_t) \cdot p_{j,t} \cdot C_{j,h,t} + p_{A,t} \cdot C_{A,h,t} + \sum_{e=1}^{E} p_{e,t} \cdot E_{e,h,t} \tag{DEAN-3}$$

$$\forall(h,t)$$

$$\sum_{t=1}^{T} p_{priv',t}^W \cdot W_{priv',t} + p_{K,T} \cdot \overline{K}_T = p_{K,1} \cdot \overline{K}_1 +$$

$$\sum_{t=1}^{T}\left\{ p_{L,t} \cdot \overline{L}_t - \tau_{priv'}^{LS} \cdot \alpha_t^{LS} - \gamma_{priv',t}^{LS} - \overline{BD}_{priv',t} \right\} \tag{DEAN-4}$$

$$p_{subs',t}^W \cdot W_{subs',t} = \gamma_{subs',t}^{LS} \quad \forall t \tag{DEAN-5}$$

$$p_{govt',t}^W \cdot W_{govt',t} = \sum_{e=1}^{E} p_{e,t} \cdot \overline{E}_{e,t} - \tau_{govt'}^{LS} \cdot \alpha_t^{LS} + TR_t \quad \forall t \tag{DEAN-6}$$

$$W_{subs',t} = \overline{W}_{subs',t} \quad \forall t; \text{ determines } \gamma_{h,t}^{LS} \tag{DEAN-7}$$

$$W_{govt',t} = \overline{W}_{govt',t} \quad \forall t; \text{ determines } \alpha_t \text{ and } \alpha_t^{LS} \tag{DEAN-8}$$

$$C_{j,'subs',t} = \left(1 - \frac{\eta_j}{Max_k\{\eta_k\}}\right) \bigg/ \left(\frac{\eta_j}{Max_k\{\eta_k\}}\right) \cdot C_{j,'priv',t} \quad \forall(j,t) \tag{DEAN-9}$$

Table 4.1 (continued)

Demographic developments and labour supply

$$\overline{L}_{t+1} = \overline{L}_t \cdot (1 + g_L) \quad \forall t \tag{DEAN-10}$$

Capital accumulation

$$\overline{K}_{t+1} = (1 - \delta_K) \cdot \left(\overline{K}_t + \iota^C \cdot I_t \right) + \iota^N \cdot I_t \quad \forall t \tag{DEAN-11}$$

$$\iota^C = \left(\frac{1}{g_L - r} \right) \cdot \left\{ \left(\frac{g_L + \delta_K}{g_L^a + \delta_K^a} \right) - \left(\frac{r + \delta_K}{r^a + \delta_K^a} \right) \right\} \tag{DEAN-12}$$

$$\iota^N = \left(\frac{-1}{g_L - r} \right) \cdot \left\{ \left(\frac{g_L + \delta_K}{g_L^a + \delta_K^a} \right) \cdot (1 + r) - \left(\frac{r + \delta_K}{r^a + \delta_K^a} \right) \cdot (1 + g_L) \right\} \tag{DEAN-13}$$

$$\overline{K}_T = (1 + g_L) \cdot \overline{K}_{T-1} \tag{DEAN-14}$$

Producers

$$Y_{j,t}^{DS} = CES(Y_{1,j,t}^{ID}, ..., Y_{J,j,t}^{ID}, K_{j,t}, L_{j,t}, ES_{1,j,t}, ..., ES_{E,j,t}; \sigma_j^1, ..., \sigma_j^V) \tag{DEAN-15}$$

$$\forall (j,t)$$

$$0 = \Pi_{j,t} = p_{j,t} \cdot Y_{j,t}^{DS} - \sum_{jj=1}^{J} (1 + \tau_{jj,j}) \cdot p_{jj,t} \cdot Y_{jj,j,t}^{ID} - (1 + \tau_{A,j}) \cdot p_{A,t} \cdot Y_{A,j,t}^{ID}$$

$$- (1 + \tau_{L,j}) \cdot p_{L,t} \cdot L_{j,t} - (1 + \tau_{K,j}) \cdot r_{K,t} \cdot K_{j,t} - \sum_{e=1}^{E} p_{e,t} \cdot E_{e,j,t} \tag{DEAN-16}$$

$$\forall (j,t)$$

International trade

$$Y_{j,t}^{TS} = CES(Y_{j,t}^{DS}, M_{j,t}; \sigma^{imp}) \quad \forall (j,t) \tag{DEAN-17}$$

$$Y_{\cdot ncm',t}^{TS} = M_{\cdot ncm',t} \quad \forall t \tag{DEAN-18}$$

$$CET(Y_{j,t}^{DD}, X_{j,t}; \sigma^{exp}) = Y_{j,t}^{TS} \quad \forall (j,t) \tag{DEAN-19}$$

$$CET(Y_{\cdot ncm',t}^{DD}, X_{\cdot ncm',t}; \sigma^{exp}) = Y_{\cdot ncm',t}^{TS} \quad \forall t \tag{DEAN-20}$$

$$\sum_{j=1}^{J} p_{x,t} \cdot \left(M_{j,t} - X_{j,t} \right) + p_{x,t} \cdot \left(M_{\cdot ncm',t} - X_{\cdot ncm',t} \right) = \sum_{h=1}^{H} \overline{BD}_{h,t} \quad \forall t \tag{DEAN-21}$$

Market clearance

$$Y_{j,t}^{DS} + M_{j,t} = Y_{j,t}^{TS} = Y_{j,t}^{DD} + X_{j,t} \quad \forall (j,t) \tag{DEAN-22}$$

$$Y_{j,t}^{DD} = \sum_{jj=1}^{J} Y_{j,jj,t}^{ID} + Y_{j,A,t}^{ID} + I_{j,t} + \sum_{h=1}^{H} C_{j,h,t} \quad \forall (j,t); \text{ determines } p_{j,t} \tag{DEAN-23}$$

Table 4.1   (continued)

$$\sum_{j=1}^{J} K_{j,t} + K_{A,t} = \bar{K}_t \quad \forall t; \text{ determines } p_{K,t} \tag{DEAN-24}$$

$$\sum_{j=1}^{J} L_{j,t} + L_{A,t} = \bar{L}_t \quad \forall t; \text{ determines } p_{L,t} \tag{DEAN-25}$$

$$S_t = \sum_{j=1}^{J} p_{j,t} \cdot I_{j,t} \quad \forall t \tag{DEAN-26}$$

Emissions and abatement

$$ES_{e,jh,t} = CES(E_{e,jh,t}^{U}, CES(E_{e,jh,t}^{A}, A_{e,jh,t}; \sigma_{e,jh}^{A}); \sigma_{e,jh}^{ES}) \quad \forall (ejh,t) \tag{DEAN-27}$$

$$E_{e,jh,t}^{A} / E_{e,jh,t} = \mu_{e,jh,t} \quad \forall (ejh,t) \tag{DEAN-28}$$

$$\sum_{jh=1}^{JH} E_{e,jh,t}^{U} + \sum_{jh=1}^{JH} E_{e,jh,t}^{A} \equiv \sum_{jh=1}^{JH} E_{e,jh,t} = \bar{E}_{e,t} \quad \forall (e,t); \text{ determines } p_{e,t} \tag{DEAN-29}$$

$$Y_{A,t} = \sum_{jj=1}^{J} Y_{A,jj,t}^{ID} + \sum_{h=1}^{H} C_{A,h,t} \equiv \sum_{jh=1}^{JH} \sum_{e=1}^{E} A_{e,jh,t} \quad \forall t; \text{ determines } p_{A,t} \tag{DEAN-30}$$

$$EM_t = (1 - \delta_{EM}) \cdot EM_{t-1} + \varepsilon_{EM} \cdot \sum_{jh=1}^{J+H} E_{'climate',jh,t} \quad \forall t \tag{DEAN-31}$$

Environmental technological progress

$$E_{e,jh,t+1} = (1 + g_L - \varphi_e) \cdot E_{e,jh,t} \quad \forall (ejh,t) \tag{DEAN-32}$$

$$\mu_{e,jh,t+1} = \mu_{e,jh,t} \cdot (1 + g_\mu) \quad \forall (ejh,t) \tag{DEAN-33}$$

$$Y_{A,t+1} = (1 + g_L + \varphi_A) \cdot Y_{A,t} \quad \forall t \tag{DEAN-34}$$

$$p_{A,t+1} = \left(\frac{1 + g_L}{1 + g_L + \varphi_A} \right) \cdot p_{A,t} \quad \forall t \tag{DEAN-35}$$

Note:
* As usual, '…' is used to indicate all items within the range as given by the items listed before and after. The domain and meaning of the indices are given in Appendix 4.I.
  A general nested CES production function with for example 4 inputs and 2 levels can be written as: $Y = (a_1 X_1^\rho + a_2 X_2^\rho + a_{34} X_{34}^\rho)^{1/\rho}$, and $X_{34} = (a_3 X_3^\psi + a_4 X_4^\psi)^{1/\psi}$ for some parameters a_1, a_2, a_{34}, a_3, a_4, where $\rho = (\sigma-1)/\sigma$ and $\psi = (\varphi-1)/\varphi$. A convenient notation is: $Y = CES(X_1, X_2, X_{34}; \sigma)$; $X_{34} = CES(X_3, X_4; \varphi)$.

4.5.1   Economic Issues

Consumers

In the description of consumer behaviour, the subsistence ('*subs.*') and surplus ('*priv.*') parts of private household consumption are treated as separate categories. However, these two parts will be aggregated in the presentation of the results, as this split is only a technical construct.

Equation (DEAN-1) gives the instantaneous utility function for household h for period t. Consumption of different goods $C_{j,h,t}$ and environmental services $ES_{e,h,t}$ are combined in a nested CES structure, using elasticities σ_h^v. This means that there are limited substitution possibilities between the different consumption goods, and that each level of consumption requires some combination of pollution permits and abatement. The auxiliary instantaneous utility $W_{h,t}$ is aggregated over time, again using CES function as shown in equation (DEAN-2).

The expenditures of the different consumers are given in equation (DEAN-3). The instantaneous utility level and price are chosen such that their product equals expenditures. The income of the consumers is given in equations (DEAN-4), (DEAN-5) and (DEAN-6). The private households (surplus part) have income from the sale of their endowments of capital goods and labour, reduced with lump sum transfers to the government and to the subsistence consumer (DEAN-4). Differences between income and expenditures for private households are reflected in the budget deficit. The subsistence consumer has only the lump sum transfer as income (DEAN-5). The government has three sources of income: sale of the pollution permits, the lump sum transfer from private households and tax revenues (DEAN-6). The lump sum transfers between the consumers are endogenously adjusted to ensure budget balance for the subsistence and government consumers; these are given in equations (DEAN-7) and (DEAN-8). The division of private household consumption between the subsistence and surplus parts is given in equation (DEAN-9).

Labour supply

Equation (DEAN-10) shows that effective labour supply grows with an exogenous rate of g_L every period. This is a combination of demographic developments and increases in labour productivity.

Capital accumulation

Capital accumulation is represented by the three equations (DEAN-11), (DEAN-12) and (DEAN-13). Investments in this period are to some extent, ι^C, productive in the same period and to some extent, ι^N, in the next period.

To account for capital stocks after the model's time horizon, the transversality condition (DEAN-14) is included in the model.

Producers
Domestic producers have a limited choice of technologies with which to produce and maximise their profits under given prices. The potential substitution between the different production technologies is captured via a nested-CES production function (DEAN-15). Inputs in this production function are labour and capital and intermediate deliveries from the other producing sectors. Each producer produces one unique output from the inputs. As full competition and constant returns to scale are assumed, no excess profits can be reaped and the maximum-profit condition (DEAN-16) diminishes to a least-cost condition.

International trade
In the Armington equation (DEAN-17) domestic supply and imports are specified to be imperfect substitutes. For non-competitive imports, there is no domestic supply, and hence the equation diminishes to (DEAN-18). Armington equations (DEAN-19) and (DEAN-20) state that domestic demand and exports are combined with a limited elasticity of transformation. The trade block is completed with the trade balance equation (DEAN-21), which is specified as an income balance for the Rest-of-the-World.

Market clearance
The market balances for produced goods, domestic demand, the capital and labour market are given in equations (DEAN-22) through (DEAN-25). Equation (DEAN-26) gives the balance between savings and investment.

4.5.2   Environmental Issues

Emissions and abatement
The environment is captured in this book purely via pollution (emissions) and abatement, and the combination of these constitutes 'environmental services'.[8] Environmental services are a combination of technically unabatable pollution, $E^U_{e,jh,t}$, technically abatable pollution, $E^A_{e,jh,t}$, and abatement $A_{e,jh,t}$, as stated in equation (DEAN-27). At the lower level, the substitution between technically abatable pollution and abatement is estimated by the 'Pollution – Abatement Substitution' (PAS) curve. At the higher level, technically unabatable pollution has to be added in a Leontief manner, to represent the part of the pollution that can only be reduced through changes in activity levels of the polluters.

The benchmark division between technically unabatable and technically abatable pollution is given in equation (DEAN-28). Note that the effective share of both parts of pollution may be different in the policy simulations, as both parts are endogenously determined in the model. It is expected that the technically abatable part will decrease much more than the technically unabatable part, as the cheapest technical measures will be cheaper than the costs of output reduction.

In equation (DEAN-29) the market balance for pollution is given. Total pollution cannot exceed the number of pollution permits issued by the government. Equation (DEAN-30) states that the demand for abatement must equal the supply of abatement. Note that the production function of abatement is already covered in equation (DEAN-15) and hence does not have to be specified separately.

For the environmental theme Climate change, the total addition to the stock of greenhouse gases until the current period is calculated in equation (DEAN-31).

Environmental technological progress
Autonomous pollution efficiency improvements result in a relative decoupling of economic growth and pollution. This is captured in equation (DEAN-32) for both producers and consumers. Equation (DEAN-33) gives the development in the technical potential for pollution reduction techniques.

Autonomous abatement efficiency improvements are represented in equation (DEAN-34). The compensating price development in equation (DEAN-35) ensures that the *value* of abatement, $p_{A,t} \cdot Y_{A,t}$, grows in the benchmark with the common growth rate g_L.

4.6   DISCUSSION AND CONCLUSIONS

The prototype forward-looking AGE model as analysed in Chapter 3 was kept as simple as possible to allow maximum focus on the mechanisms that drive the interactions between economic growth, pollution and abatement. This chapter starts with a discussion on why the forward-looking prototype model is used as the basis for the specification of the more elaborate DEAN model. It then presents some model extensions that align the model specification more with reality. These include non-unitary income elasticities, international trade via an Armington formulation, trade margins and stock mutations. The extensions of the environmental part of the model include a stock-oriented approach to greenhouse gases, public environmental expenditures and a more detailed specification of the intertemporal aspects of abatement.

The development of abatement possibilities and abatement costs over time are captured via specific parameters that govern the changes in the technical potential for pollution reduction over time, and efficiency improvements in the abatement sector. In the current specification of the model, these developments in abatement possibilities and costs are driven by exogenous parameters. Nonetheless, the model does contain endogenous diffusion of abatement technology.

The forward-looking specification with all economic and environmental extensions together give the full description of the DEAN model, which will be applied in the next chapters.

NOTES

1. Note that the assumption on the foresight behaviour of the consumer is not necessarily linked to the assumption on the savings decision; the combination as used in Chapter 3 is, however, the most common one. The reason for this is that the forward-looking model and the endogenous savings decision both depend on analysis of consumer optimisation. On a side note, it also fits with the historical development of the theories of the Solow-Swan model in the 1950s and the Cass-Koopmans-Ramsey model in the 1960s.
2. The use of CES and CET functions implies that reactions are symmetric. This may not always be in line with reality. Introducing asymmetric functions would, however, complicate the model substantially.
3. The interpretation of the conversion factor that transforms foreign prices into domestic prices, the 'price of foreign goods', as exchange rate should be done carefully; the real exchange rate is calculated as the exchange rate divided by the domestic consumer price index. See de Melo and Robinson (1989) for more details. Nonetheless, following most of the applied literature, the conversion factor is, admittedly loosely, labelled 'exchange rate' throughout this book.
4. Closure rules are very common in applied models (De Melo and Robinson, 1989; most of the single country applied models discussed in Section 2.3 adopt similar or identical closure rules), but are subject to theoretical criticism since they represent an incomplete specification of certain markets (in this case the money market).
5. This is a deviation from Gerlagh et al. (2002), where public environmental expenditures are regarded as defensive expenditures and hence are not specified as economic activity.
6. The treatment of the abatement cost curve as a continuous function, instead of as a stepwise function with discrete choices (take the measure or not) implies that partial implementation of the measure in the economy (partial diffusion) is assumed possible. This reflects a situation in which some polluters implement the measure and others don't, while for individual polluters the choice to implement a measure may be a discrete choice. This is justified as the number of polluters is large.
7. Subscripts indicate environmental theme (e), production sector (j) or consumer group (h) and time period (t). See Appendix 4.I for more details.
8. This use of the term 'environmental services' should not be confused with the notion of 'services provided by the environment' as is sometimes used in theoretical models.

APPENDIX 4.I   EXPLANATION OF SYMBOLS USED

Indices

Label	Entries	Description[*]
v_J	$1,...,V_J$	'CES-knots' in production functions
v_H	$1,...,V_H$	'CES-knots' in instantaneous utility functions
e	$1,...,E$	Environmental themes
h	$1,...,H$	Consumer groups
j and jj	$1,...,J,A$	Production sectors, including Abatement sector (A)
jh	(JxH)	Combination of production sectors and consumer groups
t	$1,...,T$	Time periods (of 5 years each)

Note: [*]The elements of the different sets are discussed in the next chapter.

Parameters

Symbol	description
δ_{EM}	Decay rate of greenhouse gas stock additions
δ_K^a	Annual depreciation rate
δ_K	Per period depreciation rate: $(1 - \delta_K) = (1 - \delta_K^a)^5$
ε_{EM}	Marginal atmospheric retention rate of greenhouse gases
φ_e^a	Annual autonomous pollution efficiency improvement for environmental theme e; assumed equal across all agents
φ_e	Per period autonomous pollution efficiency improvement for environmental theme e: $(1 + g_L - \varphi_e) = (1 + g_L^a - \varphi_e^a)^5$
φ_A^a	Annual autonomous abatement efficiency improvement
φ_A	Per period autonomous abatement efficiency improvement: $(1 + g_L + \varphi_A) = (1 + g_L^a + \varphi_A^a)^5$
η_j	Income elasticity for good j for private households and subsistence consumer
σ_h^v	Substitution elasticities between consumption goods combined in knot v_H in instantaneous utility function for consumer h
σ_j^v	Substitution elasticities between inputs combined in knot v_J in production function for sector j
$\sigma_{e,h}^A$	Substitution elasticities between pollution and abatement (PAS elasticity) for environmental theme e in instantaneous utility function for consumer h

Parameters *(continued)*

Symbol	description
$\sigma_{e,j}^{A}$	Substitution elasticities between pollution and abatement (PAS elasticity) for environmental theme e in production function for sector j
$\sigma_{e,jh}^{ES}$	Substitution elasticity between technically unabatable pollution and technically abatable pollution/abatement aggregate for environmental theme e for sector j/consumer h (always equal to zero)
σ^{exp}	Transformation elasticity between domestic demand and exports
σ^{imp}	Substitution elasticity between domestic production and imports
σ_{h}^{Util}	Intertemporal substitution elasticities in utility function for consumer h (between time periods)
$\tau_{j,h}$	Tax rate on consumption of good j by consumer h
$\tau_{jj,j}$	Tax rate on input of good jj by sector j
$\tau_{K,j}$	Tax rate on capital demand by sector j
$\tau_{L,j}$	Tax rate on labour demand by sector j
τ_{h}^{LS}	Lump sum transfer from government to consumer h, with $\sum_{h=1}^{H} \tau_{h}^{LS} = 0$
$\mu_{e,jh,t}$	Benchmark share of technically abatable emissions in total emissions for environmental theme e (technical potential parameter) for sector j/consumer h in period t
$\overline{BD}_{h,t}$	Annual budget deficit for consumer h in period t
$\overline{E}_{e,t}$	Annual endowments of pollution permits for environmental theme e in period t
g_{μ}^{a}	Exogenous annual growth rate of technical potential parameter
g_{μ}	Per period growth rate of technical potential parameter: $(1+g_{\mu}) = (1+g_{\mu}^{a})^5$
g_{L}^{a}	Exogenous annual growth rate of labour supply
g_{L}	Per period growth rate of labour supply: $(1+g_{L}) = (1+g_{L}^{a})^5$
$\overline{L}_{t}$	Exogenous annual labour supply in period t
r^{a}	Annual steady state interest rate
r	Per period steady state interest rate: $(1+r) = (1+r^{a})^5$
$\overline{W}_{'govt',t}$	Annual benchmark size of government sector in period t
$\overline{W}_{'subs.',t}$	Annual benchmark size of subsistence consumer in period t

Variables[*]

Symbol	description
α_t	Endogenous change in existing tax rates to offset changes in government income in period t
α_t^{LS}	Endogenous change in lump sum transfers to offset changes in government income in period t
$\gamma_{h,t}^{LS}$	Annual lump sum transfer from (surplus) private households to the subsistence consumer, with $\sum_{h=1}^{H} \gamma_{h,t}^{LS} = 0 \ \forall t$
$\Pi_{j,t}$	Annual (net) profits in sector j in period t (equal to zero)
$A_{e,jh,t}$	Annual demand for abatement of environmental theme e by sector j/consumer h in period t, with $\sum_{e=1}^{E} A_{e,j,t} \equiv Y_{A,j,t}^{ID}$ and $\sum_{e=1}^{E} A_{e,h,t} \equiv C_{A,h,t}$
$C_{j,h,t}$	Annual consumption of good j by consumer h in period t
$E_{e,jh,t}$	Annual total emissions of environmental theme e by sector j/consumer h in period t ($E_{e,jh,t}^{A} + E_{e,jh,t}^{U} \equiv E_{e,jh,t}$)
$E_{e,jh,t}^{A}$	Annual technically 'abatable' emissions of environmental theme e by sector j/consumer h in period t
$E_{e,jh,t}^{U}$	Annual technically 'unabatable' emissions of environmental theme e by sector j/consumer h in period t
EM_t	Level of greenhouse gas stock addition up to and including period t
$ES_{e,jh,t}$	Annual emission services of environmental theme e by sector j/consumer h in period t
$I_{j,t}$	Annual investment in sector j in period t
$\bar{K}_t$	Annual capital supply in period t
$K_{j,t}$	Annual capital demand by sector j in period t
$L_{j,t}$	Annual labour demand by sector j in period t
$M_{j,t}$	Annual imports of good j in period t
$p_{e,t}$	Equilibrium market price of pollution permits for environmental theme e in period t
$p_{j,t}$	Equilibrium market price of good j (including A) in period t
$p_{K,t}$	Equilibrium market price of capital goods in period t
$p_{L,t}$	Equilibrium market wage rate in period t
$p_{x,t}$	Equilibrium exchange rate (price of foreign goods) in period t

Variables *(continued)*

Symbol	description
$p_{h,t}^W$	Equilibrium price of the 'instantaneous utility good' (price index of consumption bundle)
$r_{K,t}$	Equilibrium market rental price of capital in period t
S_t	Annual savings in period t
TR_t	Endogenous annual tax revenues in period t
U_h	Total utility of consumer h over all periods
$W_{h,t}$	Annual, instantaneous utility level of consumer h in period t
$X_{j,t}$	Annual exports of good j in period t
$Y_{A,t}$	Annual production quantity of Abatement sector in period t (no international trade in Abatement goods)
$Y_{j,t}^{DD}$	Annual domestic demand for good j in period t
$Y_{j,t}^{DS}$	Annual production quantity (domestic supply) of sector j in period t
$Y_{jj,j,t}^{ID}$	Annual demand for input jj by sector j in period t
$Y_{j,t}^{TS}$	Annual total (Armington) supply of good j in period t

Note:
* The variables for the good '*ncm*' are not given here but are analogue to the variables for domestically produced goods, as far as applicable. The elements of the different sets are discussed in the next chapter.

APPENDIX 4.II   THE LES TRANSFORMATION

The division of consumption into a subsistence and surplus part can be achieved by the following transformation, where the time subscript is dropped for convenience.

$$C_j^{subs.} = \left(1 - \frac{\eta_j}{cst}\right) \cdot C_j \text{ and } C_j^{priv.} = \left(\frac{\eta_j}{cst}\right) \cdot C_j \qquad (A4.1)$$

Introduce Y for income and Y^{priv} for total consumption of the surplus part: $Y \equiv \Sigma_j C_j$ and $Y^{priv} \equiv \Sigma_j C_j^{priv}$. Furthermore, assume income increases with ξ per cent:

$$\frac{dY}{Y} = \xi \tag{A4.2}$$

The change in income only affects the surplus part of consumption: $dC_j^{subs} = 0$, $dC_j^{priv} = dC_j$ and $dY^{priv} = dY$. Due to the unitary income elasticities, the percentage change in surplus consumption is identical for all goods and equals

$$\frac{dC_j^{priv}}{C_j^{priv}} = \frac{dY^{priv}}{Y^{priv}} = \xi \cdot \frac{Y}{Y^{priv}} \quad \forall j \tag{A4.3}$$

For transformation function (A4.1),

$$\frac{Y}{Y^{priv}} = \frac{Y}{\sum_j \left(\frac{\eta_j}{cst}\right) \cdot C_j} = cst \cdot \frac{Y}{\sum_j \eta_j \cdot C_j} = cst \tag{A4.4}$$

as by definition (see Keller, 1980)

$$\sum_j \left\{ \eta_j \cdot \left(\frac{C_j}{Y}\right) \right\} \equiv 1 \tag{A4.5}$$

In this case, the percentage change in total consumption of good j, dC_j/C_j, equals

$$\frac{dC_j}{C_j} = \frac{dC_j^{priv}}{\left(\frac{cst}{\eta_j}\right) \cdot C_j^{priv}} = \frac{\eta_j}{cst} \cdot \frac{dC_j^{priv}}{C_j^{priv}} = \frac{\eta_j}{cst} \cdot \xi \cdot \frac{Y}{Y^{priv}} = \eta_j \cdot \xi \tag{A4.6}$$

The calculated income elasticity is

$$\left(\frac{dC_j}{C_j}\right) \Big/ \left(\frac{dY}{Y}\right) = (\eta_j \cdot \xi)/(\xi) = \eta_j \tag{A4.7}$$

APPENDIX 4.III   THE MULTI-YEAR PERIOD SPECIFICATION

When each period in the model consists of more than one year, the transfer between periods, and especially the build-up of the capital stock, has to be properly calibrated. This procedure is described in Rutherford (2001) and explained below.

In the *annual specification*, the steady state conditions imply

$$I_t = \left(\frac{g_L^a + \delta_k^a}{r^a + \delta_K^a} \right) \cdot KS_t = \left(g_L^a + \delta_k^a \right) \cdot K_t \qquad (A4.8)$$

where I_t denotes investments in period t, KS_t the annual services the current capital stock delivers to the production sectors and K_t the capital stock. The parameters that link these flows and stocks are the balanced growth rate g_L^a, depreciation rate δ_K^a and the interest rate r^a, all in annual terms. The idea is that in the steady state investments cover replacement investments ($\delta_K^a \cdot K_t$) and expansion investments ($g_L^a \cdot K_t$). Annual capital services (KS_t) equal payments to depreciation ($\delta_K^a \cdot K_t$) and profits ($r^a \cdot K_t$). An additional requirement in the steady state is that capital grows at the balanced growth rate:

$$K_{t+1} = (1 + g_L^a) \cdot K_t \qquad (A4.9)$$

Consequently, investments and capital services also grow with the balanced growth rate.

The steady state is also characterised by equilibrium conditions for prices. Firstly, the value of one unit of capital has to equal the rental price of the capital service delivered by that unit, plus the depreciated value of the remaining capital stock in the next period:

$$p_{K,t} = r_{K,t} + (1 - \delta_K^a) \cdot p_{K,t+1} \qquad (A4.10)$$

This ensures zero profit in capital supply. Secondly, in the steady state the price of capital goods is discounted with the interest rate:

$$p_{K,t+1} = \frac{p_{K,t}}{1 + r^a} \qquad (A4.11)$$

so that in real terms the price of capital goods is constant over time and we can lose the subscript for time:

$$p_K = r_K + \left(\frac{1-\delta_K^a}{1+r^a}\right) \cdot p_K = \left(\frac{1+r^a}{r^a + \delta_K^a}\right) \cdot r_K \qquad \text{(A4.12)}$$

The rental price on capital services equals the return to capital:

$$r_K = r^a + \delta_K^a \qquad \text{(A4.13)}$$

and hence

$$p_K = 1 + r^a \qquad \text{(A4.14)}$$

In the *multi-year period specification*, it is convenient to introduce *per period* (5 years) growth, depreciation and interest rates:

$$(1+g_L) = (1+g_L^a)^5, \ (1-\delta_K) = (1-\delta_K^a)^5 \ \text{and} \ (1+r) = (1+r^a)^5 \qquad \text{(A4.15)}$$

As capital services are measured in annual terms, it is logical to keep the calibration of the rental price of capital unchanged:

$$r_K = r^a + \delta_K^a \qquad \text{(A4.16)}$$

The price of capital goods can then be derived as a function of the *per period* interest and depreciation rates and the *annual* rental price of capital:

$$p_K = \left(\frac{1+r}{r+\delta_K}\right) \cdot r_K = (1+r) \cdot \left(\frac{r^a + \delta_K^a}{r+\delta_K}\right) \qquad \text{(A4.17)}$$

Assume that one unit of investment produces ι^C units of capital in the current period and ι^N units of capital in the next period. These two parameters have to be calibrated such that the equilibrium and steady state conditions still hold. The first condition on these quantities is that the capital stock generated in the next period equals this period's capital stock multiplied by the balanced growth rate for the period:

$$(K_t + \iota^C \cdot I_t) \cdot (1-\delta_K) + \iota^N \cdot I_t = K_t \cdot (1+g_L) \qquad \text{(A4.18)}$$

This can be rearranged to (see equation (A4.8))

$$K_t \cdot (g_L + \delta_K) = \left\{ \iota^C \cdot (1 - \delta_K) + \iota^N \right\} \cdot I \tag{A4.19}$$

The second condition is that the volume of capital services equals this period's return to capital, that is, the rental price of capital services times the capital stock (see equation (A4.8)):

$$KS_t = r_K \cdot (K_t + \iota^C \cdot I_t) = (r^a + \delta_K^a) \cdot (K_t + \iota^C \cdot I_t) \tag{A4.20}$$

Together, these two conditions give

$$\left(\frac{KS_t}{r^a + \delta_K^a} - \iota^C \cdot I_t \right) \cdot (g_L + \delta_K) = \left\{ \iota^C \cdot (1 - \delta_K) + \iota^N \right\} \cdot I_t \tag{A4.21}$$

The steady state condition that links investments and capital services, as specified in the annual model still holds:

$$I_t = KS_t \cdot \left(\frac{g_L^a + \delta_K^a}{r^a + \delta_K^a} \right) \tag{A4.22}$$

Hence, the condition on ι^C and ι^N can be rearranged to

$$\iota^C \cdot (1 + g_L) + \iota^N = \left(\frac{g_L + \delta_K}{g_L^a + \delta_K^a} \right) \tag{A4.23}$$

A third condition on the investment quantities is that there is zero profit in investments, which means that the value of inputs to investment equal the total value of capital produced with this investment. Per unit of investment the condition is

$$p_K \cdot \iota^C + \frac{p_K}{1+r} \cdot \iota^N = 1 \tag{A4.24}$$

Using the derived equation for the capital price (A4.17), this can be rearranged to

$$\left(\iota^C + \frac{\iota^N}{1+r} \right) \cdot (1+r) = \frac{r + \delta_K}{r^a + \delta_K^a} \tag{A4.25}$$

This implies

$$\iota^N = \left(\frac{r+\delta_K}{r^a+\delta_K^a}\right) - \iota^C \cdot (1+r) \tag{A4.26}$$

Substituting (A4.26) into (A4.23) yields

$$\iota^C \cdot (1+g_L) + \left(\frac{r+\delta_K}{r^a+\delta_K^a}\right) - \iota^C \cdot (1+r) = \left(\frac{g_L+\delta_K}{g_L^a+\delta_K^a}\right) \tag{A4.27}$$

This can be rearranged to

$$\iota^C = \left(\frac{1}{g_L-r}\right) \cdot \left\{\left(\frac{g_L+\delta_K}{g_L^a+\delta_K^a}\right) - \left(\frac{r+\delta_K}{r^a+\delta_K^a}\right)\right\} \tag{A4.28}$$

Substituting this back into condition (A4.26) and rearranging gives

$$\iota^N = \left(\frac{-1}{g_L-r}\right) \cdot \left\{\left(\frac{g_L+\delta_K}{g_L^a+\delta_K^a}\right)\cdot(1+r) - \left(\frac{r+\delta_K}{r^a+\delta_K^a}\right)\cdot(1+g_L)\right\} \tag{A4.29}$$

If the annual growth rate equals 2 per cent ($g_L^a = 0.02$), the annual depreciation rate equals 3 per cent ($\delta_K^a = 0.03$) and the interest rate equals 5 per cent ($r^a = 0.05$), then

$$\iota^C \simeq \left(\frac{1}{0.104-0.276}\right) \cdot \left\{\left(\frac{0.104+0.141}{0.02+0.03}\right) - \left(\frac{0.276+0.141}{0.05+0.03}\right)\right\} \simeq 1.81$$

and $\iota^N \simeq 2.90$.

So each unit of investment gives 1.81 units of capital that is already productive in the current period and 2.90 units of capital that is productive in the next period.

APPENDIX 4.IV A PERMIT SYSTEM FOR STOCK POLLUTANTS

In case of a stock-oriented environmental policy, the annual emissions by polluters are not directly restricted, but the total addition to the stock is.[1] The government limits the total addition to a stock by issuing 'stock addition permits'.[2] If annual emissions exceed the natural decay of the existing stock (that is, exceed the regeneration capacity of the environment), which is normally the case, the stock will increase over time, until the policy target for total stock addition is reached. In those years before the stock target is reached, emissions are effectively unbounded. The problem is then that annual emissions are unpriced until the target is reached, and that the government only collects income from the sale of the stock addition permits when the target is reached, that is, only in the last period(s).

To overcome this problem, the stock-oriented policy is carried out in two parts:

(i) The government sets up a so-called 'environmental fund' that issues emission permits to polluters.

(ii) The government issues stock addition permits when the stock addition target is reached.

Part (i) ensures that polluters have to pay annually for their emissions. The environmental fund calculates how large will be the stock addition in the final year of the model horizon stemming from this emission (depending on the decay and atmospheric retention rates). In part (ii), the environmental fund uses the proceeds from the emission permits to buy stock addition permits from the government. This procedure works well because of the assumption of perfect foresight: the environmental fund knows what price to charge for the emission permits, as it knows what the future price of the stock addition permits will be: the price for one unit of emissions will equal the costs of the stock addition permits that allow that unit to be emitted.

The perfect foresight assumption also impacts on the behaviour of private households. As the government does not receive income from the emission permits directly (these are stored in the environmental fund), the annual transfer from government to the households only reflects the government income from the sale of the stock addition permits, which is only positive if the stock addition target is reached. The private households, however, know that a large transfer will occur in the future, and respond to this by running a budget deficit in earlier periods. This budget deficit is exactly covered by the surplus of the environmental fund.

Before the stock addition permits become active, the environmental fund has an annual income from the sale of the emission permits that it lends to private households; the government itself has no income from the sale of stock addition permits. When the policy target is reached, the stock addition permits become active, and the environmental fund buys the stock addition permits from the government. The government hence earns additional income and the assumption of a fixed level of government spending implies that the government transfers these additional revenues to the private households. This allows the private households to pay back the loan they have with the environmental fund. Consequently, the environmental fund is capable of buying the stock addition permits. From this it follows that for every period the budget deficit of one sector is exactly matched by a budget surplus of another sector, so that at a macro-economic level the monetary flows are closed.

Note that the behaviour of private households is identical to their behaviour in case the government would issue emission permits: the environmental fund is used to smooth income and expenditures over time. For the interpretation of the results, the environmental fund can be aggregated with the government sector.

This set-up with an auxiliary 'environmental fund' means that the actual annual stock additions can be measured directly by looking at the amount of emission permits sold by the environmental fund. Annual emissions as well as stock additions and the current size of the stock can be directly inferred from the model results in this specification.

It should be noted that the total value of the stock addition permits can be very substantial in the period when the stock addition target is reached, as it comprises the equivalent of all previous emissions. Hence, large transfers between the government and private households are involved, and the model should be flexible enough to facilitate such large transfers. For example, if the model assumes that the environmental permit revenues can only be used for reducing existing taxes, the revenues might be larger than the existing taxes, and additional assumptions are needed for the rest of the revenues. In the DEAN model, the large transfers do not lead to any technical modelling problems, as the government redistributes the revenues to private households via a lump sum transfer of flexible size.

NOTES

1. Note that the *additions* to the stock are subject to policy. This implies that the stock is set at some exogenous constant in the base year of the model and that only domestic emissions contribute to the stock. The rationale for this approach is that national policy can only influence domestic emissions.
2. The procedure presented here is an adaptation of material from Tom Rutherford's homepage (http://nash.colorado.edu/tomruth/stock.htm).

5. Calibration of the DEAN model to The Netherlands

5.1 INTRODUCTION

The data needed to calibrate the applied general equilibrium model are twofold. Firstly, data is needed that describes the benchmark; starting year data are used to specify the initial accounting matrix. For a dynamic model, the parameters that govern the growth of the economy in the benchmark projection, in particular the growth rate of labour supply, also have to be specified. Secondly, the reactions of agents to a given impulse are determined by the substitution and income elasticities and abatement cost curves. Besides these two types of calibration data, a so-called impulse has to be specified, which represents the shock that is given to the system. The shock is specified in this book as a change in environmental policy in quantitative terms. Together with the structure of the model as laid down in the model equations, this determines the new equilibrium growth path, which can then be compared to the benchmark projection.

The choice of the base year influences the results, because the model assumes that the economy is initially on a balanced growth path. For any particular base year, business cycle effects occur and hence the economy is likely to deviate from the steady state at any given moment in time. Dynamic AGEs provide insight into the direction in which the economy is heading; they show the future development of the economy if it is undisturbed, but in reality the economy will always be disturbed. In the last few decades, more and more researchers have concluded that business cycles and the economic growth trend are related and influence each other (for an introduction to this literature see de Groot, 1998), a notion stressed long before by Schumpeter (1934). This relationship is not present in exogenous-growth AGE models like DEAN, but it plays a role in the endogenous growth literature (Aghion and Howitt, 1998).

The influence of the base year on the DEAN model results is limited by the calibration procedure for the model parameters, especially the growth rate of labour supply (g_L^a), the depreciation rate (δ_k^a) and the interest rate (r^a). These parameters are based on trend analysis for the period 1990-2000 and, as far as necessary, on the best information available from the literature and expert judgement. It is beyond the scope of this book to empirically estimate other parameters than the parameters used for abatement. As a consequence, all other parameters are calibrated using the best available information. An advantage to using 1990 as the starting year for calibration of the model, even though more recent data are available, is that analysis of realised trends since 1990 allows for an improved calibration of the model.

In the sections below, the data for the benchmark accounting matrix, the abatement cost curves and the economic and environmental parameters are discussed. The appendices contain information on the use of the accounting matrix, the complete input-output table for 1990, emissions and emission intensities by sector and realised growth rates of the main variables for the period 1990-2000.

5.2   DATA FOR THE BENCHMARK ACCOUNTING MATRIX

The base year data are taken from historical data for 1990 for The Netherlands, as reported in Dellink et al. (2001).[1] The original data are provided by Statistics Netherlands (2000) and are based on the National Accounts and environmental statistics for 1990. Appendix 5.I discusses how a social accounting matrix (SAM) can be used to represent both economic and environmental data. The emissions table is reproduced in Appendix 5.II; the main characteristics of economic activity and emissions will be described in the sections below.

The categorisation of production sectors often differs between economic and environmental accounts. Some production sectors (such as the services sub-sectors) are economically highly relevant and hence require a sufficiently disaggregated set-up in the economic accounts, while their environmental impact is relatively unimportant (and hence their representation in environmental accounts is often at a higher level of aggregation). Similarly, there are also sectors that are highly significant from an environmental perspective, but are less relevant in the economic accounts (for example, chemical sub-sectors). Moreover, for some sub-sectors Statistics Netherlands may be prohibited from providing disaggregated data for reasons of confidentiality (if there is one dominant producer in the sub-sector).

There is a series of statistics produced by Statistics Netherlands that does cover both economic and environmental accounts at a reasonable level of disaggregation, called NAMEA (Keuning, 1993). This set of statistics is readily available for more recent years. That a different data set than NAMEA is used does not mean that the data in DEAN are radically different from data in the NAMEA: the underlying data are mostly based on the same raw data as compiled by Statistics Netherlands. However, there may be some differences in definitions (mainly in the environmental accounts) and in representation and aggregation.

5.2.1   Sectoral Domestic Production and Consumption

On the production side, 27 producers of private goods are identified; this allows for a moderate degree of detail on the side of economic and environmental diversity. A more disaggregated set-up was not feasible due to data limitations. There are two household groups: private households and the government, with consumption of the former split into subsistence consumption and surplus consumption.

Some characteristics of production in The Netherlands in 1990 are given in Table 5.1. Total production value is given both in absolute amounts and as a share of total production value in the economy. The column for total consumption shows absolute and relative consumption levels for private households and government together.

The production column in Table 5.1 shows that the Non-commercial services (incl. government) sector is the largest sector in terms of production value; it comprises almost 18 per cent of total production in the economy.[2] The economic importance of this sector is even larger in terms of value added. The second largest sector is the Commercial services sector, followed by the Trade sector. Looking at total consumption the picture is slightly different: the Non-commercial services remain the largest sector (constituting 47 per cent of total consumption value), but Trade is no longer in the top three. This indicates that the Trade sector is to a large extent involved in inter-sectoral trade, as expected. For the Textiles, clothing and leather industries the consumption value is higher than the production value, reflecting low inter-sectoral trade, high imports and low exports.

The Gross Domestic Product (GDP) can be calculated as the sum of the payments for the primary production factors (the value added) including taxes. Correcting for foreign expenditures by households yields the Gross National Income (GNI). Finally, the Net National Income (NNI) is derived from GNI by subtracting depreciation. The calculated GDP in 1990 according to the DEAN is 234 billion euros; NNI equals 196 billion euros. According to Statistics Netherlands (1996), the official numbers for 1990 are 235 billion euros for GDP and 207 billion euros for NNI, respectively. The difference in NNI between the accounting matrix and the official statistics can be explained by the adjustment of the investment level in DEAN to assure that the economy is on a balanced growth path.

*Table 5.1   Sectoral economic data for The Netherlands, 1990 (in million
              euros at 1990 prices)*

Sector number and description*	Production 1990 m. €	(share)	Consumption 1990 m. €	(share)
1 Agriculture and fisheries	17154	(4.5%)	1362	(1.0%)
2 Extraction of oil and natural gas	8061	(2.1%)	122	(0.1%)
3 Other mining and quarrying	430	(0.1%)	65	(0.0%)
4 Food and food products industry	28588	(7.5%)	14390	(10.8%)
5 Textiles, clothing and leather ind.	3355	(0.9%)	5593	(4.2%)
6 Paper and board industry	3075	(0.8%)	361	(0.3%)
7 Printing industry	7453	(1.9%)	2420	(1.8%)
8 Oil refineries	8176	(2.1%)	866	(0.7%)
9 Chemical industry	15537	(4.1%)	2135	(1.6%)
10 Rubber and plastics industry	3711	(1.0%)	799	(0.6%)
11 Basic metals industry	4044	(1.1%)	476	(0.4%)
12 Metal products industry	8231	(2.1%)	116	(0.1%)
13 Machine industry	7225	(1.9%)	1324	(1.0%)
14 Electromechanical industry	9587	(2.5%)	1196	(0.9%)
15 Transport equipment industry	7633	(2.0%)	3824	(2.9%)
16 Other industries	9585	(2.5%)	3058	(2.3%)
17 Energy distribution	8120	(2.1%)	2281	(1.7%)
18 Water distribution	874	(0.2%)	447	(0.3%)
19 Construction	28359	(7.4%)	2460	(1.9%)
20 Trade and related services	54178	(14.1%)	5080	(3.8%)
21 Transport by land	8760	(2.3%)	2452	(1.8%)
22 Transport by water	2904	(0.8%)	139	(0.1%)
23 Transport by air	3276	(0.9%)	401	(0.3%)
24 Transport services	5448	(1.4%)	1527	(1.1%)
25 Commercial services	60460	(15.8%)	21074	(15.9%)
26 Non-commercial services incl. government	68191	(17.8%)	58876	(44.3%)
27 Other goods and services	922	(0.2%)	0	(0.0%)

Note: * Goods are represented by their production sector.

The data for tax categories could unfortunately not be custom-made. The categories in the model follow the categorisation in the National Accounts, and lack sufficient detail for the DEAN model. Sectoral data on taxes paid for the use of capital by firms is not distinguished from output-related taxes and import taxes are only available by the importing sector, while the DEAN model requires import taxes by imported good. The significance of the mispecification in the tax categories in the analysis may, however, be limited, as the policy simulations all comprise an equal yield tax reform.

The lump sum transfer between private households and the government consists of two opposing items. First, households pay taxes on their supply of labour, and as labour supply is fixed, this is effectively a lump sum transfer. Second, the government provides social security benefits to households. The net transfer is from households to government.

5.2.2   International Trade Flows

In most accounting matrices, competitive imports are given in a single row (often together with non-competitive imports), representing the value of imports *by importing sector*. Hence, in such a set-up, the element in the column for Agriculture and the row for Competitive imports gives total imports of goods and services by the Agricultural sector. Similarly, the column for Private households contains total consumption of imported goods in the imports row.

In the DEAN model, imports are specified *by imported good or service*. This can be represented in the accounting matrix by taking the competitive imports as a column. Each row of this column describes how much of the good is imported. Given the Armington assumption on international trade, these imports then rival with domestically produced goods and services. The non-competitive imports are still given by a single row.

To construct the imports by imported good or service in the 'imports column', a full matrix of competitive imports is provided by Statistics Netherlands. Summing all rows in this matrix gives the imports row (imports by importing sector), and summing all columns provides the required data for the imports column (imports by imported good or service).

These data are transposed to the column through a simple two-step procedure. Firstly, the full import matrix is aggregated with the matrix of (domestic) intermediate deliveries (which is commonly known as the A-matrix) to form a so-called 'total intermediate deliveries' matrix. Secondly, a column is added to the matrix displaying the imports by imported good with a negative sign. In this way, domestic production is separated from imported goods. The economic interpretation of the resulting accounting matrix is that each domestic production sector imports the competing import goods and services and then sells this to clients together with its own domestic production.

Two entries in the accounting matrix cannot be dealt with in the economic model: taxes on exports and stock changes of non-competitive imports. These relatively unimportant entries are excluded from the matrix.

5.2.3   Emissions per Environmental Theme by Sector

The environmental data for the historical year encompass the following environmental themes:

(i)   Climate change (the enhanced greenhouse effect),
(ii)   Acidification,
(iii)   Eutrophication,
(iv)   Smog formation,
(v)   Dispersion of fine dust,
(vi)   Desiccation and
(vii)   Soil contamination.

The latter two are conceptually different from the other environmental themes, as they don't entail emissions and are not specified on a sectoral basis. For these themes, the model only includes an estimate of the annual costs involved in cleaning up and restoration (see Section 5.3.8 below). Hence, they are not discussed in this section. The emission levels for the other environmental themes for 1990 are given in Table 5.2.

Table 5.2   Emission levels in 1990

	Unit*	Emission level 1990
Climate change	billion CO_2-equivalents	254.53
Acidification	million acid-equivalents	40.18
Eutrophication	million P-equivalents	192.26
Smog formation	million kilograms VOC	527.09
Dispersion of fine dust	million kilograms PM_{10}	78.62

Note: * For explanation of the aggregation into theme equivalents, see Chapter 2.

Table 5.3 presents the sectors in the economy that have a *large* or *small* share in total emission levels: 'dirty' and 'clean' sectors, respectively. Not surprisingly, Agriculture and Private households are among the largest polluters for three and five environmental themes, respectively. The agricultural sector is well known for its environmental impact, though it may seem surprising that it is also the largest polluter for climate change (caused primarily by CH_4 and to some extent by N_2O emissions). This effect is also connected to the aggregation of the sectors. There are three energy sectors in the model (Oil and gas extraction, Oil refineries, and Energy distribution) and together these account for more than a quarter of total CO_2-equivalent emissions. Private households are large polluters for all environmental themes under investigation. This is caused primarily by the sheer size of this sector.

Table 5.3 'Dirty' and 'clean' polluting sectors in absolute terms

Envir. theme	'Dirty' sectors (share*)	'Clean' sectors (share*)
Climate change	Agriculture (20.0%)	Other mining (0.0%)
	Energy distrib. (16.3%)	Printing industry (0.1%)
	Private househ. (15.0%)	Water distribution (0.1%)
Acidification	Agriculture (42.1%)	Rubber, plastics ind. (0.0%)
	Private househ. (10.1%)	Water distribution (0.0%)
	Transport by water (9.7%)	Other mining (0.1%)
Eutrophication	Agriculture (68.3%)	Other mining (0.0%)
	Private househ. (10.8%)	Rubber, plastics ind. (0.0%)
	Chemical industry (9.0%)	Water distribution (0.0%)
Smog formation	Private househ. (38.7%)	Other mining (0.0%)
	Chemical industry (6.6%)	Water distribution (0.0%)
	Construction (6.4%)	Transport services (0.1%)
Dispersion of	Private househ. (16.7%)	Oil and gas extraction (0.0%)
fine dust	Basic metals ind. (13.0%)	Rubber, plastics ind. (0.0%)
	Transp. by water (10.5%)	Water distribution (0.0%)

Note: * Share calculated as emission by sector divided by total emission in economy (per theme).

The two sectors that are listed most as small polluters are Other mining and quarrying and Water distribution, both very small sectors in economic terms (0.1 per cent and 0.2 per cent share in total production, respectively). Another 'clean' sector is the Rubber and plastics industry, where emissions are negligible for Acidification, Eutrophication and Dispersion of fine dust, but this sector has significant emissions for Climate change (especially CFCs) and Smog formation.

Some environmental themes are much more concentrated in a few sectors than the others. Even though this cannot be directly read from Table 5.3, the shares of the largest three polluting sectors give some insight into this issue. For Climate change, the shares of the largest three polluters are relatively small (just over 50 per cent of total), indicating a more or less even spread of pollution across the economy. This is in line with the intuition that energy use is widespread across all sectors. Another relatively even spread environmental theme is Dispersion of fine dust. Other environmental themes are much more concentrated. For example, Acidification and Eutrophication are concentrated to a large extent in the Agricultural sector. Regardless of whether the pollution is concentrated in some sectors or not, there are always some sectors that hardly contribute to the environmental problem (see the last column in Table 5.3), either because they are very small or because they have a low pollution intensity for that environmental theme.

Table 5.4 presents the high and low polluting sectors in relative terms. This table gives an insight into the pollution intensity of the various sectors. For producers, this intensity is calculated as the pollution in the sector divided by the production quantity; for consumers, the intensity equals pollution divided by total consumption.

Table 5.4   'Dirty' and 'clean' polluting sectors in relative terms

Envir. theme	'Dirty' sectors (factor*)	'Clean' sectors (factor*)
Climate change	Energy distribution (11.2)	Printing industry (0.0)
	Agriculture (6.5)	Commercial services (0.1)
	Transport by air (6.1)	Transport equip. ind. (0.1)
Acidification	Transport by water (18.6)	Rubber, plastics ind. (0.0)
	Agriculture (13.6)	Water distribution (0.1)
	Energy distribution (5.3)	Transport equip. ind. (0.1)
Eutrophication	Agriculture (22.1)	Water distribution (0.0)
	Transport by water (3.3)	Printing industry (0.0)
	Chemical industry (3.2)	Rubber, plastics ind. (0.0)
Smog formation	Other goods, serv. (19.9)	Other mining (0.0)
	Metal products ind. (3.1)	Energy distribution (0.0)
	Oil and gas extraction (3.1)	Water distribution (0.0)
Dispersion of	Transport by water (20.2)	Water distribution (0.0)
fine dust	Basic metals ind. (17.8)	Oil and gas extraction (0.0)
	Oil refineries (5.7)	Rubber, plastics ind. (0.0)

Note: * Factor calculated as pollution intensity of sector divided by average pollution intensity
in economy (per theme).

After the sector name, the table gives pollution intensity factors, which are defined as the pollution intensity of the sector compared to the average pollution intensity of the economy. A factor above unity means relatively high pollution intensities, a factor below unity means low pollution intensity. Table 5.4 shows for example that the production sector with the highest CO_2-equivalent emissions is Energy distribution, which has an intensity of 11.2 times the average greenhouse gas intensity. The full table with pollution intensities on which the factors in Table 5.4 are based can be found in Appendix 5.II.

The most striking difference between Table 5.3 and Table 5.4 is the role that consumers play in pollution: in absolute terms, the consumers rank among the largest polluters for all environmental themes. This does not mean that consumption is a 'dirty sector' in relative terms; on the contrary, for most themes, the pollution intensity of consumption is among the lowest of the economy. Only for Smog formation do private households emit more than average.

Note that this observation is dependent on the way emissions are attributed to the sectors: the tables above report direct emissions by the sector, not all pollution *caused* by the sector (see Chapter 3). Evidently, if pollution stemming from the production of consumer goods is attributed to consumption activity, the environmental intensity of consumption would be much higher.

One technical problem that has to be dealt with is the fact that waste handling facilities (part of the Non-commercial services) prevent substantial eutrophying emissions, mainly due to household organic waste and manure that is incinerated or dumped. In the original data, this is represented as negative emissions. These negative emissions are larger than the positive eutrophying emissions in the other parts of the Non-commercial services, and consequently the total Non-commercial services sector would have a negative emission coefficient for eutrophication. This can lead to technical problems in the model if a system of pollution permits is introduced; therefore these eutrophication 'sinks' are re-attributed to the sectors in which these emissions have originated, such as the agricultural sector and the households; see Statistics Netherlands (2000) for more details.

A calibration problem arises because the emissions stemming from consumption cannot be attributed to the different consumption goods, due to a lack of information. Therefore, the division of emissions between the subsistence and surplus parts of private households will have to be based on the share of both parts in total consumption. De facto this means that emission intensities are assumed to be identical for all consumption goods. This assumption can have a significant impact on the model outcomes, as the consumers have no opportunities of reducing their emissions via a shift from relatively dirty to cleaner goods.

5.2.4 The Abatement Sector Specification

The abatement sector is included in the accounting matrix by means of a row and a column. The row for the abatement sector specifies how large the abatement expenditures of each production sector and consumer are (see Appendices 5.I-5.III). The spending effects of abatement are represented by the column of the abatement sector in the accounting matrix.[3] As with all production sectors, the sum of inputs (the spending effects) has to equal output, and supply has to equal demand (the abatement expenditures of the sectors). In 1990, total output or supply of the abatement sector equalled almost 200 million euros, excluding the public environmental expenditures. Including these, abatement expenditures amounted to around 9.7 billion euros.

The division of abatement expenditures over the different environmental themes is based on the estimated benchmark expenditures on pollution permits. This means that sectors that are relatively large polluters of a certain theme are assumed to concentrate their abatement expenditures proportionately on this theme.

The abatement sector governs the supply of abatement activities to the polluters. The demand for abatement activities is dependent on the abatement cost curves for the environmental themes. These abatement cost curves are discussed in detail in the next section.

5.3   ABATEMENT COST CURVES FOR MAJOR ENVIRONMENTAL THEMES[4]

5.3.1   Introduction

The inventory of technical abatement measures contains many different types of reduction possibilities. End-of-pipe measures are included, as well as process-integrated options. Though the set-up of the model disregards the impact of individual abatement measures on the other inputs in the production functions, all direct environmental and economic effects of the measures are captured in this framework. If the measure leads to reduced inputs of some other good or factor, for example, in the form of energy conservation, these savings are accounted for as operational benefits, and therefore reduce the net costs of the measure. Similarly, increased inputs imply higher operational costs of the measure. The changed input is not accounted for in the production function of the polluter, but affects the production function of the Abatement sector, as this is determined by the average cost components of the measures.

The cost of an individual measure effectively reflects total net costs of adopting the measure at given prices. In this way, the methodology is consistent with the way rational polluters decide upon adoption of an abatement measure. Note that pollution can also be reduced by means of a reduction in economic activity. This is fully endogenised in the model by linking pollution to economic activity. Hence, these so-called 'volume measures' (Hueting and de Boer, 2001) should not be included in the abatement cost curves. Note that the emission reduction realised by fully implementing a measure is given as a fixed amount in physical terms. Therefore, the measures have to be interpreted as additive, and the effects of different measures can be aggregated in cumulative emission reductions.

A rational polluter, when faced with the necessity to reduce pollution, will first take the cheapest measures and then, if necessary, turn to the more costly measures, based on evaluation of private annual net costs. The marginal, and thus also the total, cost curve will therefore be monotonously non-decreasing. Except for extreme cases, not all pollution can be prevented by implementing technical measures only, that is, without reducing economic activity. Therefore, the cost curve approaches a vertical asymptote, where marginal (and total) costs approach infinity.

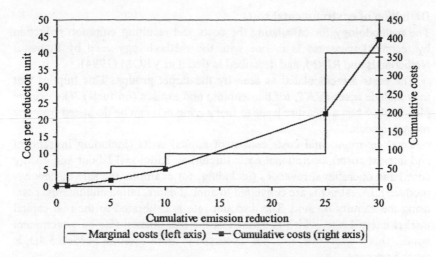

Figure 5.1   Marginal and cumulative costs of pollution reduction

The marginal cost curve of reduction will then take the shape of a step function from the origin, decreasing each time the next cheapest measure is introduced until the last, most expensive measure is reached and no further reduction is possible with technical means. The integral of the marginal cost function yields the function of total (or cumulative) reduction costs with respect to total (cumulative) pollution reduction, as schematically pictured in Figure 5.1 (using illustrative numbers). Under these assumptions the abatement cost function is convex.

For most environmental themes, the main data source was RIVM's RIM⁺ model.[5] The measures, as well as their costs and reduction effects, reflect as far as possible the technological state of the art in the early 1990s.

The themes Desiccation and Soil contamination are special cases, in the sense that they are inheritances from the past, not caused by annual emissions. The reduction costs are not those of pollution reduction but of cleaning up and restoration. For these themes, an abatement cost curve is not relevant and the model simply includes an estimate of the annual costs involved, which will be discussed in Section 5.3.8.

5.3.2   Methodology

The main issues involved in setting up abatement costs curves are discussed below. All abatement cost curves used in this book follow the same methodology.

Definition of environmental costs

The methodology for calculating the costs and resulting emission reduction by technical measures is in line with the methodology used by Statistics Netherlands and RIVM, and described in detail in VROM (1994).

The costs are calculated as seen by the target groups. This implies that they include taxes (VAT, for households) and excises (on fuels). The excises play a role when a measure leads to fuel saving that can be deducted from the reduction costs.

Total environmental costs consist of capital costs (including investment and interest costs), operational costs (including additional labour and energy costs) and operational revenues (including, for example, the sale of new by-products). Investments are converted to annual depreciation and interest costs using the annuity method. The discount rate is calibrated to the real capital market interest rate, which is defined as the real interest rate on government bonds. This interest rate, which is discussed in more detail in Section 5.4.3, is set at 5 per cent.

In 1998, the official methodology for calculating environmental was revised (VROM, 1998a). One important change was that the interest rate should be chosen differentially: the capital market interest rate should be raised with a risk premium depending on the economic sector that implements the abatement measure. RIVM has chosen not to follow this change in the official methodology, for practical reasons (Hanemaaijer, 2000). The figures that are used to calculate the abatement cost curves for the DEAN model are based on the (old) RIVM methodology and consequently, a discount rate of 5 per cent is used for all abatement measures. The cost figures do not include any transaction costs (for example, costs for implementation, enforcement or monitoring).

Negative abatement costs
Near the origin of the cost curve, the calculated costs of reduction may be negative; that is, reduction can be achieved with net savings. This is not in line with neo-classical theory and implies that certain assumptions are violated, be they assumptions on rational behaviour of the target groups, on equilibrium in the economy, on used prices and discount rates, or other assumptions. Reasons why firms do not implement cost-effective measures are discussed in Velthuijsen (1995), who focuses on energy-saving measures.

Retaining the negative abatement costs is clearly inconsistent with the assumptions behind the applied general equilibrium model: as all agents are assumed to behave rationally, these measures would immediately be implemented, regardless of the environmental policy level (in other words: these measures should have been implemented in the benchmark already).

Correcting for these negative costs is not straightforward. One could assume that the negative costs implicitly reflect hidden costs and thus total costs of the measure should be raised with the hidden cost (leading to zero net costs). However, it is arbitrary to set the hidden costs exactly equal to the negative net costs: any hidden cost larger than the negative net cost will also ensure compliance with the model assumptions. Moreover, if the measures with negative net costs should be corrected for hidden costs, the costs of other measures may also have to be corrected for hidden costs. Again, the size of the correction cannot be determined objectively.

Another option to deal with the negative net costs is to exclude these measures from the abatement cost curve. The reasoning behind this could be that these measures will automatically be implemented if a restrictive environmental policy is installed. However, this assumption is in contrast with the historical fact that a restrictive environmental policy was already active in 1990 in The Netherlands. Furthermore, removing these measures from the analysis would also mean removing the associated potential for pollution reduction. Given the fact that the estimation of these pollution reduction potentials is important for the calculation of the model, removing the negative net cost measures is undesirable.

As a practical (ad hoc) solution, the negative net costs of abatement measures are set equal to zero, which is equivalent to assuming them to be equal to the hidden cost. The model thus calculates zero costs for the emission reductions associated with these measures. The costs for the other measures are not adjusted. This assumption will presumably have only a minor influence on the model outcomes, since the simulations involve stringent emission reductions where the cost curves show unambiguously significant positive costs and since the reduction potential is calibrated correctly.

Interaction of measures

Reduction measures may interact in a number of ways. These interactions may differ substantially between different environmental problems and different processes. A detailed study of these interactions within the field of agriculture is given in Brink et al. (2001). The more general description of interactions below is based on Dellink and van der Woerd (1997) and for Climate change on de Boer and Bosch (1995). Interactions can be (i) exclusive; (ii) sequential; (iii) between themes and substances; and (iv) between measures.

Exclusiveness of measures occurs when introduction of one measure may make certain other measures inapplicable. For instance, a fuel switch from coal to gas excludes the option of coal gasification. The following method was used. The cost-effectiveness of the mutually excluding measures was calculated and the most efficient measure was then introduced into the curve. A drawback of this procedure is that a situation may occur where the total effect of the less efficient measure is higher than that of the chosen measure and that therefore the total reduction potential of abatable emissions may be underestimated.

Sometimes, a measure cannot be taken before another one is introduced (*sequentiality of measures*). For instance, a third-phase water purification cannot be realised before a second-phase purification. This may lead to a situation where a less efficient measure is taken before a more efficient one. Combining measures into packages solves this problem. Suppose that we have measure a that reduces pollution from 100 to 50 units, and measure b, that must follow measure a, reducing further from 50 to 35 units; moreover, we have a separate measure c, that reduces pollution from 100 to 40 units. The measures are then redefined as: a, $(a + b)$, and c.

Themes and substances can interact: reduction of pollution of one substance may lead to a change in the pollution of another substance. For instance, improvement of energy efficiency may lead to reduction of CO_2, NO_x and SO_2 emissions. In line with the procedures in RIM^+, a primary aim of the measure is then identified and the costs of the measure are totally attributed to that primary aim. If the measure impacts two substances within the same theme (for example, NO_x and SO_2), this procedure does not lead to double counting of the costs. However, double counting of costs may occur if a measure is defined to have a primary aim in two different themes.

Interaction between measures may also occur: the combined effect of two measures can be lower than the sum of the effects of the two separate measures. For instance, a fuel switch to low sulphur fuel and flue gas desulphurisation have, if combined, a lower effect than the sum of the effects of each measure if applied separately.

Combining measures in packages could also solve this problem. However, if many measures interact, the number of packages grows rapidly to unmanageable amounts. The procedure used is that, if measures a and b interact, and if in combination they have the effect of measure c ($= a + b$), then the measure with the lowest efficiency, say measure b, is redefined as having the effect $c - a$.

5.3.3 Climate Change

The greenhouse gases (GHGs) that cause Climate change are mainly: carbon dioxide, methane, nitrous oxide, CFCs and halons. The effects of these substances on Climate change, as well as the duration of their effects, vary. The way in which these GHGs can be aggregated into CO_2-equivalents is not unambiguous, but depends on the mix of emissions (and emission reductions). The coefficients that were chosen to aggregate the GHGs into CO_2-equivalents are described in Chapter 2; they are based on the long-term Global Warming Potentials of the substances. The construction of the abatement cost curve for Climate change is discussed in detail in de Boer (2000b).

Technical measures and costs to reduce fossil fuel use, and thus CO_2 emissions, were taken largely from the ICARUS database (Blok, 1991; Blok et al., 1991) which comprises about 300 measures ranging from more efficient energy use and co-generation to local solar power systems, and combined with measures from the MARKAL model (Okken, 1991; Okken et al., 1992).

Measures to reduce methane emissions were collected from various sources (see de Boer, 2000b) and comprise changes in the composition of animal fodder, more efficient use of manure, measures in the production and distribution of natural gas, and measures at waste dumps. The measures of changing animal fodder and more efficient management of manure are also effective in reducing nitrous oxide. The measures to reduce CFCs and halons consist of replacing them with HCFCs (with much lower warming potential) or with other substances. The resulting cost curve is depicted in Figure 5.2.

Many measures have negative net costs (corrected to zero costs, see Section 5.3.2). The reason for negative cost figures lie in considerable energy savings. Negative cost options include a number of measures in energy-intensive greenhouse agriculture; energy efficiency measures in households and transport; energy saving by intensifying aluminium recycling; introduction of co-generation in the chemical industry, the food products industry and other industries; plus a large variety of smaller energy savings in all industrial sectors, in households and in office buildings.

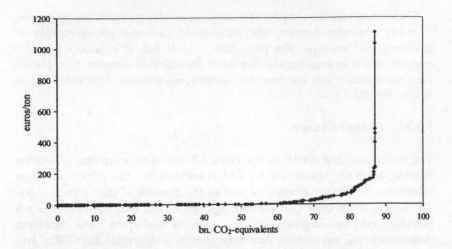

Figure 5.2   Marginal costs of reducing greenhouse gases for 1990

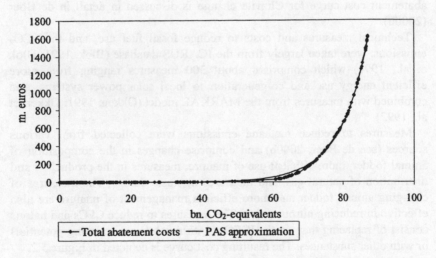

Figure 5.3   Total annual costs of reducing greenhouse gases for 1990

Measures with small, but positive net costs are situated in the middle of the curve. Apart from additional energy saving measures, they consist of CFC reduction and reduction of methane and nitrous oxide. Marginal costs are gradually rising to 0.20 euro/kg CO_2-equivalents per year with measures such as replacement of CFCs and HCFCs in cooling installations, re-use of waste heat in the ferro-metal industry, double glazing and roof insulation in houses and the use of wind and hydro power in electricity generation.

Measures with marginal costs between 0.20-0.40 euro/kg CO_2-equivalents per year include building of energy efficient houses, wall and floor insulation and the use of biogas from manure.

At the right hand side of the curve, with marginal costs rising steeply from 0.40 euro/kg CO_2-equivalents per year onwards, one finds solar energy in houses and the use of reverse osmosis in the food industry for saving fossil fuels. The effectiveness of these most expensive options is rather small.

The curve of total costs is depicted in Figure 5.3, together with the approximation by a CES curve. In total, just over 87 billion kg CO_2-equivalents can be reduced at annual costs of a little more than 1.6 billion euros.

5.3.4 Acidification

The substances that cause Acidification are NO_x, SO_2 and NH_3. The first two are mainly related to the combustion of fossil fuels, the last one to agriculture. Emissions of the three substances can be aggregated into acid-equivalents as discussed in Chapter 2: 1 kilogram NO_x = 0.022 acid-equivalents, 1 kilogram SO_2 = 0.031 acid-equivalents, and 1 kilogram NH_3 = 0.059 acid-equivalents. The measures to reduce acidification were taken from the RIM[+] database and comprise 137 options. The cost curve for reducing Acidification and the approximation with a CES function are given in Figure 5.4.

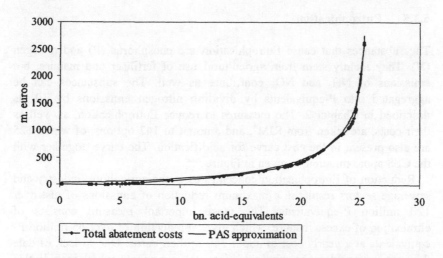

Figure 5.4   Total annual costs of reducing acidifying emissions for 1990

At the left-hand side of the curve, there are two measures with negative net reduction costs (corrected to zero costs), related to the restriction of maximum speed in traffic. Their effect on acidification is small. The next cost-effective measure is injecting manure in agricultural land, with a very substantial effect of 2.2 million acid-equivalents reduction at zero costs. Then, after a number of rather insignificant measures with respect to both costs and effects, the next sizeable measures are leanburn and flue gas circulation in gas driven engines. Thereafter follow a number of measures in oil refineries; their costs are actually underestimated as the operation and maintenance costs are unknown and therefore not included. The next sizeable measures relate to emission standards for river craft, trucks, diesel buses and tractors. An effective, but more costly measure, with a reduction in SO_2 of 3.3 million acid-equivalents, is the introduction of coal gasification/STAG for electricity generation, costing 65 million euros. Measures relating to flue gas desulphurisation in power plants and the reduction of process emissions of SO_2 in industry are effective, but costly.

Measures that reduce emissions even further than 25 million acid-equivalents include emission standards for petrol-fuelled cars, reducing the maximum speed of vans and, at very high costs and small effects, low-NO_x burners for combi-installations for electricity, and measures to reduce fuel evaporation in LPG and petrol-fuelled cars. With exclusion of the measures with the highest cost/effect ratio, 25.5 million acid-equivalents can be prevented at a total cost of 2.7 billion euros.

5.3.5   Eutrophication

The substances that cause Eutrophication are phosphorus (P) and nitrogen (N). They mainly stem from agricultural use of fertiliser and manure, but emissions of NH_3 and NO_x contribute as well. The substances can be aggregated into P-equivalents by dividing nitrogen emissions by 10, as described in Chapter 2. The measures to reduce Eutrophication, as well as their costs, are taken from RIM$^+$, and amount to 142 options, of which 125 are also present in the cost curve for acidification. The curve, together with the CES approximation, is given in Figure 5.5.

Reduction of Eutrophication concentrates in the agriculture, industry and sewerage sectors results in a maximum reduction of emissions of just over 120 million P-equivalents. The most important measure consists of elimination of excess manure, which gives a reduction of over 65 million P-equivalents at a yearly cost of about 240 million euros. Due to lack of data this measure could not be subdivided into its components, which include also dephosphating and denitrifying of wastewater from industry and households. Further steps in reduction relate to additional measures in sewerage and water purification, and one of the measures at the very end of the curve is relocation of farms: a reduction of 0.14 million P-equivalents at the fabulous cost of more than 100 million euros yearly.

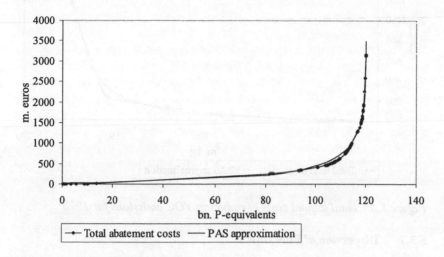

Figure 5.5 Total annual costs of reducing eutrophying emissions for 1990

5.3.6 Smog Formation

For the cost curve of Smog formation (VOCs, in particular hydrocarbons), 39 measures were identified, of which eight were deleted because they were excluded by other measures, while on two occasions measures had to be combined due to sequentiality. This results in 29 points on the curve. The cost curve and its approximation by a CES curve are given in Figure 5.6.

The measures with the best cost-effectiveness at the left-hand side of the curve are mainly identified in VROM's KWS-2000 programme and relate to households, the construction sectors, industry, services and the energy sector. About 150 million kilograms can be reduced at relatively low costs of about 215 million euros yearly. The measures at the right-hand side are mainly within the target group of traffic and transportation, and are mostly not primarily aimed at VOC reduction. They include emission standards for river craft, locomotives and LPG vans and measures to prevent fuel evaporation. The total reduction potential amounts to somewhat more than 180 million kilograms, at total costs of about 1.66 billion euros.

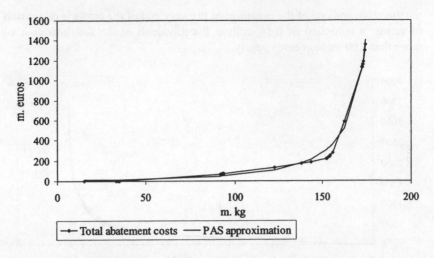

Figure 5.6   Total annual costs of reducing VOC emissions for 1990

5.3.7   Dispersion of Fine Dust

Dispersion of fine dust to air is measured by the emissions of fine particles (PM_{10}) into air. Like VOCs, they contribute to local air pollution.

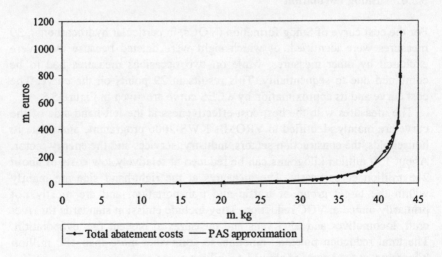

Figure 5.7   Total annual costs of reducing emissions of fine particles to air for 1990

The curve contains 36 measures, starting with three measures that are relatively cheap and specifically aimed at reducing PM_{10} pollution (for example, filters to capture fine particles). Furthermore the curve contains measures that are primarily aimed at reducing NO_x, but also reduce emissions of fine particles. As shown in Figure 5.7, the curve can produce a reduction of almost 44 million kilograms of PM_{10} at a cost of around 1.15 billion euros annually.

5.3.8 Public Environmental Expenditures

As argued above, for the environmental themes Desiccation and Soil contamination no abatement cost curves are constructed. For the estimation of the annual costs to reduce the arid/dehydrated area, use was made of a study of policy scenarios (RIZA, 1996). The scenarios are each composed of a variety of measures, but due to data shortage it was not possible to carry out the analysis on a measure-by-measure basis. Measures of the scenarios include a variety of local small-scale projects such as adaptation of the water system, depoldering, extraction of drinking water, extraction of industrial water and reducing irrigation water use. Full and sustained rehydration, which is the long-run policy goal, is best represented by the scenario Reversing the Trend 2045 (Trendbreuk 2045). In this scenario, the time horizon is extended as compared to the other scenarios, which leads to a smoothing out of the cost differences. Table 5.5 depicts the annual costs of rehydration. The ad-hoc assumption is made that these costs will have to be borne throughout the model horizon.

Table 5.5   Annual costs for Desiccation and Soil contamination

	Annual costs (Million €/yr)
Desiccation	250
Soil contamination	8800
Total public environmental expenditures	9050

In Dellink and van der Woerd (1997) a draft version of the RIZA data was used. Some of the costs of the measures have been revised in the final version; consequently, total costs for this environmental theme have been changed from 390 million euros per year to 250 million (RIZA, 1996). Note that all abatement costs for the environmental theme Desiccation are assumed to be public costs. In reality, some of the costs will be borne by private sectors. In 1990 this constitutes a relatively small portion of all costs; it has become more important in later years.

Estimation of the cost curve of cleaning up contaminated soils from the past is a heroic, if not absurd, effort. Data are weak or lacking and the estimation should be interpreted, at most, as an indication of the order of magnitude.

The first and possibly largest problem is that no complete inventory of contaminated locations is available. Although after the first cleaning up operation, at Lekkerkerk in 1980, a policy was formulated to clean up all contaminated locations within one generation, a more realistic policy has since been followed to complete the inventory of all contaminated locations within one generation. In recent years, the number of suspect locations has grown by a factor of 200 from about 3000 to 600,000. The 600,000 locations were, admittedly and necessarily, only roughly categorised into three classes: not severely contaminated, not urgent severely contaminated, and urgent severely contaminated.

The bodies involved in cleaning up soil contamination are various, but for an estimation of the costs a restriction was made to locations under the responsibility of provinces, with some additional information on private cleaning costs. These cost estimates were then extrapolated to other locations. Not only the types of contamination differ, but also the cleaning techniques and their effectiveness. Apart from isolation (which is not really cleaning up) one can distinguish, among others, bio restoration, air ventilation, steam stripping, thermal cleaning, floatation, land farming, bio-reactors, and extraction plus biological cleaning of silt. The range of costs shows a factor 30 or more between the cheapest and the most expensive techniques. The estimation of costs for complete cleaning of all contaminated sites to full, multifunctional, 'sustainable' use is in the range of 105-205 billion euros (total, not yearly costs). More details on this estimate can be found in Dellink and van der Woerd (1997). To convert total costs into annual costs, an everlasting annuity payment is calculated at 5 per cent interest. This leads to rounded annual payments of 8800 million euros (as shown in Table 5.5).

5.3.9   Discussion

The cost curves presented in this chapter are estimates with weaknesses. They are an approximation to which various improvements can be made.

Firstly, the data bases that were used are incomplete. In particular, the pollution reduction measures of the RIM⁺ model are acknowledged by RIVM itself to require further completion and updating, be it within the structure of RIM⁺ or within some other new structure. It seems that the reduction measures that were used for Climate change are more comprehensive. Aside from the completeness of the data, the accuracy is unknown.

Secondly, the costs of some measures were double-counted. There is an overlap in measures with respect to Climate change and to Acidification (in particular energy saving measures) and with respect to Acidification and Eutrophication (measures on nitrogen). A measure can be seen as the primary aim for the perspective of one theme, but the same measure may also have an impact on another theme. In the methodology used, the environmental effects of the measure are all taken into account, but the costs of that measure may be double-counted. It requires further study to correct this flaw in the analysis, given the stylised modelling structure. More detailed studies that focus on a particular subject do provide some options that prevent double-counting (for example, Brink et al., 2001).

Thirdly, excises and (for households) VAT are included in the prices. From a macro-economic viewpoint one might argue that factor prices should be used. However, the sectors in the model react on prices as perceived by them, so including excises and VAT is correct. Moreover, to the extent that revenues of emission charges replace taxes, excises and VAT should diminish. But as excises and VAT are an integral part of the cost curves, they are built in and cannot be discarded as such. This leads to price distortions that are difficult to justify.

Fourthly, the estimations of future costs are based on certain macro-economic scenarios. These scenarios are the central economic projections of CPB Netherlands Bureau for Economic Policy Analysis and they are not necessarily consistent with the DEAN model. Moreover, these scenarios are exogenous and hence not influenced by the environmental policies investigated. For instance, they use the original relative prices. In an ideal case, the scenario used to calculate the future costs of the reduction measures should be fully endogenous: the costs of the measures should be calculated *within* the model. This would, however, lead to circular references in the model: the economic results depend on the costs of the measures and the costs of the measures depend on the economic results. Therefore, the exogenous scenarios are accepted as they are, leading to distortions in the estimation of the abatement costs that cannot be predicted.

The incompleteness and the double-counting result in overestimation of the costs of reduction. Whether the assumptions on the interest rate, the inclusion of excises and VAT and the exogenous underlying scenario lead to a structural bias is unclear, but all points mentioned above lead to inaccuracy. Although the estimated cost curves are based on the best available information, an improvement of the estimates can be achieved by further research. How to deal correctly with the double-counting also requires attention in future research.

5.4   ECONOMIC PARAMETER VALUES

5.4.1   Labour Supply Growth Rate

International empirical literature, for example, Jones (1995), suggests that the average long-term growth rate of the economy can be assumed to be stable over time. In DEAN model terms, this translates into an exogenous, constant annual growth rate of the effective labour supply, as this is the driving force of economic growth. This increase in effective labour supply is a combined effect of demographic developments, that is, increases in the number of workers, and increased labour productivity, that is, increases in production per worker.

Preliminary analysis of realised economic growth rates, as reported in Appendix 5.III, shows that on average, GDP growth was above 2 per cent per year, while increases in effective labour supply were just below 2 per cent. Therefore, an annual labour supply growth rate and hence also a GDP growth rate of 2 per cent seems justified.

5.4.2   Depreciation Rate of Capital

In principle, the benchmark accounting data on depreciation can be used directly to calculate the annual depreciation rate of capital. However, the economic situation in The Netherlands was not very favourable in 1990. This is reflected in relatively low savings and investments.[6] Moreover, depreciation data in the National Accounts are notorious for their low quality. Therefore, an indirect approach is adopted, using the steady state relationship between investments and capital as discussed in Appendix 4.III:

$$I_{steady\ state} = \left(\frac{g_L^a + \delta_K^a}{r^a + \delta_K^a} \right) \cdot K_{steady\ state} \qquad (5.1)$$

To reduce the impact of the choice of the base year on the results, the depreciation rate is a rounded average of the depreciation rates for 1990 and 1995 as calculated with equation (5.1). For 1990, the depreciation rate equals 2.75 per cent and for 1995, 3.6 per cent. To avoid a false sense of accuracy, a rounded annual depreciation rate of 3 per cent is used in the model. In order to keep the assumption in the model that the economy starts from a steady state, the investments provided for the base year are recalculated, using equation (5.1). Differences between the calibrated steady state investments and the investment levels from the data are corrected in the accounting matrix by recalculating the consumption of private households. Effectively, the savings rate of households is changed to reflect the steady state. Total production values of different production sectors and the composite of profits and depreciation per sector are unchanged.

5.4.3   Interest Rate

The annual interest rate is calibrated to the long-term (10 year) interest rate on government bonds, as these have no risk premium. This interest rate has steadily declined to below 5 per cent in the 1990s (De Nederlandsche Bank, 2002). For practical reasons, a stable annual interest rate of 5 per cent is used. The higher interest rate as it prevailed in 1990 is rejected, as it does not reflect current interest rate expectations. This same annual interest rate is used in the calculations of the abatement costs.

5.4.4   Substitution Elasticities for the Utility Functions

The substitution elasticities in the instantaneous utility function govern the trade-off of different consumption goods. The nesting structure for this function is kept relatively simple, as reflected in Figure 5.8. At the lowest level, the different consumption goods are aggregated into four categories: 'food', 'transport', 'services' and 'other'. Then, at the higher level ('demand') there are some substitution possibilities between these four categories. Finally, the total aggregate of consumption goods is coupled with environmental services (the composition of emissions and abatement) in a Leontief function. The values and nesting structure are taken from Statistics Netherlands (1991) and are given in Table 5.6.

Table 5.6   Substitution elasticities for consumers

	Demand (σ_h^{top})	Food (σ_h^{food})	Transport (σ_h^{trans})	Services (σ_h^{serv})	Other (σ_h^{other})	Intertemp. (σ_h^{Util})
Private househ. (surplus part)	0.5	0.8	0.5	0.9	0.5	0.5
Subsistence	0	0	0	0	0	0
Government	0	0	0	0	0	0
Rest-of-the-World	0	0	0	0	0	0

These elasticities are for a static model, and represent adaptation possibilities for the medium term, normally interpreted to consist of several (3-5) years. Hence, they can be directly used in the DEAN model, as each period consists of 5 years. There is no need to recalibrate the elasticities. The intertemporal elasticity of substitution has to be calibrated only for the

Private households (surplus part), as the other consumers (Subsistence, Government and Rest-of-the-World) are assumed to have no forward-looking behaviour. The value for private households equals 0.5, based on Hall (1988).

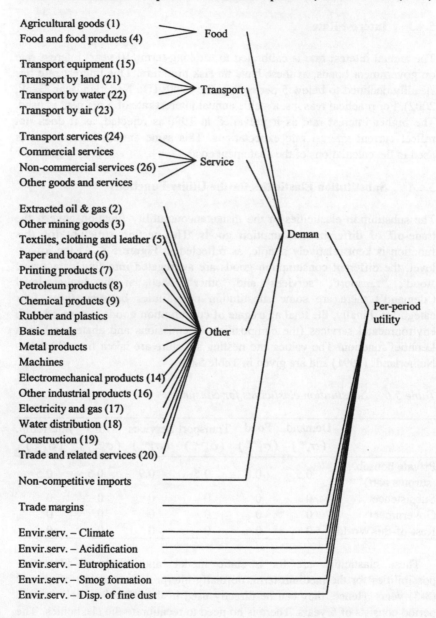

Agricultural goods (1)
Food and food products (4) — Food

Transport equipment (15)
Transport by land (21)
Transport by water (22) — Transport
Transport by air (23)

Transport services (24)
Commercial services
Non-commercial services (26) — Service
Other goods and services

Extracted oil & gas (2)
Other mining goods (3)
Textiles, clothing and leather (5)
Paper and board (6)
Printing products (7)
Petroleum products (8)
Chemical products (9)
Rubber and plastics
Basic metals — Other
Metal products
Machines
Electromechanical products (14)
Other industrial products (16)
Electricity and gas (17)
Water distribution (18)
Construction (19)
Trade and related services (20)

Non-competitive imports

Trade margins

Envir.serv. – Climate
Envir.serv. – Acidification
Envir.serv. – Eutrophication
Envir.serv. – Smog formation
Envir.serv. – Disp. of fine dust

Deman

Per-period
utility

Figure 5.8 Nesting structure of instantaneous utility function

5.4.5   Income Elasticities

The income elasticities for the private households are based on Statistics Netherlands (1991). They are reproduced in Table 5.7.

Table 5.7   Income elasticities and subsistence shares for the private households.

Sector number and description of goods	Income elasticity	Subsistence share
1 Agricultural goods	0.48	0.660
2 Extracted oil and natural gas	0.38	0.730
3 Other mining products	0.38	0.730
4 Food and food products	0.44	0.688
5 Textiles, clothing and leather	0.88	0.376
6 Paper and board	0.38	0.730
7 Printing products	0.70	0.504
8 Refined oil	1.33	0.057
9 Chemicals	0.88	0.376
10 Rubber and plastics	1.00	0.291
11 Basic metals	0.59	0.582
12 Metal products	1.10	0.220
13 Machines	1.01	0.284
14 Electromechanical products	1.01	0.284
15 Transport equipment	1.41	0.000
16 Other industrial products	1.11	0.213
17 Energy distribution	0.27	0.809
18 Water distribution	0.20	0.858
19 Construction	1.25	0.113
20 Trade and related services	1.40	0.007
21 Transport by land	0.39	0.723
22 Transport by water	0.39	0.723
23 Transport by air	0.39	0.723
24 Transport services	0.39	0.723
25 Commercial services	0.79	0.440
26 Non-commercial services	0.76	0.461
27 Other goods and services	not consumed	

The income elasticities of private households are used to partition private households into a surplus private households consumer and an auxiliary 'subsistence consumer' (see Section 4.2.1). After partition, the private households (surplus part) will have an income elasticity equal to 1 for all consumption goods (this follows directly from the choice of a nested CES utility function). The other consumers, Subsistence, Government and Rest-of-the-World, have fixed incomes and hence their income elasticities are irrelevant.

5.4.6 Substitution Elasticities for the Production Functions

Table 5.8 gives the substitution elasticities used in the production function, based on Statistics Netherlands (1991).

Table 5.8 Substitution elasticities for production sectors

Sector number and description	Production (σ_j^{top})	Intermediates (σ_j^{intm})	Prim. factors (σ_j^{prim})
1 Agriculture and fisheries	0.4	0.1	0.3
2 Extraction of oil and natural gas	0.9	0.5	0.5
3 Other mining and quarrying	2	1.3	0.8
4 Food and food products industry	0.4	0.2	0.2
5 Textiles, clothing, leather ind.	0.4	0.2	0.2
6 Paper and board industry	0.5	0.2	0.3
7 Printing industry	1.4	0.6	0.9
8 Oil refineries	0.9	0.5	0.5
9 Chemical industry	0.3	0.2	0.1
10 Rubber and plastics industry	0.3	0.2	0.1
11 Basic metals industry	0	0	0
12 Metal products industry	0.7	0.2	0.4
13 Machine industry	0.7	0.2	0.4
14 Electromechanical industry	0.6	0.6	0
15 Transport equipment industry	0.3	0	0.3
16 Other industries	1.2	0.6	0.6
17 Energy distribution	0.1	0.1	0
18 Water distribution	0.1	0.1	0
19 Construction	1	0.3	0.7
20 Trade and related services	1.8	0.7	1.1
21 Transport by land	0.7	0.3	0.4
22 Transport by water	0.7	0.3	0.4
23 Transport by air	0.7	0.3	0.4
24 Transport services	0.7	0.3	0.4
25 Commercial services	1.5	0.7	0.9
26 Non-commercial services	0	0	0
27 Other goods and services	0	0	0

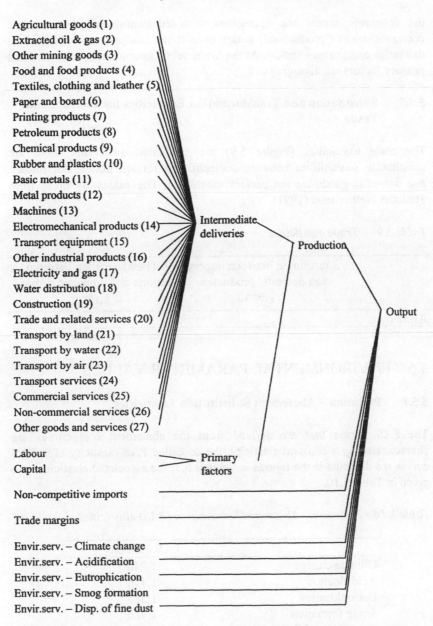

Agricultural goods (1)
Extracted oil & gas (2)
Other mining goods (3)
Food and food products (4)
Textiles, clothing and leather (5)
Paper and board (6)
Printing products (7)
Petroleum products (8)
Chemical products (9)
Rubber and plastics (10)
Basic metals (11)
Metal products (12)
Machines (13)
Electromechanical products (14)
Transport equipment (15)
Other industrial products (16)
Electricity and gas (17)
Water distribution (18)
Construction (19)
Trade and related services (20)
Transport by land (21)
Transport by water (22)
Transport by air (23)
Transport services (24)
Commercial services (25)
Non-commercial services (26)
Other goods and services (27)

Intermediate deliveries

Production

Output

Labour
Capital

Primary factors

Non-competitive imports

Trade margins

Envir.serv. – Climate change
Envir.serv. – Acidification
Envir.serv. – Eutrophication
Envir.serv. – Smog formation
Envir.serv. – Disp. of fine dust

Figure 5.9   Nesting structure of production function

The production functions follow Statistics Netherlands (1991) and consist of a nested CES function with three levels (see Figure 5.9). At the top level, the economic inputs are aggregated with environmental services. The economic inputs ('production') in turn consist of a composite of intermediate deliveries and primary factors. At the lower level, intermediate deliveries and primary factors are disaggregated.

5.4.7 Substitution and Transformation Elasticities for International Trade

The trade elasticities (Figure 5.9) are calibrated such that there are substitution possibilities between domestic and foreign goods, but foreign and domestic goods are not perfect substitutes. The values are taken from Statistics Netherlands (1991).

Table 5.9   Trade elasticities

	Substitution between imports and domestic production (σ^{imp})	Transformation between exports and domestic demand (σ^{exp})
Armington	3	3

5.5   ENVIRONMENTAL PARAMETER VALUES

5.5.1   Pollution – Abatement Substitution Elasticities

The PAS curves that are derived from the abatement cost curves are characterised by a constant elasticity, the so-called PAS elasticity. The PAS curves are depicted in the figures in Section 5.3; the associated elasticities are given in Table 5.10.

Table 5.10   Pollution – Abatement Substitution (PAS) elasticities

	PAS elasticity
Climate change	1.240
Acidification	1.416
Eutrophication	1.388
Smog formation	1.186
Dispersion of fine dust	1.264

Source: Own calculations based on abatement cost curves described in Section 5.3.

5.5.2   Benchmark Prices of Emission Permits

The benchmark prices of emission permits are derived from the PAS approximation of the abatement cost curves described above. Derivation of the benchmark permit prices is based on duality theory: if the substitution between the volumes of two inputs is given by a CES function, then the associated relative prices are also given by a CES function. More details on this duality can be found in Diewert (1974).

The benchmark prices for 1990 are shown in Table 5.11. For Climate change, the price of the stock addition permits equals zero in the benchmark, since there is no restrictive Climate policy in the benchmark.

Table 5.11   Benchmark prices of emission permits for 1990

	p_E	
Climate change	0	€/ton CO_2-equivalent
Acidification	4.29	€/acid-equivalent
Eutrophication	0.62	€/P-equivalent
Smog formation	0.14	€/kilogram
Dispersion of fine dust	0.12	€/kilogram

Source: Own calculations based on abatement cost curves described in Section 5.3.

5.5.3   Autonomous Pollution Efficiency Improvement Parameter

The autonomous pollution efficiency improvement parameter (φ_e) describes the difference between the benchmark growth rate of the economy, g_L, and the growth rate of emissions, g_e, in the benchmark projection: $g_e = g_L - \varphi_e$. This difference may be the result of pure free efficiency improvements as some sort of 'manna from heaven', but it also captures the impacts of any abatement activities in the benchmark projection. Note that in the policy simulations, the development in emissions will differ from the benchmark projection, as environmental policy requires additional emission reductions.

The autonomous pollution efficiency improvements can be calibrated using the realised pollution levels for the period 1990 to 2000 by first calculating the average annual growth rate of emissions and then calculating $\varphi_e = g_L - g_e$.

Unfortunately, the information is not sufficient to properly calibrate this parameter on a sectoral level. Therefore, the parameter is assumed to be equal for all sectors and calibrated by observing the average growth rate of pollution between 1990 and 2000. The resulting figures are represented in

Table 5.12. These numbers are rounded to reflect the limited accuracy used in the calibration of this parameter.

Table 5.12   Annual growth rates of emissions and annual autonomous pollution efficiency improvements (percentages)

	annual growth rate of emissions 1990-2000	φ_e 1990	φ_e 2030 and after
Climate change	+0.3	1.7	2.0
Acidification	-4.1	6.1	2.0
Eutrophication	-3.5	5.5	2.0
Smog formation	-5.7	7.7	2.0
Dispers. of fine dust	-6.4	8.4	2.0

Source: Own calculations based on RIVM (2002b).

It is unrealistic to assume that high autonomous pollution efficiency improvements can be sustained in a growing economy without additional abatement efforts. Therefore, the ad-hoc assumption is made that the φ_e gradually changes over time to the common benchmark growth rate g_L, such that benchmark emissions are stabilised in 2030 and beyond. So for the eight five-year periods between 1990 to 2030 φ_e is calculated as $\varphi_{e,t} = (1 - t/8) \cdot \varphi_{e,1990} + (t/8) \cdot g_L$ and for all periods after 2030 as $\varphi_{e,t} = g_L$.

5.5.4   Technical Potential for Pollution Reduction Parameter

The technical potential for pollution reduction cannot be specified on a sectoral basis due to lack of data. The economy-wide technical potential for emission reduction in environmental theme e for 1990, $\mu_{e,1990}$, can be directly derived from the abatement cost curves described in Section 5.3. A convenient way to represent the technical potential is by calculating the share of technically abatable emissions in total emissions. This 'technically abatable share' equals the technical potential divided by the level of emissions and can be represented as a percentage. Comparing the technically abatable share with the required emission reduction in percentages gives a good insight into the ease with which a policy target can be met by technical abatement measures. The technical potential for pollution reduction may change over time: $\mu_{e,t+1} = \mu_{e,t} \cdot (1 + g_{\mu,e})$. The parameter $g_{\mu,e}$ governs the exogenous growth of the technical potential for pollution reduction for environmental theme e and is based on a comparison of the abatement cost curves for 1990 and 1995.

The abatement cost curves for 1995 are taken from Hofkes et al. (2002). A possible complication is that the abatement cost curves for 1995 do not include those measures that were implemented between 1990 and 1995. In contrast, the DEAN model assumes these measures remain in the curve (see Chapter 4) and are part of the benchmark level of abatement. Moreover, the relatively large decreases in technical potential as reported by Hofkes et al. (2002) are partially caused by differences in the way the raw data on reduction techniques are gathered. Therefore, a negative growth rate of the technical potential is rejected and the technical potential is assumed to grow at the same speed as emissions, that is, the technically abatable share stays constant over time. The resulting values are shown in Table 5.13. As this is a very meagre base for calibrating an important parameter, the growth rate of the technical potential for pollution reduction will have to be subjected to sensitivity analysis.

Table 5.13   *Annual growth rate of the technical potential for pollution reduction*

	technical potential 1990 ($\mu_{e,1990}$) absolute[*]/(percentage)	annual growth rate of technical potential ($g_{\mu,e}$) (percentage)
Climate change	105.37 (41.4)	0.2
Acidification	25.44 (63.3)	0
Eutrophication	119.97 (62.4)	0
Smog formation	181.32 (34.4)	0.1
Dispers. of fine dust	42.85 (54.5)	0

Note: [*] For units see Table 5.2.

5.5.5   Autonomous Abatement Efficiency Improvement Parameter

The autonomous improvements in abatement efficiency are reflected in decreasing real abatement costs over time. A major problem in calibrating this parameter is that the underlying technical measures are very diverse. Moreover, empirical studies on development of abatement costs over time are mostly on a highly detailed and disaggregated level, that is, they describe the development of costs of one or at most of a few specific techniques. As a consequence, it is too far-fetched to empirically calibrate the autonomous abatement efficiency parameter on a disaggregated level.

Honig et al. (2000) carried out a study to obtain a tentative estimate of the decrease of environmental costs over time as the result of decreasing real marginal abatement costs. They conclude that a reduction of total abatement costs of 10 per cent in 20 years is not unlikely. Using the bold assumption that this 10 per cent decrease in 20 years applies to all abatement costs and all periods, the autonomous abatement efficiency improvement, φ_A, is calibrated to 0.5 per cent per year.

Table 5.14   Annual autonomous abatement efficiency improvement

	φ_A
All measures	0.5%

5.5.6   Decay Factor and Retention Rate for Climate Change

To calculate the net addition to the stock of greenhouse gases from the emissions, two parameters are needed: (i) the annual decay factor that governs how much of the stock in year t will still be present in the atmosphere in year $t+1$, and (ii) the marginal atmospheric retention rate that determines how much one unit of emissions adds to the stock of greenhouse gases. As not all emissions remain in the atmosphere, this rate is smaller than unity.

Both the annual decay factor and the atmospheric retention rate are taken from the DICE model (Nordhaus, 1994) and equal 0.00866 and 0.64, respectively. These parameters are only correct for CO_2 and imply a bias for other GHGs. For example, CH_4 decays faster than CO_2: according to Metz et al. (2001), the lifetime of CH_4 is 12 years, for N_2O 114 years and for CO_2 it is variable and roughly between 50 and 200 years. For CFCs, the lifetimes are much greater than for CO_2.

The problem is that the emissions are given in CO_2-equivalents, and individual GHGs are not modelled. Consequently, one parameter value is used for the aggregate emissions in CO_2-equivalents. Using the parameter values from DICE leads to an inaccuracy in the calculation of the GHG stock addition. As this inaccuracy affects both benchmark development and policy scenarios, the impact on the model results is likely to be minor. It is recognised that this modelling of Climate change can be improved; nonetheless, the working of the mechanisms related to GHGs as stock pollutants can be revealed with this simplified specification.

5.5.7   Environmental Policy Targets

Dutch environmental policy targets are based on the National Environmental Policy Plan 4 (VROM, 2001). This document is co-authored by several Dutch ministries and is the latest in a series of comprehensive environmental policy plans. For most environmental problems the emission targets are set for the year 2030. As these targets are specified at the level of individual pollutants, they have to be adapted to targets for environmental themes. For Climate change, the target is specified for emission levels, not for the associated stock of CO_2-equivalents.

A complication is that policy targets are not readily available for all pollutants that are captured in the themes. For instance, no target for halons could be found, while these are included in the theme Climate change. For Eutrophication, no target for 2030 could be found and a target of 75 per cent reduction is assumed, based on expert judgement. The targets for the environmental themes are a weighted average of the available targets, extrapolated for those substances that have no policy target (that is, identical reduction percentages) and rounded to avoid a misleading feeling of accuracy. The targets for 2030 can be found in Table 5.15.

Table 5.15   Policy targets for environmental themes in The Netherlands for 2010 and 2030

	reduction target 2010 (% change compared to 1990)[a]	reduction target 2030 (% change compared to 1990)[b]
Climate change[c]	-8	-50
Acidification	-75	-85
Eutrophication	-65	-75[d]
Smog formation	-75	-85
Dispers. of fine dust	-75[e]	-90

Notes:
[a] *Source*: NEPP3, except for Dispersion of fine dust.
[b] *Source*: NEPP4, except for Eutrophication.
[c] Targets are for emissions of greenhouse gases, not for the associated stock.
[d] Expert judgement.
[e] Based on targets for related themes.

Table 5.15 also contains intermediate targets for 2010. These are based, as far as possible, on the National Environmental Policy Plan 3 (VROM, 1998b). NEPP4 explicitly states that the targets as laid down in NEPP3 still stand. For Climate change, the target for 2010 is based on the Kyoto Protocol. For Dispersion of fine dust, no target for 2010 could be found. The target is set at a reduction of 75 per cent, equal to the required reductions for the related theme Smog formation.

As the table shows, including the intermediate targets for 2010 implies that the path between introduction of the policy and 2030 is non-linear. For some themes, relatively more pollution has to be reduced before 2010 (for example,

Acidification), while for other themes (in particular Climate change) the emphasis of environmental policy is on the periods between 2010 and 2030.

5.6   DISCUSSION AND CONCLUSIONS

This chapter presents the calibration of the DEAN model to The Netherlands, using 1990 as starting year. Detailed data on the economy and on emissions are available for 1990, although reliable disaggregated data that is consistent for both economic and environmental variables is still scarce. Attributing emissions to different consumption goods is not possible due to lack of data; this has consequences for the behaviour of private households, as they are not able to reduce their emissions by switching between different consumption goods. Major data limitations also lead to a high level of aggregation in the calibration of the abatement cost curves. As discussed in Section 5.3.9, many refinements can be made to the abatement cost curves, both methodologically and with respect to the data. This warrants further study, but that task goes beyond the scope of this book. Nonetheless, the current procedure and data do give insight into the bottom-up possibilities for pollution abatement, and its limitations.

The choice of 1990 as starting year for the model, even though more recent data are available, allows for a calibration of some major model parameters using a trend analysis for the period 1990-2000. In this way, the influence of the choice of the base year on model outcomes, a common problem in dynamic models like DEAN that do not capture business cycle effects, is restricted.

NOTES

1. Consequently, this section draws heavily on Dellink et al. (2001). Note that Statistics Netherlands has adjusted some numbers since then, as reported in Hofkes et al. (2002). Therefore, the numbers used here may differ from the ones in Dellink et al. (2001).
2. If intra-sectoral deliveries within a sector are included in the analysis, the Commercial services sector is the largest. These intra-sectoral deliveries amount to 19 billion euros for the Commercial services and to 4 billion euros for Non-commercial services.
3. These spending effects differ from the shares used in Gerlagh et al. (2002). The main difference is the inclusion of capital in the spending effects in the calibration of DEAN.
4. This section draws heavily on Dellink and Van der Woerd (1997) and Dellink et al. (2001).
5. RIM$^+$ contains emission coefficients and emission factors for various economic sectors, as well as technical reduction measures with their costs and their effects on emissions. This model has been abandoned by RIVM, without an economy-wide replacement model being available.
6. It is an empirical fact that savings and investment volumes vary widely between different years.

APPENDIX 5.I   DESCRIPTION OF THE INITIAL EQUILIBRIUM USING A SAM

In this Appendix, a description of the initial equilibrium is given and a Social Accounting Matrix (SAM) that conveniently describes the initial equilibrium is presented. All conditions that constitute the initial equilibrium can be translated into conditions on the SAM. Table A5.1 gives an often-used schematic SAM.

Table A5.1   A schematic SAM

	Goods	Producers	Consumers	Total
Goods		*Inputs*	*Consumption*	*Demand*
Producers	*Outputs*			*Revenues*
Consumers	*Endowments*	*Transfers*		*Income*
Total	*Supply*	*Expenditures*	*Expenditures*	

In this SAM, producers can produce more than one good, and each good can be produced by different production sectors. If the classification of goods and producers is made such that each good has one unique producer which only produces that good, there is direct correspondence between producers and goods. This is common in input-output tables and this approach is also adopted here. An alternative presentation of the economy is given by the adjusted SAM, where goods and producers are aggregated. Table A5.2 gives the adjusted SAM for an open economy.

In the base accounting matrix, all prices are normalised to unity (without loss of generality). The reason for this is that macro-economic statistics are normally only accounted in value terms. In aggregated models, physical quantities cannot be derived in a straightforward way, as this entails summing apples and pears, so some price normalisation has to be applied and quantities defined to match prices. Equating all benchmark prices to unity is called the Harberger convention.

All rows have to add up to zero to ensure market clearance (where supply is valued positive and demand is valued negative). In the columns for producers, the value of outputs (the quantity on the diagonal of the matrix) has to equal the value of inputs including tax payments, so each column has to sum to zero; this is known as the zero-profit condition. In the columns for consumers the value of consumption has to equal the value of the endowments (including tax revenues, transfers and budget surplus) in order to ensure income balance. If prices differ from unity in policy simulations, then one must multiply all entries in a row with the associated price (each

Table A5.3   An augmented SAM

	Y1	Y2	YA	X	M	Priv.	Subs.	Gov.	sum	Prices
Y1	Y_1	$-Y^{ID}_{1,2}$	$-Y^{ID}_{1,A}$	$-X_1$	M_1	$-C_{1,Priv}$	$-C_{1,Subs}$	$-C_{1,Gov}$	0	1
Y2	$-Y^{ID}_{2,1}$	Y_2	$-Y^{ID}_{2,A}$	$-X_2$	M_2	$-C_{2,Priv}$	$-C_{2,Subs}$	$-C_{2,Gov}$	0	1
YA	$-Y^{ID}_{A,1}$	$-Y^{ID}_{A,2}$	Y_A	$-X_A$	M_A	$-C_{APriv}$	$-C_{ASubs}$	$-C_{AGov}$	0	1
NCM	$-M_{ncm,1}$	$-M_{ncm,2}$	$-M_{ncm,A}$	$-M_{ncm,X}$	M_{ncm}	$-M_{ncmPriv}$	$-M_{ncmSubs}$	$-M_{ncmGov}$	0	1
L	$-L_1$	$-L_2$	$-L_A$			$\bar{L}$			0	1
K	$-K_1$	$-K_2$	$-K_A$			$\bar{K}$			0	1
τ	$-\tau_{z,11}\,Z$ $(z{=}K,L,ji)$	$-\tau_{z,22}\,Z$ $(z{=}K,L,ji)$	$-\tau_{z,AA}\,Z$ $(z{=}K,L,ji)$			$-\tau_{zPP}\,Z$ $(z{=}K,L,ji)$	$-\tau_{zSS}\,Z$ $(z{=}K,L,ji)$	TR	0	1
τ^{LS}						τ^{LS}		$-\tau^{LS}$	0	1
τ^{SUB}						$-\tau^{SUB}$	τ^{SUB}		0	1
Trade				X	$-M$	BD			0	0
E	$-E_{e,1}$ $(e{=}theme)$	$-E_{e,2}$ $(e{=}theme)$	$-E_{eA}$ $(e{=}theme)$			$-E_{ePr}$ $(e{=}theme)$	$-E_{eSubs}$ $(e{=}theme)$	$\bar{E}_{eGov}$ $(e{=}theme)$	0	0
sum	0	0	0	0	0	0	0	0	0	0

row has its own associated price) in order to get the zero-profit and the income-balance conditions.

The accounting matrix presented in Table A5.2 can easily be augmented to include import by imported good instead of by importing sector (transpose competitive imports to a column, while keeping non-competitive imports, NCM, as a single row), the subsistence consumer (split the column for the private households), the abatement producer (include an additional row and column) and pollution (include additional rows for each environmental theme; the revenues are accounted in the column for the government sector; prices are zero in the benchmark).

Table A5.3 gives the augmented accounting matrix, using the notation of Chapter 4.

Table A5.2   A schematic adjusted SAM

	Producer1	Producer2	Exports	Private households	Government	Rest of the World	Col. sum	Prices
Producer1	Output	– Intermed. deliveries	– Exports	– Consumption	– Consumption		0	1
Producer2	– Intermed. deliveries	Output	– Exports	– Consumption	– Consumption		0	1
Imports	– Imports	– Imports	– Transit of goods	– Imports	– Imports	Total imports	0	1
Labour	– Labour demand	– Labour demand		Labour supply			0	1
Capital	– Capital demand	– Capital demand		Capital stock			0	1
Taxes	– Taxes on output & inputs	– Taxes on output & inputs	– Taxes on exports	– Taxes on cons. & endow.	Tax revenues		0	1
Transfers				Lump sum transfers	– Lump sum transfers		0	1
Budget surplus			Total exports	– Budget surplus	Budget surplus	– Total imports	0	1
Row sum	0	0	0	0	0	1	0	

APPENDIX 5.II ENVIRONMENTAL INPUT DATA FOR THE NETHERLANDS, 1990

Table A5.4 Sectoral emissions in The Netherlands, 1990

	Climate change (bn. CO_2-eq.)	Acidification (m. acid-eq.)	Eutrophication (m. P-eq.)	Smog formation (m. kg VOC)	Disp. of fine dust (m. kg PM_{10})
Agriculture and fisheries	50.91	16.92	131.30	9.96	7.69
Extraction of oil, nat. gas	13.21	0.08	0.08	23.56	0.02
Other mining, quarrying	0.10	0.02	0.02	0.00	0.09
Food, food products ind.	5.93	0.33	5.75	10.59	7.46
Textiles and related ind.	0.53	0.05	0.25	2.53	0.18
Paper and board industry	1.68	0.08	1.79	3.80	0.04
Printing industry	0.15	0.04	0.04	15.02	0.09
Oil refineries	9.77	2.39	0.63	15.92	6.61
Chemical industry	26.55	1.70	17.30	34.79	4.52
Rubber and plastics ind.	8.83	0.01	0.02	7.85	0.02
Basic metals industry	6.90	0.64	0.54	6.80	10.18
Metal products industry	1.55	0.18	0.37	24.25	0.60
Machine industry	0.56	0.05	0.08	2.42	0.45
Electromechanical industry	1.96	0.09	0.15	8.01	0.49
Transport equipment ind.	0.46	0.04	0.06	15.97	1.18
Other industries	4.58	0.76	0.90	10.86	2.20
Energy distribution	41.49	3.11	2.36	0.84	1.52
Water distribution	0.18	0.00	0.00	0.11	0.00
Construction	1.86	0.48	0.58	33.47	1.77
Trade and related services	4.07	0.56	0.69	30.04	1.05
Transport by land	6.41	2.01	2.46	8.80	5.81
Transport by water	6.21	3.91	3.33	1.16	8.28
Transport by air	9.14	0.80	0.92	0.69	0.19
Transport services	0.46	0.10	0.13	0.69	2.10
Commercial services	3.44	0.82	0.87	23.61	1.75
Non-commercial services	8.20	0.83	0.81	13.81	1.07
Other goods and services	1.30	0.12	0.15	17.34	0.16
Private households	38.10	4.05	20.69	204.19	13.11
Total	254.53	40.18	192.26	527.09	78.62

Table A5.5   Sectoral pollution intensities^a in The Netherlands, 1990

	Climate change (bn. CO_2-eq./bn. €)	Acidifi-cation (m. acid-eq./bn. €)	Eutrophi-cation (m. P-eq./bn. €)	Smog formation (m. kg VOC/bn. €)	Disp. of fine dust (m. kg PM_{10}/bn. €)
Agriculture and fisheries	2.97	0.99	7.65	0.58	0.45
Extraction of oil, nat. gas	1.64	0.01	0.01	2.92	0.00
Other mining, quarrying	0.24	0.05	0.04	0.00	0.22
Food, food products ind.	0.21	0.01	0.20	0.37	0.26
Textiles and related ind.	0.16	0.01	0.07	0.75	0.05
Paper and board industry	0.55	0.03	0.58	1.23	0.01
Printing industry	0.02	0.00	0.01	2.02	0.01
Oil refineries	1.20	0.29	0.08	1.95	0.81
Chemical industry	1.71	0.11	1.11	2.24	0.29
Rubber and plastics ind.	2.38	0.00	0.01	2.12	0.01
Basic metals industry	1.71	0.16	0.13	1.68	2.52
Metal products industry	0.19	0.02	0.04	2.95	0.07
Machine industry	0.08	0.01	0.01	0.34	0.06
Electromechanical ind.	0.20	0.01	0.02	0.84	0.05
Transport equipment ind.	0.06	0.00	0.01	2.09	0.15
Other industries	0.48	0.08	0.09	1.13	0.23
Energy distribution	5.11	0.38	0.29	0.10	0.19
Water distribution	0.20	0.00	0.00	0.12	0.00
Construction	0.07	0.02	0.02	1.18	0.06
Trade and related services	0.08	0.01	0.01	0.55	0.02
Transport by land	0.73	0.23	0.28	1.00	0.66
Transport by water	2.14	1.34	1.15	0.40	2.85
Transport by air	2.79	0.24	0.28	0.21	0.06
Transport services	0.08	0.02	0.02	0.13	0.39
Commercial services	0.06	0.01	0.01	0.39	0.03
Non-commercial services	0.12	0.01	0.01	0.20	0.02
Other goods and services	1.41	0.13	0.17	18.81	0.17
Private households^b	0.33	0.04	0.18	1.77	0.11

Notes:
[a]   The pollution intensities for production sectors are calculated as emissions divided by total output.
[b]   The intensities for private households are based on total consumption value in billion euros and are not directly comparable to pollution intensities for production sectors.

APPENDIX 5.III   REALISED GROWTH RATES FOR THE PERIOD 1990-2000

This appendix presents and discusses the realised annual growth rates for economic and environmental variables for the period 1990-2000. The economic growth rates are based on own calculations using the social accounting matrices (SAMs) provided by Statistics Netherlands. The SAM for 2000 contains provisional data and does not contain data on emissions. Therefore, the environmental growth rates are based on data taken from RIVM (2002b). The main numbers are shown in Table A5.6; a more detailed description of these data is given in Dellink (2002).

Table A5.6   Realised average annual growth rates for period 1990-2000

	1990-1995	1995-2000	1990-2000
GDP	1.79	3.78	2.78
NNI	1.24	3.58	2.40
Production Agriculture	-2.58	-2.13	-2.36
Production Industry	0.46	2.45	1.45
Production Services	2.59	4.70	3.64
Labour supply	1.43	2.41	1.92
Capital supply	1.03	4.86	2.93
Tax income Government	5.53	4.94	5.23
Savings	1.03	4.86	2.93
Emissions Climate change	0.84	-0.22	0.31
Emissions Acidification	-4.17	-4.09	-4.13
Emissions Eutrophication	-1.78	-5.11	-3.46
Emissions Smog formation	-5.99	-5.35	-5.67
Emissions Dispersion of fine dust	-6.89	-5.98	-6.43

Economic data for 1990 and 1995 are available from Dellink et al. (2001) and Hofkes et al. (2002) and merely have to be reorganised. Data for 2000 are delivered by de Boer (2002), but are provisional. No attempt is made to correct for any changes in definitions between the data for 1995 and 2000, due to a lack of information on the definitions for the 2000 data. The data for 1995 and 2000 are in constant prices of 1990, using the consumer price index for deflation of the data (Statistics Netherlands, 2002). The use of one common price index for all economic flows is imprecise, and hence the numbers should be used only on a highly aggregated level and with limited confidence in their exactness.

Many measurement problems arise concerning data and model calibration. Though the data source can be called reliable, regular corrections on older data by Statistics Netherlands shows that the raw numbers provided are surrounded with uncertainties. This applies especially to the environmental data. Some sectoral growth rates that are derived from the data are dubious, even though the original IO tables for 1990 and 1995 have been corrected for changes in definitions in consultation with Statistics Netherlands. The decline in the agricultural sector may be exaggerated because of the use of one price index, as it is likely that price levels for agricultural products increased less than average.

Looking at the growth rates of GDP and NNI, the conclusion holds that the later years of the 1990s were relatively high-growth years, compared to the preceding period. Throughout the decade, economic growth originates primarily in the services sector, while agriculture declines.

The emission intensities can be read from the table by comparing the growth rates of the economy with the growth rates of emissions. For all environmental themes except Climate change, absolute levels of emissions have declined throughout the decade. This means that an absolute decoupling of economic growth and environmental pressure is established for these themes. For Climate change, only a relative decoupling occurs: the absolute level of emissions increases, at least in the first half of the decade, but the emission intensity decreases.

The aggregated presentation of the data in Table A5.7 does not reveal all the interesting details from analysing the SAMs for the different years. Some of these details, which cannot be read from Table A5.7, are discussed below. According to the data, the agricultural sector showed a decrease in its tax payments of 15 per cent per year, while tax payments by the services sector increased by 7 per cent per year. Though a full evaluation of these numbers is beyond the scope of this appendix, it is likely that these numbers reflect problems with the statistics rather than actual developments. There is, however, also an economic interpretation for the big decrease in tax payments by the agricultural sector. The sector is characterised by a lack of economic growth and a decrease in capital use, which point to an unfavourable economic position. Given the tax system in The Netherlands, where firms can deduct operational losses from their taxes, a decrease in tax payments is then not unlikely. The raw data support this interpretation: agricultural taxes on production in the original IO table are negative for 1995.

Rather surprising is the decrease in government expenditures of consumption goods: these decrease with almost 7 per cent for industrial goods and more than 4 per cent for services. These negative growth rates are present in the original IO tables and seem to be connected to some missing data for government consumption in the 1995 table.

The data for 2000 have not been corrected for changes in definitions, and may therefore deviate from the data for 1990 and 1995. Nonetheless, most growth rates seem reasonable. The only calculated growth rate that is dubious is the decrease in consumption of industrial goods by private households: these expenditures decrease by almost 60 per cent over 5 years, while the rest of the economy is growing. The explanation for this is simple: the adjustment of the investments to the assumption of a steady state implies that some expenditures have been shifted from consumption to savings, and this affects industrial consumption the most. The original data show a steady 2 per cent annual increase in consumption of industrial goods over the period 1995-2000.

6. Dynamic empirical analysis of environmental policy in The Netherlands using DEAN

6.1 INTRODUCTION

In this chapter, the DEAN model as described in Chapter 4 is used for empirical analysis of the impact of environmental policy on the economy of The Netherlands. The data used for this empirical analysis are presented in Chapter 5. The analysis of the economic costs of environmental policy in The Netherlands as carried out in this chapter will focus on the interactions between economic growth, sectoral structure, international trade, pollution and abatement. The influence of the timing of environmental policy on these interactions is also investigated. The model set-up enables the attribution of the economic costs to different environmental themes. Moreover, the direct costs of implementation of emission reduction measures can be compared to the indirect economic effects of environmental policy. Hence, the analysis in this chapter is used to answer the empirical research questions 3-5 as formulated in Chapter 1.

Section 6.2 describes the benchmark projection, to which the policy simulations can be compared, and the environmental policy impulses that determine the different scenarios. Section 6.3 presents the results of the model simulations for the base specification of the DEAN model. Section 6.4 compares the different policy scenarios. In Section 6.5, the robustness of these results is tested by performing a range of sensitivity analyses. The chapter concludes in Section 6.6 with a discussion and conclusions from the simulations. The GAMS source code for the base specification of the DEAN model is available from the website of Wageningen University: http://www.socialsciences.wur.nl/enr/gams.

6.2 INPUTS TO THE MODEL

6.2.1 Description of the Benchmark Projection

In order to properly understand the results of the model simulations, it is important to understand how the benchmark projection develops. The values of the variables for the base year 1990 were given in the previous chapter. The volumes of economic variables, including sectoral production and consumption, grow at the speed of the balanced growth rate, which is 2 per cent. For Gross Domestic Product (GDP) and Net National Income (NNI), the resulting benchmark projection is represented in Figure 6.1. All results are in constant 1990 prices. As only relative prices matter, the price of the consumption bundle for the private households, that is, a consumer price index, for 1990 is chosen as numeraire ($p^W_{priv',1990}$ in model terms).

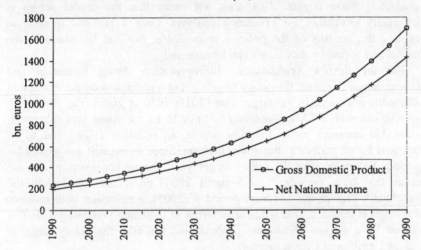

Figure 6.1   Development of GDP and NNI in the benchmark projection

For emissions, the benchmark projection follows a different path. The growth rate of emissions is lower than the growth rate of the economy, due to autonomous pollution efficiency improvements, which vary per theme. The resulting growth paths for emissions are shown in Section 6.2.2, Figures 6.2a to 6.2d and Figure 6.3.

6.2.2 The Policy Scenarios

Three policy scenarios are constructed and analysed: *NEPP2030*, *Delay* and *NEPP2010*. The term NEPP refers to the basis for the policy targets: the fourth National Environmental Policy Plan of The Netherlands (VROM, 2001). In all three scenarios, the national emission targets are set for each environmental theme, as discussed in Section 5.5.7. The only difference between the scenarios is the timing of the environmental policy. In the *NEPP2030* scenario, the policy targets have to be met in the year 2030. In the *Delay* scenario, the same targets are set, with a delay of 10 years. The *NEPP2010* scenario consists of the targets from *NEPP2030*, with additional intermediate targets for the year 2010.

It should be noted that these policy targets are actual policy targets for The Netherlands. Though these targets are undoubtedly based on thorough analysis, they are not necessarily efficient. The DEAN model cannot assess the efficiency of these targets, as the model does not capture the welfare benefits of the policies (see Section 3.5). The analysis presented here aims at assessing the economic costs of the exogenous targets, not at explaining or evaluating these targets. This does not mean that the model set-up is inherently unsuitable for efficiency analysis. Once a realistic module to capture the benefits of the policies is available, this can be added to the model and optimal policy levels can be assessed.

For the themes Acidification, Eutrophication, Smog formation and Dispersion of fine dust, the policy targets act as a restriction on the maximum allowable emissions in the target year (2010, 2030 or 2040). For the policy simulations with DEAN, these targets have to be translated into maximum allowable emission paths. In other words, an emission ceiling has to be imposed for all periods in the model horizon. Since no explicit goals exist for periods before or after the policy target year, the ad hoc assumptions are made that (i) in periods 1 to 3 (until 2004) emissions can follow the benchmark projection;[1] (ii) from period 4 (2005), a reduction path towards the target is imposed, that is linear in terms of reduction percentages, as this allows for a gradual adjustment process; and (iii) after the policy target is reached, emissions cannot increase.

The benchmark emissions for Acidification, Eutrophication, Smog formation and Dispersion of fine dust are decreasing over time, and stabilise after 2030. This development is determined by specification of autonomous pollution efficiency improvements and the constant growth rate of the economy. Figures 6.2a-d show the benchmark development of emissions and the number of emission permits auctioned by the government for the different scenarios for (a) Acidification, (b) Eutrophication, (c) Smog formation and (d) Dispersion of fine dust.

It should be emphasised that the environmental quality that is reached at the end of the model horizon differs between the scenarios. For environmental themes that have stock characteristics, especially Acidification and Eutrophication, environmental quality at the end of the twenty-first century depends not only on emissions in the last period, but also on emission levels in earlier periods (see Chapter 2).

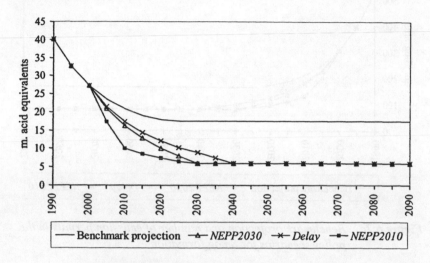

Figure 6.2a   Benchmark projection and number of emission permits in the policy scenarios for Acidification

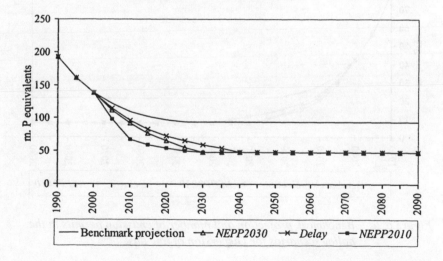

Figure 6.2b   Benchmark projection and number of emission permits in the policy scenarios for Eutrophication

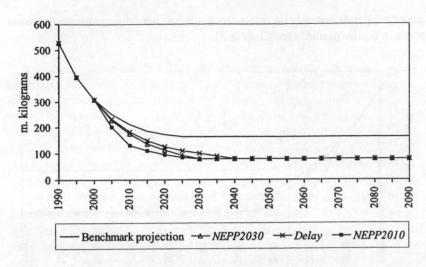

Figure 6.2c   Benchmark projection and number of emission permits in the policy scenarios for Smog formation

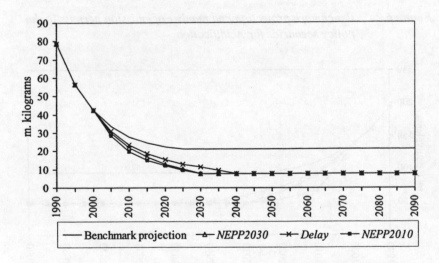

Figure 6.2d   Benchmark projection and number of emission permits in the policy scenarios for Dispersion of fine dust

For the environmental themes Smog formation and Dispersion of fine dust, the duration of environmental effects of emissions is much smaller, and therefore long-term environmental quality for these themes does not depend as much on earlier emissions. Total emission reductions are largest in the

NEPP2010 scenario and smallest in the *Delay* scenario, implying a better environmental quality in the *NEPP2010* scenario for Acidification and Eutrophication.

For Climate change, the emission target as laid down in the environmental policy plans is specified in terms of emission reductions. This target is, however, not imposed in the scenarios, but translated into a target for total allowable addition to the stock of greenhouse gases (GHGs) over the model horizon, to allow flexibility in timing of emission reductions.[2] The emission reduction target for the target year gives insufficient information to calculate the stock addition target, as the emissions in other years are in principle unrestricted. Therefore, a two-step approach is used. Firstly, a proposed path of GHG emissions is formulated that is consistent with the emission policy target of *NEPP2030*, analogue to the maximum allowable emission paths for the other environmental themes (that is, a linear reduction path between 2005 and 2030 and constant emissions thereafter). This path is presented in Figure 6.3, together with the benchmark development of GHG emissions.

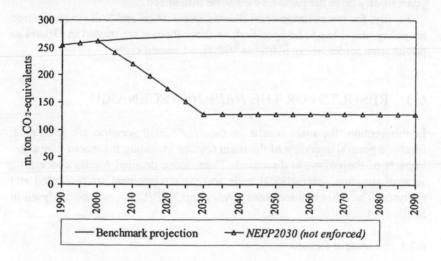

Figure 6.3   Benchmark projection and proposed emission reductions for Climate change

Secondly, the stock addition over the model horizon that would result from this emission path is calculated. This calculated stock addition is then taken as the maximum allowable stock addition in the *NEPP2030* scenario. It should be stressed that the proposed emission path is not imposed: emissions can fluctuate over time, as long as the stock addition target is not exceeded. For the *Delay* scenario and *NEPP2010* scenario, the same maximum allowable stock addition is imposed as in the *NEPP2030* scenario, so that greenhouse gas concentrations at the end of the model horizon are identical across the scenarios.

Table 6.1 shows the maximum allowable stock addition of GHGs that results from the proposed emission paths depicted in Figure 6.3.

Table 6.1   Maximum stock additions of GHGs in bn. ton CO_2-equivalents

	Benchmark projection	*NEPP2030* scenario	*Delay* scenario	*NEPP2010* scenario
Max. stock addition	12.65	7.06	7.06	7.06

In the first three periods (1990-2004) no new environmental policy is introduced. In addition, it is assumed that before 2005 there are no substitution possibilities between emissions and abatement. Hence, these periods serve as a reference. The rationale for this assumption is that these years mostly lie in the past and cannot be influenced.

Finally, for the environmental themes Desiccation and Soil contamination no policy target has to be specified, as these themes are treated in DEAN as public environmental expenditures with fixed annual costs.

6.3   RESULTS FOR THE *NEPP2030* SCENARIO

In this section, the main results of the *NEPP2030* scenario are presented. Firstly, a general overview of the main results, including the macro-economic impacts of the policy, is discussed. Then, more detailed results concerning sectoral structure, international trade and the environment are presented and analysed. The other two scenarios, *Delay* and *NEPP2010*, will be analysed in Section 6.4.

6.3.1   General Results

The impact of the *NEPP2030* scenario on the main economic and environmental variables is presented in Table 6.2. In 1990, emissions do not have to decrease compared to the benchmark projection; hence, GDP is hardly affected. The composition of Gross and Net National Income does, however, change in this first year: consumption by private households increases by 1 per cent while savings, and hence investments, decrease by almost 2 per cent compared to the benchmark.

Table 6.2   *Results of the* NEPP2030 *scenario for the base specification of DEAN*

	1990	2010	2030	2050
Macro-economic results (% change in volumes compared to benchmark)				
GDP	-0.02	-1.35	-8.45	-10.21
NNI	0.33	-0.26	-6.26	-8.55
Total private consumption	0.96	1.10	-6.12	-10.35
Total production	-0.25	-2.05	-16.00	-16.47
Savings/investment	-1.85	-7.11	-20.00	-19.00
International trade results (% change in volumes compared to benchmark)				
Total imports	-0.51	-3.04	-23.19	-23.02
Total exports	-0.50	-2.99	-22.90	-23.12
Trade balance (in % GDP)	0.99	1.01	1.09	1.11
Sectoral[a] results (% change in volumes compared to benchmark)				
Private consumption Agriculture	0.44	-0.08	-6.88	-9.30
Private consumption Industry	0.89	0.91	-8.80	-12.05
Private consumption Services	1.06	1.34	-3.23	-8.57
Sectoral production Agriculture	-1.09	-7.46	-32.64	-34.58
Sectoral production Industry	-0.60	-3.25	-35.05	-30.64
Sectoral production Services	0.09	-0.64	0.49	-3.74
Sectoral production Abatement services	-0.03	4.23	16.59	15.81
Environmental results (% change in volumes compared to benchmark)				
Emissions Climate change	-1.06	-13.36	-45.24	-50.06
Emissions Acidification	0.00	-21.84	-65.52	-65.52
Emissions Eutrophication	0.00	-16.40	-49.21	-49.21
Emissions Smog formation	0.00	-17.32	-51.96	-51.96
Emissions Dispersion of fine dust	0.00	-20.98	-62.93	-62.93
Prices of main variables (constant 1990 prices)				
Exchange rate index (benchmark = 1)	1.00	1.01	0.82	0.89
Price of abatement services (bm. = 1)	1.00	1.00	0.68	0.78
Price Climate change[b] (€/ton CO_2-eq.)	2.2	7.1	17.0	45.0
Price Acidification (€/acid-eq.)	3.9	25.9	929.7	1092.2
Price Eutrophication (€/P-eq.)	0.6	2.5	7.5	11.3
Price Smog formation (€/kilogram)	0.1	1.4	1277.0	1360.2
Price Disp. fine dust (€/kilogram)	0.1	0.9	82.4	103.8

Notes:
[a]   The 27 production sectors are grouped into three categories.
[b]   Expressed in terms of emissions.

This indicates that consumers are anticipating a stricter future environmental policy and reacting by placing more emphasis on current consumption and accepting lower consumption levels in later periods.[3] The higher consumption levels do not imply that production levels are also higher. The negative impact of lower investments on the demand for produced goods outweighs the positive impact of increased demand by the private households.

Over time, the negative impact of the environmental policy on the economy becomes more significant. By 2050, GDP has dropped 10 per cent compared to the benchmark projection. The lower savings induce a lower growth rate in the economy and it is therefore not surprising that the long-run levels of NNI, consumption and production are all well below the benchmark. Note that though investments decrease substantially, the capital stock is still growing in absolute terms.[4]

The results for international trade are influenced by two assumptions: (i) foreign goods are imperfect substitutes for domestically produced goods, and (ii) the deficit on the trade balance is exogenously given. Aggregate imports and aggregate exports have to move in the same direction and decrease with the declining income of private households. The trade balance as a percentage of GDP increases because of the decrease in GDP. The flexible exchange rate adjusts to clear this international trade market. There are two influences on the real exchange rate as reported in Table 6.2. Firstly, the price of foreign goods may be adjusted: appreciation or depreciation. Secondly, the domestic price level may change (changes in the consumer price index that is used as numeraire). The real exchange rate is the ratio between the price of foreign goods and the domestic consumer price index.

One of the strong points of the AGE framework that forms the basis of the DEAN model is that it allows a detailed analysis of the impact of the policy on different sectors in the economy. In Table 6.2 the sectors are aggregated into three categories; a more detailed sectoral analysis follows in Section 6.3.2. In the first few periods, the costs of environmental policy have the largest impact on the agricultural sector. Though consumption of agricultural products does increase in 1990, the production volume of the sector drops significantly right from the first period. This is because, on the one hand, the agricultural sector is characterised by relatively large emissions: 20 per cent of greenhouse gas emissions, 42 per cent of acidifying emissions and 68 per cent of eutrophying emissions are attributed to Agriculture. On the other hand, the contribution of Agriculture to GDP is relatively small. In some periods, losses in production are greater in the industrial sectors, due to the relative importance of the environmental theme Smog formation and due to the decrease in demand for industrial products for investments. The production of the services sectors follow a more complicated pattern and will be analysed in Section 6.3.2.

The demand for abatement services increases significantly as environmental policy becomes stricter. The numbers may seem small, but one has to remember that by far the largest part of the demand for abatement services (98 per cent in the benchmark) is constituted by the government sector for public environmental expenditures. The demand for abatement services in 2010 by the other sectors is five times higher in the *NEPP2030* scenario compared to the benchmark. As environmental permits become more expensive it is efficient to spend more on abatement and reduce the level of emissions. However, marginal abatement costs are also increasing, as more emissions are abated. In the end, there is a new equilibrium where marginal abatement costs equal the price of environmental permits and polluters are indifferent between buying more pollution permits, demanding more abatement services or adjusting the activity level.

The decrease in emissions is in accordance with environmental policy. For Climate change, the path of emission reductions is endogenous, that is, determined by the individual polluters, not imposed by government. Emissions are, however, bounded by the restriction on the total allowable addition to the stock of GHGs. Some emissions are reduced in 1990, even though the assumption is made that between 1990 and 2000 no technical abatement measures are available. The 1 per cent reduction in GHG emissions is therefore fully achieved via a restructuring of the economy, that is, via the reduction of agricultural and industrial production. For the other environmental themes, the path of emission reduction is exogenously given, and therefore the numbers in the table reflect the difference between benchmark emissions and the number of emission permits auctioned by the government as shown in Figure 6.2.

The decline in emissions is much larger than the decline in GDP, and absolute economic growth levels are positive. Therefore, the conclusion can be drawn that a decoupling of economic growth and environmental pressure is possible, given the availability of the abatement measures.

The permit prices for 1990 are in line with the benchmark, as there is as yet no reduction in the number of permits. After the introduction of the environmental policy, permit prices start to increase rapidly, especially for Acidification and Smog formation. Note that the permit prices are not directly comparable across the environmental themes, as emissions for each theme are expressed in different units. The permit prices for Climate change can be reported either as the price of one kilogram of stock addition or as the price of one kilogram of emissions. These two prices differ as one kilogram of CO_2-equivalent emissions leads to less than one additional kilogram stock of CO_2-equivalents, given a calibrated marginal retention rate of less than unity. In Table 6.2 the Climate change permit prices are given in euro per ton of emissions of CO_2-equivalents. Total expenditures on Climate change permits do not depend on the way the permit prices are represented. The development of the permit prices will be analysed in more detail in Section 6.3.4.

To obtain more insight into the economic transition paths that are induced by the environmental policy, it is useful to look at the development of GDP and NNI. These are shown in Figure 6.4. Both measures of the size of the economy are closely related, and their development is very similar. For all periods, the impact of the policy is more negative on GDP than on NNI. As the capital stock falls below the benchmark projection, there is less depreciation and hence the gap between GDP and NNI diminishes.

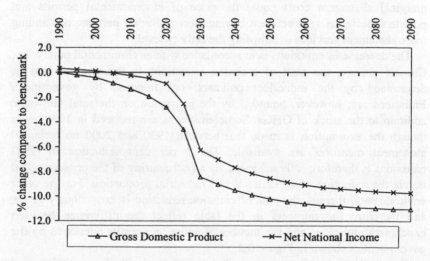

Figure 6.4   Results of the NEPP2030 *scenario on the development of GDP and NNI for the base specification of DEAN*

Though the private households have perfect foresight on the future level of environmental policy and know the future prices of environmental permits, the paths of GDP and NNI are not completely smooth. The extent to which consumers switch between current and future consumption is driven by the constant intertemporal elasticity of substitution (this CIES equals 0.5 for the private households). The properties of the CIES utility function imply that the further the consumers shift their consumption away from the original equilibrium, the less they can fulfil their preferences and the larger the disutility associated with this shift. Therefore, the costs, in terms of a decrease in utility, increase more than proportionately if more consumption is shifted intertemporally. In effect, the development of GDP and NNI over time reflects a combination of the required emission reductions and a temporary slowdown of economic growth.

The drop in GDP growth does not mean that absolute GDP levels are declining. Whereas in the benchmark the growth rate of GDP equals 2 per cent, the economic growth rate in the *NEPP2030* scenario remains above 1 per cent throughout the model horizon. In fact, the growth rate of the economy comes very close to the benchmark level in the second half of the century, implying that the environmental policy, which has constant emission reduction percentages in the long run, has only a temporary effect on the growth rate of the economy. The decrease in the absolute level of GDP is, however, lasting. This is in line with neo-classical growth theory which shows that the steady state *growth rate* is not influenced by the level of policy, but by the *levels* of consumption, capital stock and other economic variables are (Barro and Sala-i-Martin, 1995).

Extrapolating the GDP curve, one might draw the conclusion that a structural reduction of emissions of 50 per cent or more for all environmental themes available in the DEAN model will lead to an economy that is structurally around 10-11 per cent below what it would have been without the environmental policy. Since the monetarised benefits of this environmental policy are not analysed here, it is impossible to say whether these costs are justified.

6.3.2   Sectoral Results

The impacts of environmental policy on individual sectors is likely to be much more diverse than the macro-economic results suggest. In the AGE approach, a reduction of activity in one sector will always mean that the primary factors, including labour, are re-allocated to other sectors, in order to satisfy the market equilibrium constraints: if total supply of the primary factor is exogenously given, total demand is also given, and the associated price will adapt. It is therefore more useful to interpret the sectoral results in terms of a shift between sectors rather than an isolated change in one sector.

There are indeed some noteworthy differences between the sectors. These arise from different pollution intensities, substitution possibilities and income elasticities of the various goods and services. A shift will occur from relatively polluting sectors to relatively clean sectors. This shift is even more important in the DEAN model than in most other models, as the opportunities for reducing emissions via technical abatement measures is limited in DEAN.

Figure 6.5 shows how the *NEPP2030* scenario impacts the production volumes of various production sectors. The sector Other goods and services is by far the most severely hit by the environmental policy. This small sector

(0.2 per cent of total production in the economy), which comprises many heterogeneous subsectors, almost completely ceases production after the environmental policy is introduced. The main reasons for this are that a relatively large share of VOC emissions is attributed to this sector (see Table 5.4) and that the calibrated substitution elasticities for the production function of this sector equal zero.

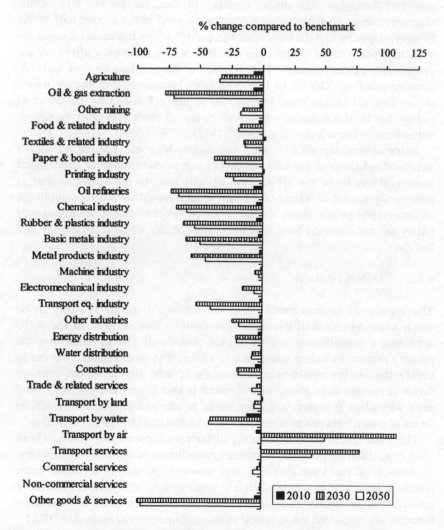

Figure 6.5   Results of the NEPP2030 *scenario on sectoral production volumes for the base specification of DEAN*

The other sectors that have high VOC intensities, the Metal products industry and Oil and gas extraction, also observe very substantial reductions in production. As far as the other sectors are concerned, it is mainly the 'hardcore' industrial sectors, such as Oil refineries, Chemical industry and Basic metal industry that are hardest hit by the policy.

The services-related sectors are relatively well off. In general they have a favourable ratio between value added generated in the sector and emissions. Therefore, restructuring of the economy will be from the 'dirty' industrial sectors to the 'clean' services sectors. The Commercial and Non-commercial services sectors together make up one-third of all production in the economy. These relatively clean sectors are hardly affected by the environmental policy, indicating that for them the negative impact of the policy is almost fully mitigated by the positive impact of the restructuring of the economy.

The only two sectors that gain substantially from the environmental policy are Transport by air and Transport services. The results for these sectors seem rather counter-intuitive and are directly connected to the relatively low VOC emissions in these sectors. The ratio between generated value added and VOC emissions is much higher for Transport by air than for Transport by land or Transport by water.[5] The VOC emissions attributed to Transport by air are 0.13 per cent of total VOC emissions. For Transport services, a similar share applies.

The increase in production of Transport by air and Transport services, together representing less than 2.5 per cent of total production in the economy, significantly influences the results for the whole category Services, as shown in Table 6.2. More detailed analysis of these sectors below shows that the production increases for these two sectors are primarily driven by an increase in exports, not by an increase in consumption. Moreover, the two sectors are closely connected: a large part of the inputs for Transport by air comes from Transport services.

The sectoral results for consumption by private households, as shown in Figure 6.6, are more uniform. Comparing Figure 6.6 with Figure 6.5 shows that the reduction in consumption levels is on average much smaller; the largest decrease is in the consumption of petrol (sector Oil refineries). The sector is characterised by a relatively small share in total consumption value and a high income elasticity of 1.33.

One noticeable difference between the figures for production and consumption is the timing of the reductions. In 2010, consumption levels for most goods are above the benchmark, while production levels are below the benchmark. For production, the reductions are mostly larger in 2030 than in 2050, while for consumption the reverse holds. This effect can only be explained by the role of capital investments. Firstly, the reduction in investments is directly linked to lower savings, implying that higher consumption means lower investments. Secondly, lower investments have a negative impact on production, through a reduced demand for produced investment goods.

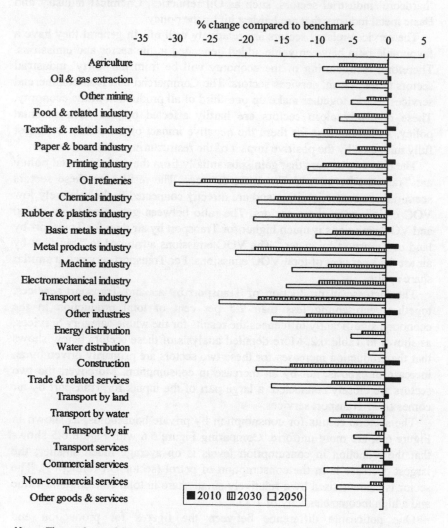

% change compared to benchmark

Note: The products of the sector Other goods and services are not consumed; these products largely consist of imported goods used as intermediate inputs for domestic producers.

Figure 6.6   Results of the NEPP2030 *scenario on sectoral consumption volumes of private households for the base specification of* DEAN

After 2030, investments are well below the benchmark level, but the difference from the benchmark diminishes. This explains the differences in the impacts of the policy on production and consumption.

Food and related products (19 per cent), Commercial services (25 per cent) and Non-commercial services (10 per cent) together make up more than 50 per cent of total expenditures by private households. Consumption of these goods and services decreases relatively little. For Food products, this can be explained by its 'necessary good' nature (the income elasticity is estimated to be 0.44). For the services sectors, the income elasticities are higher, but still below unity. Most industrial products have an income elasticity above unity, which helps explain why consumption of these goods decreases relatively much.

6.3.3   International Trade Results

The budget balance of the private households determines the aggregates of sectoral imports and exports. There is, however, scope for sectoral variation in both imports and exports. These sectoral results are shown in Figure 6.7.

The sectoral pattern of imports roughly resembles the pattern of domestic consumption: a moderate reduction throughout, with some variation across sectors. There are two exceptions: Transport by air and, to a lesser extent, Transport services. These two sectors have increasing imports (though the absolute numbers are small) combined with substantially increasing exports. There seems to be no straightforward explanation for this increase in transfer trade.[6]

For the industrial sectors, the decrease in exports is larger than the decrease in imports. For services, the exports increase while imports decrease (except for the two transport sectors discussed above). This allows for a large restructuring of the domestic economy in terms of production, while keeping the changes in domestic consumption relatively small. Domestic emissions can be reduced significantly through this 'leakage effect'. For local pollutants, this does not have to be a problem. For transboundary environmental problems, such a transfer of emissions to a different geographical location may partially or even fully mitigate the environmental effect of the domestic emission reductions.

In policy discussions, the prevailing argument against unilateral environmental policy is that it would affect the competitive position of the domestic production sectors. In standard AGE models, including DEAN, this effect is dominated by the ability to specialise in clean production sectors.[7] The model results show a severe loss in competitive position in the relatively dirty production sectors, where production losses are substantial. But these are 'compensated' by increasing exports of relatively clean sectors. One element that is, however, ignored by DEAN and similar models is that a quick implementation of more stringent environmental policy will lead to significant adjustment costs, especially in the relatively dirty production sectors, where changes in production volumes are largest. Consequently, the abstraction from adjustment costs leads to an underestimation of costs, and hence loss of competitive position for domestic producers.

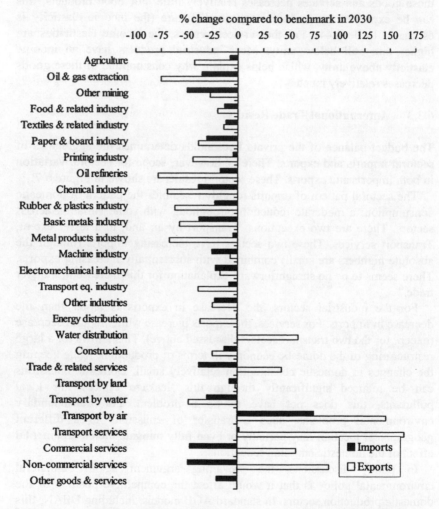

Figure 6.7   Results of the NEPP2030 *scenario on sectoral import and export volumes in the year 2030 for the base specification of DEAN*

6.3.4   Environmental Results

For each environmental theme, the reduction in emissions can be broken up into (i) a reduction in emissions via the implementation of technical abatement measures, and (ii) a reduction in emissions due to economic restructuring. The concept of 'technically abatable emissions', that can be reduced by technical abatement measures, and 'technically unabatable emissions' that cannot, is very helpful in analysing the emission reductions in more detail, though, as explained below, the reduction in technically unabatable emissions does not correspond directly to the reduction in emissions due to economic restructuring.

The ratio between technically abatable and technically unabatable emissions differs between the environmental themes. For instance, almost two-thirds of acidifying emissions can be reduced via technical abatement measures, while only roughly one-third of VOC emissions can be reduced in this way. Total emission reduction is a weighted average of reduction percentages of technically abatable and technically unabatable emissions. Figure 6.8 shows the reduction in technically abatable emissions.

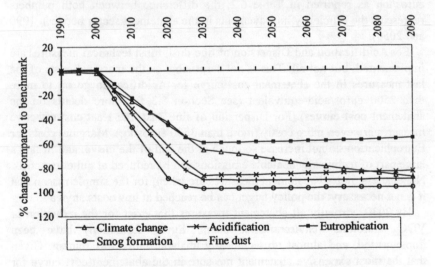

Figure 6.8   Results of the NEPP2030 scenario on the development of technically abatable emissions for the base specification of DEAN

It should be noted that the assumption is made that abatement options are fixed to the benchmark projection for the first three periods (1990-2004). Changes in economic activity that occur in these early periods influence all emissions and therefore also the technically abatable emissions. This influence is caused by the direct link between economic activity and the demand for environmental services, that is, the aggregate of technically abatable emissions and abatement services. For sectors that decrease production, the demand for environmental services decreases and as there are no substitution possibilities between technically abatable emissions and abatement in these early periods, the volume of technically abatable emissions must also decrease. Consequently, technically abatable emissions react on economic restructuring. For all themes, the technically abatable emissions decrease rapidly from the moment the environmental policy is introduced.

The technically abatable emissions for Climate change follow a different path to the technically abatable emissions for other themes, and reflect the path of total GHG emissions. Technically abatable GHG emissions are already substantially reduced in 2005, and then keep on decreasing. In 2050, almost 75 per cent of emissions that can be reduced by technical abatement measures are reduced. In the abatement cost curve for 1990, that would mean marginal costs of around 70 euros/ton (compare the permit price of 45 euros/ton as reported in Table 6.2; the difference between both numbers represents the efficiency improvements in the abatement sector between 1990 and 2050).

For Acidification and Dispersion of fine dust, most technical measures are implemented, but not all. This is not surprising, as the marginal costs of the last measures in the abatement cost curve for Acidification go up to more than 2500 euros/acid-equivalent (see Section 5.3 for more details on the abatement cost curves). For Dispersion of fine dust, the least cost-effective measures are even more costly (more than 3500 euros/kg). Marginal costs for Eutrophication do not increase so much at the end of the curve, and in fact a large part of technically abatable emissions can be reduced at quite low costs. Nonetheless, not all abatement measures are taken, for the simple reason that it is not necessary: the policy target can be reached at low costs anyway.

By 2030, virtually all abatement measures that exist for the reduction of VOC emissions (environmental theme Smog formation) have been implemented, and almost no technically abatable emissions remain. Given that the most expensive abatement measure in the abatement cost curve for Smog formation has marginal costs of less than 250 euros/kg, and that the permit price rises to well above 1000 euros/kg, it is not surprising that technically abatable emissions are reduced as quickly as possible.

Figure 6.9 presents the reductions in technically unabatable emissions. For producers, these are a fixed proportion of their production quantity; for consumers, they are coupled to consumption quantity. For all environmental themes, the reductions in technically unabatable emissions are much smaller than the reductions in technically abatable emissions. This confirms the intuition that implementing technical abatement measures is in most cases cheaper than a restructuring of the economy that reduces emissions, even though an economic restructuring will influence emissions of all environmental themes, while abatement only affects one theme. The differences between the themes with respect to the reduction in technically unabatable emissions are caused by the different spread of emissions over the sectors.

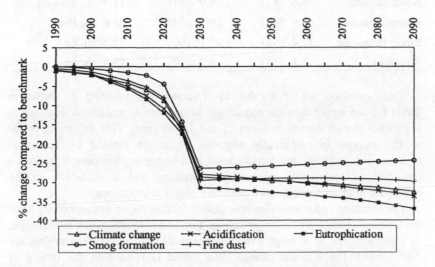

Figure 6.9 Results of the NEPP2030 *scenario on the development of technically unabatable emissions for the base specification of DEAN*

The changes in emissions due to economic restructuring and due to implementation of technical measures can be derived from the changes in technically abatable and technically unabatable emissions. The impact of technical measures on emissions is not equal to the changes in technically abatable emissions, since the technically abatable emissions are influenced by changes in economic activity. Sectoral changes in emissions due to economic restructuring are directly proportional to the changes in the activity level of the sector. Summing these sectoral changes in emissions due to economic restructuring gives the economy-wide change in emissions caused by economic restructuring. The emission reductions due to the implementation of technical measures can then be derived as the rest of total emission reductions. The absolute emission reductions of the two parts, and their share in total emission reductions, are presented in Table 6.3.

Table 6.3   *Contributing parts to emission reductions in the year 2030 in the*
                NEPP2030 scenario for the base specification of DEAN

	Technical measures		Economic restructuring		Total	
	abs.	(%)	abs.	(%)	abs.	Unit
Climate change	46.1	(38)	76.1	(62)	122.3	m. ton CO_2-eq.
Acidification	6.6	(57)	4.9	(43)	11.5	m. acid-eq.
Eutrophication	16.9	(36)	29.7	(64)	46.6	m. P-eq.
Smog formation	42.4	(50)	43.1	(50)	85.5	m. kg
Fine dust	7.1	(53)	6.2	(47)	13.3	m. kg

Total emission reductions due to economic restructuring as shown in
Table 6.3 are larger than the reductions in unabatable emissions depicted in
Figure 6.9 (for all themes between 25 and 35 per cent). This difference is due
to the change in technically abatable emissions caused by economic
restructuring: reducing the activity level of a sector implies *ceteris paribus* a
reduction in technically unabatable emissions and a reduction in the
combination of abatement and technically abatable emissions.

The emission reductions due to economic restructuring are especially large
for Climate change and Eutrophication. For Eutrophication this is expected,
as emissions are to a large extent concentrated in a few sectors (mainly
Agriculture). For Climate change, this effect is related to the timing of
emission reductions: emission reductions are to some extent postponed to
later periods, thereby reducing the need to implement technical measures in
2030. Note that the relatively small contribution of technical measures to the
reduction of emissions for Climate change and Eutrophication can also be
inferred from Figure 6.8. For Smog formation, the contribution of technical
measures is limited, even though virtually all available technical measures
are implemented. These are, however, insufficient to achieve the emission
reduction target and therefore large emission reductions through economic
restructuring are required.

These results show that the upper limit on technical abatement, the
technical potential for emission reduction for each environmental theme, has
major impacts on the model results. Since the costs of economic restructuring
are relatively high compared to the marginal abatement costs for most of the
available abatement measures, the low technical potential for emission
reduction for Smog formation implies that emission permits for this theme
are relatively expensive. The price of Smog formation permits is further
increased by the fact that a relatively large part of VOC emissions is

attributed to Private households. As households' emissions are, at least in the current version of the model, coupled to total consumption (see Section 5.2.3) and not to consumption of individual goods, households cannot reduce their VOC emissions by substituting from one consumption good to another. Moreover, the LES structure implies that part of the emissions of private households are connected to the 'subsistence part', to reflect the non-unitary income elasticities. This subsistence part of private households has a fixed size and hence the emissions attributed to this part (28 m. kg in the year 2030) cannot be reduced at all.

The environmental permit prices in euro per theme equivalent are not directly comparable across environmental themes, as the physical units differ. Therefore, it makes sense to express total environmental permit values in billion euros. These permit values give insight into the economic costs of environmental policy per environmental theme. This is possible because the model calculates a cost-effective equilibrium, where marginal abatement costs equal permit prices and equal marginal costs of economic restructuring. The resulting permit values for selected years and, for comparability, the public environmental expenditures are reported in Table 6.4.

Table 6.4   Environmental permit values in the NEPP2030 *scenario for the base specification of DEAN (undiscounted values in billion euros)*

	1990	2010	2030	2050
Climate change	0.55	1.64	2.52	6.07
Acidification	0.16	0.42	5.60	6.58
Eutrophication	0.11	0.23	0.36	0.54
Smog formation	0.07	0.25	100.96	107.54
Dispersion of fine dust	0.01	0.02	0.65	0.82
Desiccation*	0.25	0.37	0.37	0.64
Soil contamination*	8.77	13.04	13.15	22.42
Total environmental expenditures	9.92	15.98	123.62	144.62
in percentage of GDP	*4%*	*5%*	*26%*	*21%*

Note: * Government expenditures, not permit revenues.

Table 6.4 reveals that in the long run the permit value for Smog formation is more dominant than the reported permit prices in Table 6.2 suggest. The likelihood that such a result will become reality is rather low. If the permit prices are rising as dramatically as shown in these simulations, consumers will substitute away from VOC-intensive consumption goods to other consumption goods, though this substitution may be limited by the availability of substitute consumption goods and the income elasticities of the VOC-intensive goods. This effect is not present in the model. Moreover, polluters will react on the high permit price for Smog formation by investigating new technologies (or new applications of existing technologies) to reduce their VOC emissions and avoid paying the expensive permits. The base specification of the DEAN model does not capture such endogenous innovation effects; these will be investigated in the next chapter. The results do, however, show the potential threat of current Smog formation policy for the economy if no additional effort is placed on researching VOC-reducing technologies. One more option that might prevent the results of the DEAN simulations becoming reality is that the government will auction more VOC permits to prevent the severe economic impacts.

It should be noted that for the emission-related environmental themes, the private environmental permit expenditures are also accounted as income for the government, and recycled to the private households. For Desiccation and Soil contamination, the environmental expenditures are a demand for abatement services (by the government). As all other economic activities, these abatement services generate value added and hence contribute to GDP. The macro-economic costs of environmental policy are therefore smaller than Table 6.4 suggests.

Over time, the Climate change permits become more and more expensive, which is in line with the declining GHG emission levels for later periods. Expressed as a percentage of GDP, the costs of Climate change permits increase from 0.2 per cent in 1990 to 0.9 per cent in 2050.

The 'cheapest' environmental theme is Eutrophication. There are several reasons why the permits for this theme are relatively cheap. Firstly, the emissions are concentrated in a few sectors (more than two-thirds are attributed to the Agricultural sector), implying that a restructuring of the economy to reduce emissions is relatively easy. Secondly, the substitution elasticity between emissions and abatement (the PAS elasticity) is higher than for other themes, indicating relatively easy abatement options. Thirdly, a relatively large share of eutrophying emissions can be reduced via low-cost technical abatement measures. Fourthly, the policy target in percentages of emissions is not as stringent as for most other themes.

Total costs for Soil contamination dominate environmental expenditures in the first decades, constituting a little less than 4 per cent of GDP. The public environmental expenditures on Desiccation and Soil contamination are exogenously given and are assumed to increase by 2 per cent per year. As expenditures on the other environmental themes increase much more, especially around 2030, the relative importance of Soil contamination decreases over time.

6.4 COMPARING THE *DELAY* AND *NEPP2010* SCENARIOS WITH *NEPP2030*

In order to analyse the impact of the timing of environmental policy on the economy and on abatement, two alternative scenarios are analysed. These alternative scenarios are described in Section 6.2.2 above. In the *Delay* scenario, the policy targets of *NEPP2030* are implemented with a delay of 10 years, that is, in 2040. This means that the adjustment path to the target is longer, and policy targets for the period 2000-2040 are less ambitious. It is expected that the delay in policy implementation will reduce the economic costs of the policy.

Instead of slowing down implementation of environmental policy, government can also choose to implement intermediate targets in 2010: the *NEPP2010* scenario. These intermediate targets are more stringent than the linear adjustment path to the 2030 target implies (compare Figure 6.2). Hence, the short-term economic costs of environmental policy are expected to be larger. The alternative scenarios have no impact on the target for Climate change, as the allowed addition to the stock of GHGs is equal across the scenarios.

6.4.1 General Results

Table 6.5 presents the main results for the *Delay* scenario. The main difference between the numbers in Table 6.5 and the numbers for the *NEPP2030* scenario in Table 6.2 is clearly in the column for 2030. This is also the period where the difference between policy levels is the largest between the two scenarios. Perhaps more interesting than the large differences for 2030 are the adjustment processes that emerge before the policy is implemented (1990-2000). As can be seen by comparing the results for NNI, private consumption and capital investment, the tendency to place more emphasis on current consumption at the expense of future consumption is less strong in the *Delay* scenario than in *NEPP2030*.

In 2010, the situation is even more pronounced: the decreases in capital investment are substantially smaller than in the *NEPP2030* scenario, combined with smaller increases in private consumption and smaller losses in GDP. One can directly observe the slower adjustment path of environmental policy by comparing the emission reductions between the two policy scenarios.

In 2050, the GDP loss is still more than 0.5 per cent point less than in the *NEPP2030* scenario. Production losses are also smaller in the *Delay* scenario, and due to higher growth rates in the first half of the century consumption losses can be limited as well.

Table 6.5   Results of the Delay *scenario for the base specification of DEAN*

	1990	2010	2030	2050
Macro-economic results (% change in volumes compared to benchmark)				
GDP	-0.01	-0.92	-3.52	-9.52
NNI	0.21	-0.24	-1.68	-7.76
Total private consumption	0.62	0.56	0.02	-9.01
Total production	-0.23	-1.51	-6.20	-16.20
Savings/investment	-1.19	-4.51	-13.28	-18.84
International trade results (% change in volumes compared to benchmark)				
Total imports	-0.48	-2.35	-9.44	-23.01
Total exports	-0.47	-2.32	-9.29	-22.99
Trade balance (in % GDP)	0.99	1.00	1.03	1.10
Sectoral[a] results (% change in volumes compared to benchmark)				
Private consumption Agriculture	0.23	-0.28	-1.89	-8.58
Private consumption Industry	0.56	0.40	-0.73	-11.00
Private consumption Services	0.70	0.76	0.89	-6.91
Sectoral production Agriculture	-1.18	-6.09	-17.53	-33.82
Sectoral production Industry	-0.50	-2.37	-11.13	-31.47
Sectoral production Services	0.06	-0.45	-1.36	-2.64
Sectoral production Abatement services	-0.04	4.23	11.09	17.17
Environmental results (% change in volumes compared to benchmark)				
Emissions Climate change	-1.16	-14.75	-33.37	-51.77
Emissions Acidification	0.00	-16.38	-49.14	-65.52
Emissions Eutrophication	0.00	-12.30	-36.90	-49.21
Emissions Smog formation	0.00	-12.99	-38.97	-51.96
Emissions Dispersion of fine dust	0.00	-15.73	-47.20	-62.93
Prices of main variables (constant 1990 prices)				
Exchange rate index (benchmark = 1)	1.00	1.01	0.99	0.87
Price of abatement services (bm. = 1)	1.00	1.00	0.95	0.75
Price Climate change[b] (€/ton CO_2-eq.)	2.5	7.9	24.7	54.1
Price Acidification (€/acid-eq.)	3.9	20.0	230.9	1101.7
Price Eutrophication (€/P-eq.)	0.6	2.1	9.7	11.4
Price Smog formation (€/kilogram)	0.1	1.0	183.2	1493.4
Price Fine dust (€/kilogram)	0.1	0.8	10.6	106.4

Notes:
[a]   The 27 production sectors are grouped into three categories.
[b]   Expressed in terms of emissions.

Table 6.6   Results of the NEPP2010 scenario for the base specification of
DEAN

	1990	2010	2030	2050
Macro-economic results (% change in volumes compared to benchmark)				
GDP	-0.03	-2.59	-9.06	-10.49
NNI	0.55	-0.93	-7.01	-8.86
Total private consumption	1.60	0.89	-7.46	-10.86
Total production	-0.31	-5.14	-16.25	-16.59
Savings/investment	-3.08	-11.38	-19.90	-19.11
International trade results (% change in volumes compared to benchmark)				
Total imports	-0.61	-7.95	-23.23	-23.00
Total exports	-0.60	-7.83	-23.11	-23.17
Trade balance (in % GDP)	0.99	1.02	1.09	1.11
Sectoral[a] results (% change in volumes compared to benchmark)				
Private consumption Agriculture	0.83	-1.29	-7.61	-9.57
Private consumption Industry	1.52	0.16	-9.83	-12.45
Private consumption Services	1.73	1.75	-4.92	-9.21
Sectoral production Agriculture	-1.05	-16.32	-33.14	-34.89
Sectoral production Industry	-0.83	-9.55	-34.09	-30.35
Sectoral production Services	0.16	-0.72	-0.71	-4.17
Sectoral production Abatement services	-0.03	9.35	15.47	15.10
Environmental results (% change in volumes compared to benchmark)				
Emissions Climate change	-0.98	-17.98	-43.23	-48.78
Emissions Acidification	0.00	-51.85	-65.52	-65.52
Emissions Eutrophication	0.00	-38.85	-49.21	-49.21
Emissions Smog formation	0.00	-37.44	-51.96	-51.96
Emissions Dispersion of fine dust	0.00	-29.76	-62.93	-62.93
Prices of main variables (constant 1990 prices)				
Exchange rate index (benchmark = 1)	1.00	0.99	0.84	0.89
Price of abatement services (bm. = 1)	1.00	0.95	0.70	0.79
Price Climate change[b] (€/ton CO_2-eq.)	2.0	6.3	14.4	39.3
Price Acidification (€/acid-eq.)	3.9	196.1	912.7	1096.2
Price Eutrophication (€/P-eq.)	0.6	7.2	7.6	11.3
Price Smog formation (€/kilogram)	0.1	99.2	1182.8	1308.7
Price Fine dust (€/kilogram)	0.1	1.1	77.6	103.5

Notes:
[a]   The 27 production sectors are grouped into three categories.
[b]   Expressed in terms of emissions.

The slower adjustment path does, however, lead to a lower growth rate of the economy in 2050. Hence, the alternative scenario is characterised by lower economic costs in the first half of the century, but also by a longer period of economic adjustment costs.

Most permit prices are, in the short run, lower in the *Delay* scenario than in the *NEPP2030* scenario; in the long run, the permit prices are slightly higher than in the *NEPP2030* scenario. For Climate change, the permit prices are persistently above the respective level in the *NEPP2030* scenario. This is coupled with significantly smaller emission reductions in 2030 and somewhat larger emission reductions in other periods. Clearly, the less stringent target in 2030 for the other environmental themes means that it is less easy to reduce GHG emissions in that period. Hence, the pressure on the market for Climate permits is higher throughout the century.

The main economic and environmental results for the *NEPP2010* scenario are shown in Table 6.6. As expected, the loss in GDP and NNI, production and capital investments in the year 2010 are significantly worse than when the intermediate targets are not imposed. The production of Abatement services increases by almost 10 per cent in 2010 if the intermediate targets are imposed, while the increase is around 4 per cent if the intermediate targets are not imposed. Detailed analysis of sectoral abatement demand reveals that the demand for abatement services by the polluting sectors (excluding government) increases to 9 times the benchmark projection in the *NEPP2010* scenario. The higher demand for abatement services in 2010 is, however, coupled with relatively smaller demand in later periods.

To a large extent, the differences between the *NEPP2010* and *NEPP2030* scenarios are opposite to those between the *Delay* and *NEPP2030* scenarios. When the *NEPP2010* policy targets are implemented, GDP levels are more severely affected in 2010 and 2030, and to a lesser extent in 2050.

Figure 6.10 displays the development of GDP for the different policy scenarios. The largest decrease in GDP throughout the model horizon is in the *NEPP2010* scenario, while the GDP losses are the smallest in the *Delay* scenario. As expected, the *NEPP2030* scenario lies between these two alternatives. The graph also shows that the impacts of environmental policy on the development of GDP are relatively smooth, though there is a break in the curves in 2030 for *NEPP2030* and *NEPP2010* and in 2040 for the *Delay* scenario. This indicates that the growth rates of the economy are not evolving as smoothly as the levels. It is not difficult to recognise the parallel between the development of the implemented environmental policy and the GDP graph: the reductions are small for the first few periods, then rapidly decrease and after 2030/2040 they stabilise.

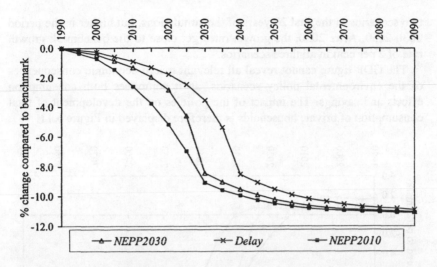

Figure 6.10 Results of the policy scenarios on the development of GDP for the base specification of DEAN

In the long run, the GDP losses converge for all three scenarios to around 11 per cent below the benchmark projection, and the growth rate of GDP is restored at 2 per cent. This implies that a temporary difference in environmental policy will lead to a temporary difference in economic costs. The implications of the scenarios on environmental quality are, however, permanently different between the scenarios, as greenhouse gases, acidifying emissions and eutrophying emissions have the characteristics of stock pollutants.

Table 6.7 Average annual growth rates of GDP in percentages for selected periods in the different policy scenarios for the base specification of DEAN

	1990-2010	2010-2030	2030-2050	2050-2070
NEPP2030	1.93	1.62	1.90	1.97
Delay	1.95	1.86	1.67	1.97
NEPP2010	1.86	1.65	1.92	1.97

The average annual growth rates of GDP per 20 years are given in Table 6.7. In line with the observations above, the *NEPP2030* scenario has the lowest average growth rate in the period 2010-2030, while in the *Delay* scenario the slowdown of economic growth occurs mostly between 2030 and 2050. In the *NEPP2010* scenario, the growth rate is lower than for the other two scenarios in the first 20 years of the simulations, but higher in the period 2030-2050. After 2050, the growth rates get close to the benchmark growth rate of 2 per cent in all three scenarios.

The GDP figure cannot reveal all relevant macro-economic consequences of the environmental policy scenarios, as it comprises both consumption effects and savings. The impact of the policies on the development of total consumption of private households is therefore displayed in Figure 6.11.

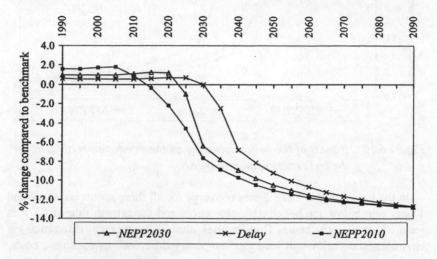

Figure 6.11   Results of the policy scenarios on the development of total consumption of private households for the base specification of DEAN

The intermediate targets imposed in the *NEPP2010* scenario induce an intertemporal shift in consumption that is stronger than in the *NEPP2030* scenario, while the *Delay* scenario leads to a less strong intertemporal shift. Apparently, the more stringent environmental policy will be, and the quicker it will be implemented, the more emphasis consumers place on current consumption at the expense of future consumption. The shift in consumption over time is, however, a temporary phenomenon: in the long run, total consumption levels converge for all three scenarios to around 13 per cent below the benchmark projection at the end of the century.

6.4.2   Sectoral Results

Figure 6.12 presents the impact of the different policy scenarios on sectoral production volumes for the year 2050. The figure shows that the sectoral impacts are quite similar across the different scenarios. By 2050, in all three scenarios strict environmental targets are imposed, leading to substantial production losses in most sectors.

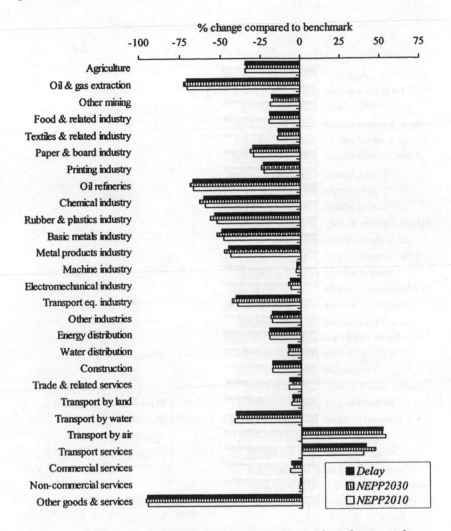

Figure 6.12   Results of the policy scenarios on sectoral production volumes in the year 2050 for the base specification of DEAN

Total production losses are slightly lower in the *Delay* scenario than in the other two scenarios (compare Table 6.5 with Table 6.2 and Table 6.6), but for most production sectors, especially in agriculture and industry, the losses are larger in the *Delay* scenario than in the other two scenarios. This illustrates how a purely macro-economic analysis can lead to different insights compared to a more detailed sectoral analysis.

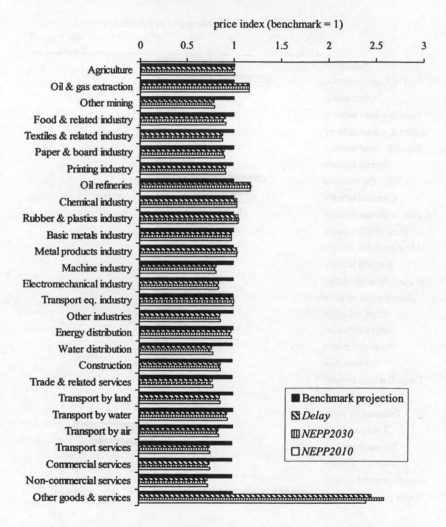

Figure 6.13   Results of the policy scenarios on sectoral output price indices in the year 2050 for the base specification of DEAN

Figure 6.13 displays the prices for produced goods for the different policy scenarios. In the benchmark projection, all prices are normalised to unity (the Harberger convention). The implementation of the stricter environmental policy leads to increases in output prices of relatively dirty production sectors, and lower prices for relatively clean products. As the CGE model can only calculate relative prices, that is, there is no money illusion, these prices are all relative to the consumer price index. The price increase of dirty products reflects the increased cost of production as well as the reduced demand for these goods. The price increase is the largest for the sector Other goods and services, in line with the drastic reduction in production volume (compare Figure 6.12). Relative prices between the different produced goods hardly differ between the different scenarios, except for Other goods and services.

6.4.3 International Trade Results

The increasing costs of production due to environmental policy lead to higher domestic prices and hence the restriction on the trade balance must be accommodated by an adjustment of the exchange rate. A substantial increase in the price of foreign goods, that is, a substantial depreciation of the domestic currency, is needed to keep the trade balance in line. This suggests that there is considerable pressure to reduce the budget surplus to be able to import more goods and/or export less. Given the fact that The Netherlands is part of the euro currency union, the assumption that the exchange rate fully adjusts while the trade balance is unchanged may not be realistic. The implications of this assumption are analysed in the next chapter. Exchange rate adjustments with major trade partners such as the United Kingdom, the United States and Japan are, however, not unrealistic.

Figure 6.14 shows that the depreciation does not mean that the real exchange rate increases: the increase in domestic prices is larger than the increase in the price of foreign goods, especially from 2020 onwards. De facto, imports become cheaper compared to domestically produced goods and domestically produced goods can only be sold at relatively low prices on the international markets. This shows that the competitive position of domestic producers decreases as a result of the environmental policies.

The depreciation of the domestic currency is caused by a positive correlation between exports and domestic environmental intensity. For Climate change, the correlation coefficient between sectoral export intensity (exports divided by value added) and sectoral emission intensity (also in terms of value added) is 0.27. For Smog formation, the correlation is 0.67. The only theme for which there is no positive correlation between exports and domestic emissions is Eutrophication. The economic interpretation of this is that the domestic economy specialises in relatively dirty goods. As these dirty goods become more expensive when a stringent environmental policy is implemented, a depreciation of the domestic currency is needed to partially counter the loss in competitive position of these exporting sectors.

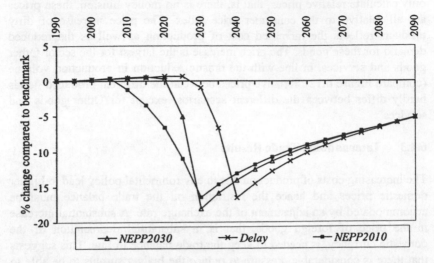

*Figure 6.14   Results of the policy scenarios on the development of the real
              exchange rate for the base specification of DEAN*

6.4.4   Environmental Results

The division of emission reductions into reductions due to economic restructuring and due to implementation of technical measures is shown in Table 6.8 for the year 2050 for the different scenarios. Though the absolute numbers may differ between the different scenarios, the shares of both parts are very similar over the scenarios. This indicates that only the absolute amounts of emission reductions realised through implementation of technical measures depend on total emission reduction, not on shares. The division between both parts is determined by equating the marginal costs of both ways to reduce emissions.

Comparing the numbers for scenario *NEPP2030* in Table 6.8 (for the year 2050) with the numbers for the same scenario for the year 2030 in Table 6.3 shows that the percentages are similar, indicating a stable share of both parts over time. The only exception is Climate change, where the contribution of technical measures increases over time (38 per cent in 2030 versus 42 per cent in 2050). This effect can also be seen in Figure 6.8 and is related to the flexibility in the timing of greenhouse gas emission reductions (more emphasis on later reductions).

*Table 6.8 Contributing parts to emission reductions in the year 2050 in the different policy scenarios for the base specification of DEAN**

	NEPP2030		Delay		NEPP2010	
	Technical measures	Economic restruct.	Technical measures	Economic restruct.	Technical measures	Economic restruct.
	Abs. (%)	Abs. (%)	Abs. (%)	Abs. (%)	Abs. (%)	Abs. (%)
Climate change	57 (42)	79 (58)	61 (43)	79 (57)	54 (41)	78 (59)
Acidification	6 (55)	5 (45)	6 (55)	5 (45)	6 (54)	5 (46)
Eutrophication	16 (34)	31 (66)	16 (35)	30 (65)	15 (33)	31 (67)
Smog formation	43 (51)	42 (49)	43 (51)	42 (49)	43 (51)	42 (49)
Disp. of fine dust	7 (54)	6 (46)	7 (54)	6 (46)	7 (54)	6 (46)

Note: * For units see Table 6.3.

The expenditures on abatement differ widely between sectors, as shown in Figure 6.15. This is the case in the benchmark, but it is even more pronounced in the policy simulations. Moreover, different scenarios have different impacts on sectoral abatement. For example, in the year 2030 the agricultural sector has a higher demand for abatement services in the *NEPP2030* scenario than in the other scenarios, while the Chemical industry has the highest abatement level in the *Delay* scenario.

The demand for abatement services by the government sector is not displayed in Figure 6.15, as it is much larger than the numbers for the other sectors and constant over the scenarios. Total demand for abatement services in 2030 amounts to around 29 billion euros (*NEPP2030* scenario) including government demand, or 4.6 billion euros if government demand is excluded. This is a substantial figure, but only a small fraction of GDP (in the *NEPP2030* scenario GDP is around 475 billion euros in 2030). It is also less than the total economic costs of the environmental policy: almost 8.5 per cent of GDP or 44 billion euros. This shows the importance of having a good economic model to calculate total direct and indirect costs of emission policies and not focusing purely on bottom-up data from abatement cost curves.

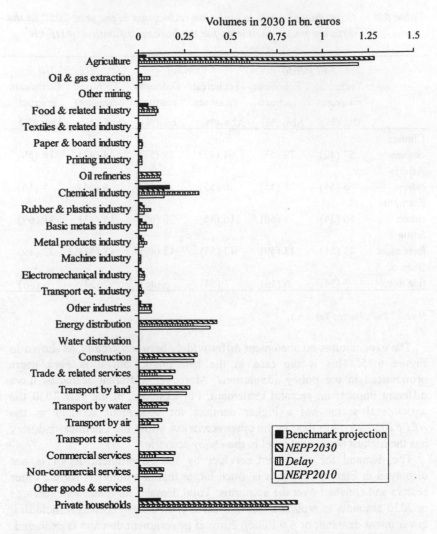

*Figure 6.15   Results of the policy scenarios on the demand for abatement
                services in the year 2030 for the base specification of DEAN*

Figure 6.16 shows the endogenous path of emission reductions for
greenhouse gases. At first glance, it may seem surprising that the emission
path of GHGs is similar to the paths of the other environmental themes.
Moreover, even though the policy target in terms of the maximum allowable
stock addition is identical across the policy scenarios, the scenarios give
differences in the optimal path of GHG emissions that resemble the

differences in emission paths between the scenarios for the other environmental themes. This result is primarily caused by economic restructuring induced by the other themes.

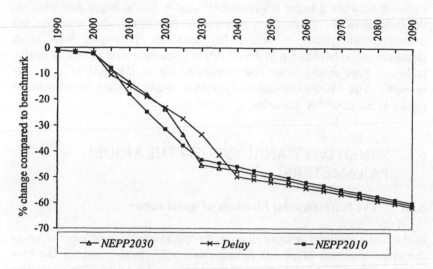

Figure 6.16   Results of the policy scenarios on GHG emissions for the base specification of DEAN

In the *Delay* scenario, the economy adapts more slowly to the environmental policy, and hence it makes sense for the polluters to time their GHG emission reductions to coincide with that development. The path of GHG emissions is determined by a discounted minimisation of the costs of technical abatement measures, the costs of environmental permits and the costs of economic restructuring, that is, balancing the marginal costs of the different options. The relatively small abatement efforts in the earlier periods are encountered in many studies on the timing of greenhouse gas emission reductions (see Metz et al., 2001).

There is one major difference between the emission path for Climate change and the paths for the other environmental themes, and that is that GHG emissions keep on decreasing in the long run, while the emissions for the other themes stabilise. This is due to the fact that Climate change policy allows flexibility in the timing of the emissions, while for the other environmental themes this flexibility is not available.

The DEAN model cannot be used to assess whether the economic costs of environmental policy are justified, as the benefits of the policy, in terms of better environmental quality, are not taken into account (see the discussion in earlier chapters). Hence, the optimal level of environmental policy cannot be inferred and the analysis has to be confined to an evaluation of the cost-effectiveness of exogenously given scenarios. This also means that the model cannot give an appraisal which of these scenarios is preferred, as they entail a trade-off between a better environmental quality and a larger economy.[8] In the *Delay* scenario, the economy is better off than in the other scenarios, but environmental quality is worse (at least for pollutants with stock characteristics). In contrast, in the *NEPP2010* scenario environmental quality is higher than in the other two scenarios, but at the cost of a smaller economy. The *NEPP2030* scenario provides results that are in between the results of the other two scenarios.

6.5   SENSITIVITY ANALYSIS ON THE MODEL PARAMETERS[9]

6.5.1   The Intertemporal Elasticity of Substitution

In the first sensitivity analysis, the intertemporal elasticity of substitution in the utility function of private households, σ_{priv}^{Util}, is changed. In the base specification of the model, this parameter has a value of 0.5. The alternative values investigated are 0.6 and 0.4, respectively. A higher intertemporal elasticity of substitution means that households are more flexible in their decisions to consume now or in the future. A lower elasticity implies the opposite: the disutility from a forced intertemporal shift in consumption is larger than in the base specification.

The main results for this sensitivity analysis are represented in Table 6.9. The values shown are for the *NEPP2030* scenario and for the year 2030. Though the parameter under investigation is expected to have the most impact on the growth rates of variables, some observations can already be made by looking at the results for a single year.

Firstly, a higher intertemporal substitution elasticity leads to a larger reduction in GDP. This turns out to apply to all periods, and is connected to the larger impact of environmental policy on investments. In the model with a high intertemporal substitution elasticity more emphasis is placed on current consumption, thereby reducing the growth rate of the economy and hence reducing future GDP levels. Secondly, a higher intertemporal elasticity of substitution leads to a smaller increase in abatement. The production of the Abatement services sector increases less than in the base specification, though the effect is small.

This effect is connected to the first effect: since the future economy is smaller in the specification with a high intertemporal substitution elasticity,

Table 6.9   Results of the NEPP2030 scenario for the year 2030 for alternative values of the intertemporal elasticity of substitution

	Base spec.	High σ_{priv}^{Util}	Low σ_{priv}^{Util}
Macro-economic results (% change in volumes compared to benchmark)			
GDP	-8.45	-8.85	-7.93
NNI	-6.26	-6.60	-5.84
Total private consumption	-6.12	-6.57	-5.62
Total production	-16.00	-16.19	-15.73
Savings / investment	-20.00	-20.71	-18.94
International trade results (% change in volumes compared to benchmark)			
Total imports	-23.19	-23.37	-22.92
Total exports	-22.90	-23.05	-22.69
Trade balance (in % GDP)	1.09	1.09	1.08
Sectoral results (% change in volumes compared to benchmark)			
Private consumption Agriculture	-6.88	-7.14	-6.59
Private consumption Industry	-8.80	-9.12	-8.46
Private consumption Services	-3.23	-3.82	-2.55
Sectoral production Agriculture	-32.64	-32.94	-32.27
Sectoral production Industry	-35.05	-34.75	-35.40
Sectoral production Services	0.49	-0.09	1.23
Sectoral production Abatement services	16.59	16.20	17.09
Environmental results (% change in volumes compared to benchmark)			
Emissions Climate change	-45.24	-44.97	-45.60
Emissions Acidification	-65.52	-65.52	-65.52
Emissions Eutrophication	-49.21	-49.21	-49.21
Emissions Smog formation	-51.96	-51.96	-51.96
Emissions Dispersion of fine dust	-62.93	-62.93	-62.93
Prices of main variables (constant 1990 prices)			
Exchange rate index (benchmark = 1)	0.82	0.83	0.81
Price of abatement services (bm. = 1)	0.68	0.69	0.66
Price Climate change (€/ton CO_2-eq.)	17.0	16.8	17.3
Price Acidification (€/acid-eq.)	929.7	915.1	946.6
Price Eutrophication (€/P-eq.)	7.5	7.5	7.5
Price Smog formation (€/kilogram)	1277.0	1232.3	1332.0
Price Fine dust (€/kilogram)	82.4	80.0	85.8

the demand for emission permits is smaller and there is less need for abatement. This is also reflected in the lower prices for the emission permits.

The results for the model specification with a lower intertemporal elasticity of substitution show that the mechanisms are more or less symmetric with respect to the value of this parameter. A lower intertemporal substitution elasticity implies smaller GDP losses in 2030, combined with more abatement and higher prices for the emission permits.

As the different values for the intertemporal elasticity of substitution primarily affect the optimal path of consumption, the results for one year will not give sufficient information on the impact of the parameter on model outcomes. Therefore, the path of total consumption of private households, in percentage change compared to the benchmark, is presented in Figure 6.17. The figure shows that the higher the value of the intertemporal substitution elasticity, the higher total consumption is in the first three decades. This comes at the expense of future consumption, as expected.

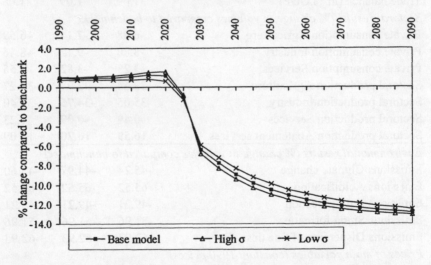

Figure 6.17   Results of the NEPP2030 *scenario on the development of total consumption of private households for the base specification and alternative values of the intertemporal elasticity of substitution*

A change in the value of the intertemporal elasticity of substitution may also affect the sectoral composition of the economy, especially for consumption. Figure 6.18 shows that this effect is clearly dominated by the impact of the parameter on total consumption.

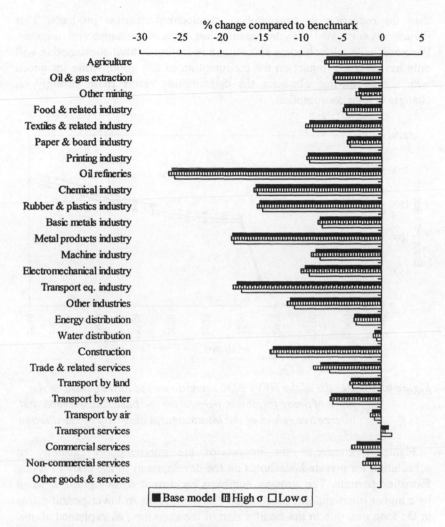

*Figure 6.18   Results of the NEPP2030 scenario on sectoral consumption
volumes of private households in the year 2030 for the base
specification and alternative values of the intertemporal
elasticity of substitution*

For all sectors, the lowest consumption volume, that is, the largest
decrease or smallest increase compared to the benchmark projection, occurs
in the specification with a high intertemporal substitution elasticity. The
magnitudes of the differences between the specifications do vary by sector.
For example, the reduction in consumption of basic metal products varies less

than the reduction in consumption of electromechanical products. This variation is correlated with the income elasticities of the consumption goods. For goods with a low income elasticity, a reduction in total consumption will only have a small impact on the consumption of this good, while for goods with a high income elasticity the consumption reacts more strongly on changes in total consumption.

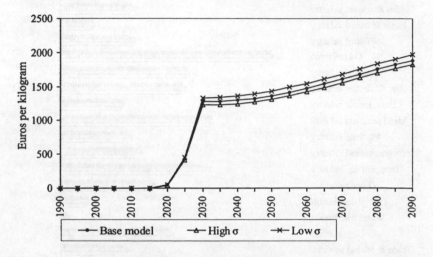

Figure 6.19   Results of the NEPP2030 *scenario on the development of the price of Smog formation permits for the base specification and alternative values of the intertemporal elasticity of substitution*

Figure 6.19 reveals the impact of the intertemporal elasticity of substitution for private households on the development of the price of Smog formation permits. The stronger emphasis on current consumption, induced by a higher intertemporal substitution elasticity, leads to lower permit prices in the long run, due to the smaller size of the economy, as explained above. For all periods, the permit price for the high elasticity is below the level in the base specification, while the opposite is true for a low elasticity. This shows that the intertemporal elasticity of substitution does influence the development path of the economy, more or less as a scaling parameter.

6.5.2 The Technical Potential for Emission Reduction

One parameter that is expected to have significant effects on model outcomes is the technical potential for emission reduction, μ. Increasing this technical potential means that more abatement via implementation of technical measures is possible. Since this form of emission reduction is almost always cheaper than the costs of economic restructuring, the likely impact of increasing the technical potential is that economic costs of environmental policy are smaller.

In the base specification, the technical potential, expressed as share of total emissions that can be abated via technical abatement measures, equals 0.414 for Climate change, 0.633 for Acidification, 0.624 for Eutrophication, 0.344 for Smog formation and 0.545 for Dispersion of fine dust. In the sensitivity analysis, one of these values is increased by 0.05. So first, the value for Climate change is increased to 0.464, keeping the values for the other themes on their original level. Sensitivity analyses on the technical potential for Acidification, Eutrophication, Smog formation and Dispersion of fine dust are carried out in a similar fashion.

Table 6.10 presents the results for the base specification and for the alternative values of the technical potentials for the *NEPP2030* scenario for the year 2030. The only parameter that influences GDP substantially is the technical potential for VOC emission reductions.[10]

This clearly shows the sensitivity of the model results for the modelling of this environmental theme. Increasing the scope for emission reductions via technical abatement measures effectively means less emission reductions via economic restructuring.

For a highly binding constraint such as that which the environmental policy for Smog formation constitutes, any additional abatement opportunity leads to a substantial decrease in the economic costs of the environmental policy. For the other environmental themes, the increase in technical potential matters much less, as the restrictions on emissions are less binding for these themes than for Smog formation. This confirms the conclusion that the significant reduction in the long-run level of GDP can be attributed largely to the environmental theme Smog formation. In reality, it is likely that these high economic costs of environmental policy will induce innovations that can reduce VOC emissions further at relatively low costs. Hence, the results of the sensitivity analysis may be considered to be as realistic as the base specification.

From an empirical point of view, the insensitivity of the model results for changes in the specification of Climate change may seem surprising. Most of the environmental-economic literature focuses on Climate change, which is deemed to be the most important environmental problem society is facing.

Table 6.10   Results of the NEPP2030 scenario for the year 2030 for
alternative values of the technical potentials for emission
reduction per environmental theme

	Base specification	High μ Climate change	High μ Acidification	High μ Eutrophication	High μ Smog form.	High μ Fine dust
Macro-economic results (% change in volumes compared to benchmark)						
GDP	-8.45	-8.43	-8.37	-8.46	-6.06	-8.44
NNI	-6.26	-6.24	-6.21	-6.27	-4.40	-6.26
Total priv. consumption	-6.12	-6.09	-6.10	-6.13	-4.17	-6.12
Total production	-16.00	-15.97	-15.74	-16.02	-12.51	-15.96
Savings/investment	-20.00	-20.00	-19.77	-20.03	-14.79	-19.98
International trade results (% change in volumes compared to benchmark)						
Total imports	-23.19	-23.14	-22.81	-23.23	-18.99	-23.12
Total exports	-22.90	-22.85	-22.52	-22.94	-18.79	-22.84
Trade balance (% GDP)	1.09	1.09	1.08	1.09	1.06	1.09
Sectoral results (% change in volumes compared to benchmark)						
Private cons. Agriculture	-6.88	-6.86	-6.48	-6.92	-5.84	-6.90
Private cons. Industry	-8.80	-8.77	-8.73	-8.82	-6.31	-8.80
Private cons. Services	-3.23	-3.20	-3.28	-3.23	-1.83	-3.23
Production Agriculture	-32.64	-32.64	-29.81	-32.90	-29.63	-32.82
Production Industry	-35.05	-35.10	-35.16	-35.06	-25.84	-35.08
Production Services	0.49	0.58	0.81	0.47	-0.52	0.59
Prod. Abatement services	16.59	16.42	16.72	16.69	18.19	16.62
Environmental results (% change in volumes compared to benchmark)						
Emissions Climate ch.	-45.24	-44.53	-44.44	-45.29	-44.81	-45.24
Emissions Acidification	-65.52	-65.52	-65.52	-65.52	-65.52	-65.52
Emissions Eutrophication	-49.21	-49.21	-49.21	-49.21	-49.21	-49.21
Emissions Smog form.	-51.96	-51.96	-51.96	-51.96	-51.96	-51.96
Emissions Fine dust	-62.93	-62.93	-62.93	-62.93	-62.93	-62.93
Prices of main variables (constant 1990 prices)						
Exchange rate index	0.82	0.82	0.82	0.82	0.90	0.82
Price abatement services	0.68	0.68	0.68	0.68	0.77	0.68
Price Climate change	17.0	14.4	17.8	16.9	23.1	17.0
Price Acidification	929.7	954.1	687.9	947.5	982.7	956.3
Price Eutrophication	7.5	7.5	9.4	6.7	10.9	7.5
Price Smog formation	1277.0	1280.5	1278.5	1277.3	926.2	1279.4
Price Fine dust	82.4	83.6	146.5	82.1	200.6	22.5

In national models like DEAN, however, regional pollutants have relatively more weight. Moreover, the significance of the environmental theme Smog formation is caused primarily by a lack of available technologies to reduce VOC emissions. There seems to be a feedback mechanism inducing environmental technicians to put most of their effort into specifying reduction measures for those environmental themes that are in the centre of attention of policy makers. In the 1980s, acid rain was the 'hot topic', and many technical abatement measures for acidifying substances were specified and partially implemented. In the 1990s, the focus shifted towards Climate change, both for scientists and policy makers. The number of technical abatement options available in the abatement cost curves discussed in Chapter 5 confirms the lack of options for reducing VOC emissions: the curve for Climate change contains 335 measures, the curve for Acidification 137 measures and the curve for Smog formation 29 measures.

The fact that Smog formation may cause serious problems, in terms of environmental and economic effects, may not come as a surprise for environmental policy makers in The Netherlands. The annual 'State of the environment', published by RIVM (2002a), mentions that current VOC policies in The Netherlands will not reduce VOC emissions enough to reach the EU target in 2010. RIVM (2002a) also indicates that the environmental effects are important: around 1700 deaths in The Netherlands in 2000 can be attributed to the theme Smog formation. Actual VOC abatement expenditures have risen from around 40 m. euros in 1990 to 240 m. euros in 2000 (Brink, 2003).

An increase in technical potential for a certain environmental theme is likely to result in a lower associated permit price. As shown in Table 6.10, this is indeed the case. The permit price for Dispersion of fine dust is most sensitive to changes in the technical potential. Increasing the technical potential for PM_{10} emission reductions reduces the economic costs of Dispersion of fine dust policy substantially. Given the presence of other environmental policies this has, however, no major impact on the total economy.

The prices of Dispersion of fine dust and Eutrophication permits are also sensitive to the parameter value of the technical potential for the other environmental themes: an increase in technical potential for Acidification or Smog formation leads to an increase in the permit price for Eutrophication and Dispersion of fine dust. This implies that the higher technical potential induces less reduction in production of the sectors that are also environmentally intensive with respect to Eutrophication and Dispersion of fine dust. In other words, there is a complementarity between these environmental themes so that reducing the implicit strictness of policy for one theme increases the implicit strictness of policy for the other theme.

Figure 6.20 shows how the sensitivity analyses impact the development of GDP over time. In line with the observations made above, the only sensitivity analysis that leads to a clearly different GDP curve is the one for Smog formation. For the other environmental themes, there is hardly any difference with the base specification. For Smog formation, the curvature of the GDP curve is not affected as much as the level: the decrease in GDP in the sensitivity analysis is about a quarter less than in the base specification. This holds for all periods.

Figure 6.21 displays the sectoral effects of the sensitivity analysis for production volumes in 2030. The most prominent differences are seen in the transport sectors, though the higher technical potential for VOC emission reductions also leads to changes in sector structure for the other sectors. As discussed above, the base specification of the model leads to a substantial increase in production of Transport by air and Transport services. It was argued that these results are connected to the specification of the environmental theme Smog formation. Figure 6.21 shows that this is indeed the case: increasing the technical potential for the theme Smog formation leads to much smaller increases in production for these two sectors.

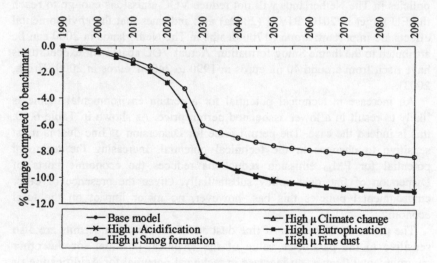

Figure 6.20   Results of the NEPP2030 scenario on the development of GDP
for the base specification and alternative values of the
technical potentials for emission reduction per environmental
theme

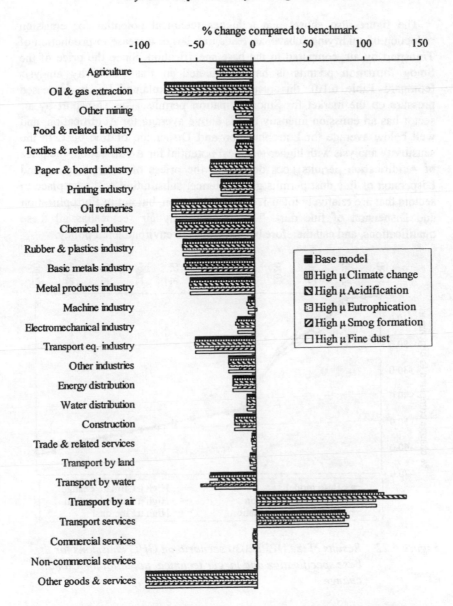

% change compared to benchmark

Legend:
- Base model
- High μ Climate change
- High μ Acidification
- High μ Eutrophication
- High μ Smog formation
- High μ Fine dust

*Figure 6.21   Results of the NEPP2030 scenario on sectoral production
volumes in the year 2030 for the base specification and
alternative values of the technical potentials for emission
reduction per environmental theme*

The figure also shows that a higher technical potential for emission reduction of acidifying substances leads to a larger increase in production of Transport by air, compared to the base specification. Since the price of the Smog formation permits is hardly affected in this sensitivity analysis (compare Table 6.10), this result cannot be explained by an increased pressure on the market for Smog formation permits. The Transport by air sector has an emission intensity that is above average for Acidification, and well below average for Eutrophication and Dispersion of fine dust. In the sensitivity analysis with higher technical potential for Acidification, the price of Acidification permits goes down and the prices of Eutrophication and Dispersion of fine dust permits go up. Hence, substitution will take place to sectors that are relatively intensive in Acidification, but not in Eutrophication and Dispersion of fine dust. The Transport by air sector has all these qualifications, and can therefore benefit from the environmental policy.

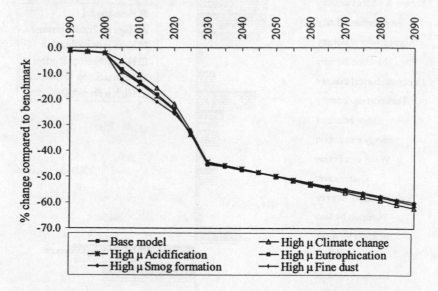

Figure 6.22   Results of the NEPP2030 *scenario on GHG emissions for the base specification and larger technical potential for Climate change*

Figure 6.22 shows how an increase in the technical potential for greenhouse gas reduction influences optimal timing of GHG emission reductions. The higher potential means that the costs of emission reductions are somewhat smaller, as a larger number of relatively cheap technical abatement options are available. This means that it is less problematic to have substantial reduction percentages in later periods, and thus fewer emissions have to be reduced in early periods. However, the effects are not very big.

The influence of the technical potential on the development of technically abatable emissions is depicted for Smog formation in Figure 6.23. Figure 6.24 gives the corresponding results for technically unabatable emissions. Figure 6.23 clearly shows that the additional opportunities to reduce emissions via technical abatement measures are almost completely used. While in the base specification around 97 per cent of all technical abatement measures are implemented, in the sensitivity analysis this is 96 per cent. In absolute terms, the emission reduction in the year 2050 is 59 kilotons in the base specification, and 67 kilotons in the sensitivity analysis.

The additional abatement via technical measures means that fewer emissions have to be reduced via economic restructuring. This is clearly visible in Figure 6.24: reductions of technically unabatable emissions are roughly 20 per cent in the sensitivity analysis, 5 percentage points less than in the base specification. For 2050, these 5 percentage points are equal to 8 kilotons (19 kilotons reduction versus 27 kilotons). By adding the reductions for technically abatable and technically unabatable emissions, it can easily be verified that total VOC emission reductions are equal in the base specification and sensitivity analysis: 86 kilotons.

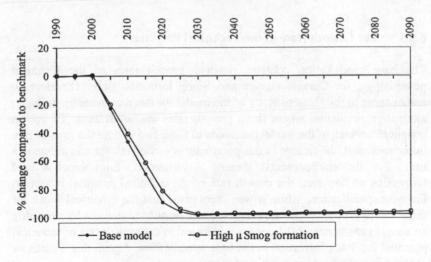

Figure 6.23   Results of the NEPP2030 scenario on the development of technically abatable VOC emissions for the base specification and larger technical potentials for emission reduction for Smog formation

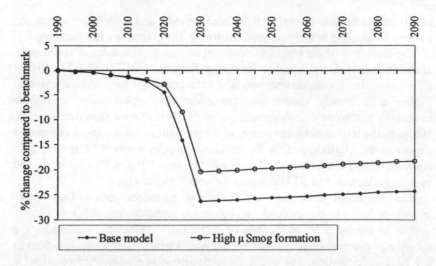

Figure 6.24   Results of the NEPP2030 scenario on the development of
technically unabatable VOC emissions for the base
specification and larger technical potentials for emission
reduction for Smog formation

6.5.3   The Growth Rate of the Technical Potential

The base specification contains positive growth rates of the technical potential, g_{i}, for Climate change and Smog formation only. Therefore, it makes sense to test the sensitivity of the model for this parameter by doing an alternative simulation where these growth rates are set at zero. To get an insight into which of the model outcomes of these two themes the growth rate influences most, the change in this parameter is carried out for one theme at a time. For the environmental themes Acidification, Eutrophication and Dispersion of fine dust, the growth rate of the technical potential is zero in the base specification, while it was recognised that the empirical basis for these values is poor. These are subjected to a sensitivity analysis by assuming an annual growth rate of 0.1 per cent, identical to the growth rate of technical potential for Smog formation in the base specification. Again, this sensitivity analysis is carried out per individual theme.

   The results of these changes in the growth rates of the technical potential per environmental theme are shown in Table 6.11. Decreasing the growth rate of the technical potential for Climate change or Smog formation leads to a lower level of GDP, at least in the year 2030. This effect is much stronger for Smog formation than for Climate change.

Table 6.11 Results of the NEPP2030 *scenario for the year 2030 for alternative values of the growth rates of the technical potential per environmental theme*

	Base specification	Zero g_μ Climate change	High g_μ Acidification	High g_μ Eutrophication	Zero g_μ Smog form.	High g_μ Fine dust
Macro-economic results (% change in volumes compared to benchmark)						
GDP	-8.45	-8.47	-8.40	-8.45	-9.17	-8.44
NNI	-6.26	-6.29	-6.23	-6.26	-6.80	-6.26
Total private cons.	-6.12	-6.18	-6.11	-6.13	-6.65	-6.12
Total production	-16.00	-16.05	-15.86	-16.01	-16.92	-15.97
Savings/investment	-20.00	-19.99	-19.86	-20.01	-21.69	-19.99
International trade results (% change in volumes compared to benchmark)						
Total imports	-23.19	-23.28	-22.98	-23.21	-24.18	-23.14
Total exports	-22.90	-23.00	-22.69	-22.92	-23.87	-22.86
Trade bal. (% GDP)	1.09	1.09	1.09	1.09	1.09	1.09
Sectoral results (% change in volumes compared to benchmark)						
Priv. cons. Agriculture	-6.88	-6.94	-6.66	-6.90	-7.18	-6.90
Priv. cons. Industry	-8.80	-8.86	-8.77	-8.81	-9.46	-8.80
Priv. cons. Services	-3.23	-3.28	-3.26	-3.23	-3.63	-3.23
Prod. Agriculture	-32.64	-32.67	-31.05	-32.76	-34.22	-32.76
Prod. Industry	-35.05	-34.98	-35.10	-35.06	-37.56	-35.07
Prod. Services	0.49	0.34	0.66	0.48	0.87	0.56
Prod. Abatement serv.	16.59	16.97	16.72	16.64	16.04	16.62
Environmental results (% change in volumes compared to benchmark)						
Emis. Climate change	-45.24	-46.77	-44.92	-45.25	-44.86	-45.24
Emis. Acidification	-65.52	-65.52	-65.52	-65.52	-65.52	-65.52
Emis. Eutrophication	-49.21	-49.21	-49.21	-49.21	-49.21	-49.21
Emis. Smog formation	-51.96	-51.96	-51.96	-51.96	-51.96	-51.96
Emis. Fine dust	-62.93	-62.93	-62.93	-62.93	-62.93	-62.93
Prices of main variables (constant 1990 prices)						
Exchange rate index	0.82	0.82	0.82	0.82	0.80	0.82
Price abatement serv.	0.68	0.68	0.68	0.68	0.65	0.68
Price Climate change	17.0	22.1	17.6	16.9	15.2	17.0
Price Acidification	929.7	886.3	794.3	939.2	923.3	947.2
Price Eutrophication	7.5	7.5	8.5	7.1	6.5	7.5
Price Smog formation	1277.0	1270.1	1277.8	1277.2	1358.1	1278.6
Price Fine dust	82.4	80.2	113.5	82.3	68.0	41.7

For Acidification, the sensitivity analysis leads to a smaller impact of environmental policy on GDP. Increasing the growth of the technical potential for the other environmental themes hardly affects GDP levels at all. The other macro-economic indicators are in line with these observations. Therefore, the conclusion of the previous sensitivity analysis also applies here: only the specification of Smog formation in the model influences the results significantly. Note that this does not imply that if Smog formation were less dominant the other environmental themes would still have no impact on the outcomes. The general mechanism is that if there is a dominant environmental theme, then the specification is less sensitive for other environmental themes, within a certain range.

The change in growth rate of the technical potential for emission reduction also influences the prices of the emission permits. A reduction in the growth of the technical potential for Climate change and Smog formation leads to higher permit prices, and a larger technical potential leads to lower permit prices. Moreover, the lower (higher) permit price for the environmental theme for which the sensitivity analysis is carried out is accompanied by a higher (lower) price of the other environmental permits. This is in line with the results of the previous sensitivity analysis. Perhaps more remarkable is that a decrease in the growth rate of technical potential for Smog formation has a bigger impact on the price of Eutrophication permits than an increase in the growth rate of the technical potential for Eutrophication itself.

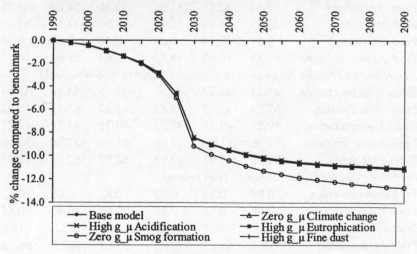

Figure 6.25   Results of the NEPP2030 *scenario on the development of GDP for the base specification and alternative values of the growth rates of technical potentials for emission reduction per environmental theme*

Figure 6.25 shows how the sensitivity analyses of the growth rates of the technical potential for emission reduction influence the development of GDP. As the lower growth rate effectively reduces the technical potential for emission reduction for Smog formation, the GDP levels are persistently below the levels of the base specification. The sensitivity analyses of the other environmental themes do not lead to substantial changes in GDP development.

Figure 6.26 shows that the absence of growth in the potential for greenhouse gas emission reduction via technical abatement measures leads to an increase in GHG abatement for each period: the percentages of emission reduction via technical abatement measures are clearly larger in the sensitivity analysis than in the base specification.

Similarly, emission reduction percentages via economic restructuring are somewhat lower, as shown in Figure 6.27. In absolute amounts, the positive technical potential growth parameter for Climate change leads to 5 billion CO_2-equivalents additional emissions via economic restructuring for the year 2050. This is offset by 4 billion CO_2-equivalents extra emission reduction via technical abatement measures. As the path of emission reductions over time is also influenced by the sensitivity analysis, these changes do not add up to zero. On balance, fewer emissions are reduced in 2050 in the sensitivity analysis than in the base specification.

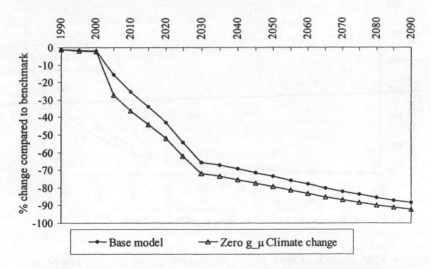

Figure 6.26   Results of the NEPP2030 *scenario on the development of technically abatable GHG emissions for the base specification and zero growth rate of technical potential for emission reduction for Climate change*

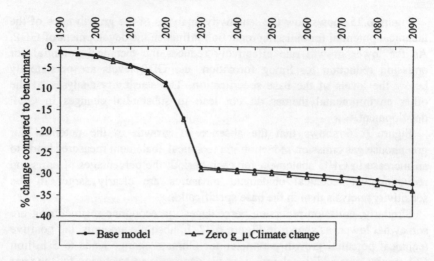

Figure 6.27   Results of the NEPP2030 scenario on the development of
*   technically unabatable GHG emissions for the base*
*   specification and zero growth rate of technical potential for*
*   emission reduction for Climate change*

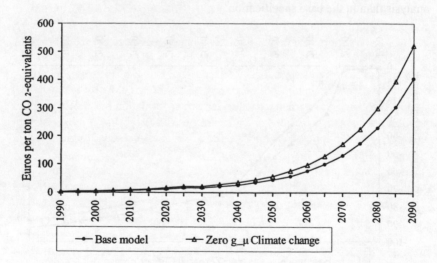

Figure 6.28   Results of the NEPP2030 scenario on the development of the
*   price of Climate change permits for the base specification and*
*   zero growth rate of technical potential for emission reduction*
*   for Climate change*

Figure 6.28 shows the development of the price of Climate change permits over time for the base specification and the sensitivity analysis on Climate change. As the potential for emission reduction via technical abatement measures is reduced in the sensitivity analysis, the economic costs of Climate change policy increase. For each period, the price of GHG permits is 30 per cent above the base specification. The relative price of the permits over time, that is, the permit price in period t compared to the permit price in period t-1, is unaffected by the sensitivity analysis. This is a direct result of the flexibility of the path of GHG emission reductions over time: the discounted costs of climate policy are constant over time.

6.5.4   The Autonomous Pollution Efficiency Improvements

Increasing the autonomous pollution efficiency improvements, φ_e, implies that the required emission reductions decrease, as the emissions in the benchmark projection are smaller. This is tested by increasing the value of φ_e by 3 percentage points for the starting year 1990. The change in this parameter over time as modelled in the base specification is not altered, that is, after the year 2030 emissions are still stabilised in the benchmark. The alternative values for the sensitivity analysis are 0.020 for Climate change, 0.064 for Acidification, 0.058 for Eutrophication, 0.080 for Smog formation and 0.087 for Dispersion of fine dust.

Table 6.12 shows how these alternative values influence the model results. As the increase in autonomous pollution efficiency improvements reduces the need for emission reduction, the sensitivity analyses lead to lower economic costs of the environmental policies. Just as in the previous two sensitivity analyses, a change in parameter value for Smog formation has a clear impact on GDP, a change in parameter value for Acidification has a small impact and a change in parameter values for the other environmental themes hardly changes GDP levels.

At a sectoral level, the sensitivity analysis on the specification for Acidification leads to a difference in the production loss for Agriculture. As Agriculture is responsible for 42 per cent of all acidifying emissions, this sector will react strongly to any changes in the specification of Acidification. The specification of Smog formation influences all model variables, including the production losses for all three categories of production sectors. Moreover, higher autonomous pollution efficiency improvements for Smog formation lead to an increase in the demand for Abatement services that is larger than in the base specification. For the sensitivity analysis on the other environmental themes, the increased autonomous pollution efficiency improvements lead to smaller increases in abatement demand compared to the base specification.

Table 6.12   Results of the NEPP2030 *scenario for the year 2030 for alternative values of the autonomous pollution efficiency improvements per environmental theme*

	Base specifi- cation	High φ Climate change	High φ Acidifi- cation	High φ Eutrophi- cation	High φ Smog form	High φ Fine dust
Macro-economic results (% change in volumes compared to benchmark)						
GDP	-8.45	-8.43	-8.36	-8.44	-6.56	-8.44
NNI	-6.26	-6.23	-6.20	-6.25	-4.79	-6.26
Total private cons.	-6.12	-6.06	-6.07	-6.12	-4.58	-6.12
Total production	-16.00	-15.96	-15.75	-15.99	-13.30	-15.96
Savings/investment	-20.00	-20.07	-19.79	-19.99	-15.90	-19.98
International trade results (% change in volumes compared to benchmark)						
Total imports	-23.19	-23.13	-22.82	-23.19	-20.05	-23.13
Total exports	-22.90	-22.84	-22.54	-22.91	-19.83	-22.84
Trade balance (% GDP)	1.09	1.09	1.08	1.09	1.06	1.09
Sectoral results (% change in volumes compared to benchmark)						
Private cons. Agriculture	-6.88	-6.83	-6.54	-6.85	-6.05	-6.90
Private cons. Industry	-8.80	-8.74	-8.71	-8.80	-6.83	-8.79
Private cons. Services	-3.23	-3.16	-3.24	-3.22	-2.12	-3.23
Production Agriculture	-32.64	-32.66	-30.39	-32.24	-30.15	-32.80
Production Industry	-35.05	-35.14	-35.15	-35.02	-27.88	-35.07
Production Services	0.49	0.62	0.84	0.44	-0.35	0.58
Prod. Abatement serv.	16.59	16.01	16.05	16.53	16.96	16.58
Environmental results (% change in volumes compared to benchmark)						
Emis. Climate change	-45.24	-42.33	-44.55	-45.25	-44.79	-45.23
Emis. Acidification	-65.52	-65.52	-63.32	-65.52	-65.52	-65.52
Emis. Eutrophication	-49.21	-49.21	-49.21	-45.98	-49.21	-49.21
Emis. Smog formation	-51.96	-51.96	-51.96	-51.96	-48.86	-51.96
Emis. Fine dust	-62.93	-62.93	-62.93	-62.93	-62.93	-60.52
Prices of main variables (constant 1990 prices)						
Exchange rate index	0.82	0.82	0.82	0.82	0.88	0.82
Price abatement services	0.68	0.68	0.68	0.68	0.75	0.68
Price Climate change	17.0	13.7	17.8	17.0	21.4	17.0
Price Acidification	929.7	966.4	757.3	937.8	973.6	953.7
Price Eutrophication	7.5	7.5	8.8	5.9	10.1	7.5
Price Smog formation	1277.0	1282.3	1276.3	1278.2	1008.0	1279.1
Price Fine dust	82.4	84.1	122.8	82.0	160.6	27.6

This effect is rather small and is related to the changes in the sector structure of the economy. In the sensitivity analysis for Smog formation, it is optimal to keep the production losses in the industrial sectors limited, by implementing more abatement measures and accepting lower production levels in services to keep total emissions within the bounds set by environmental policy.

In contrast to the earlier sensitivity analyses, the increase in the autonomous pollution efficiency improvements reduces the required emission reduction percentages, as can be seen in the 'environmental results' block of Table 6.12. The effects on the prices of the emission permits are similar to the earlier sensitivity analyses: the permit price for the theme that is subject to sensitivity analysis is reduced, while the permit prices for the other environmental themes go up. This is most clear for the price of Dispersion of fine dust permits in the sensitivity analyses for Acidification or Smog formation.

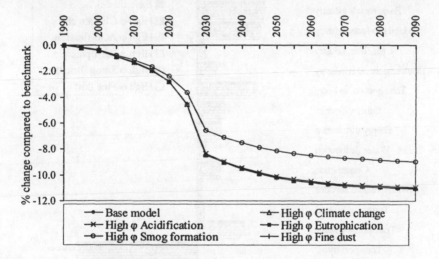

Figure 6.29   Results of the NEPP2030 *scenario on the development of GDP for the base specification and alternative values of the autonomous pollution efficiency improvements per environmental theme*

The development of the sensitivity analyses on the level of GDP is shown in Figure 6.29, where the results are again shown as percentage changes compared to the benchmark projection using the *NEPP2030* scenario.

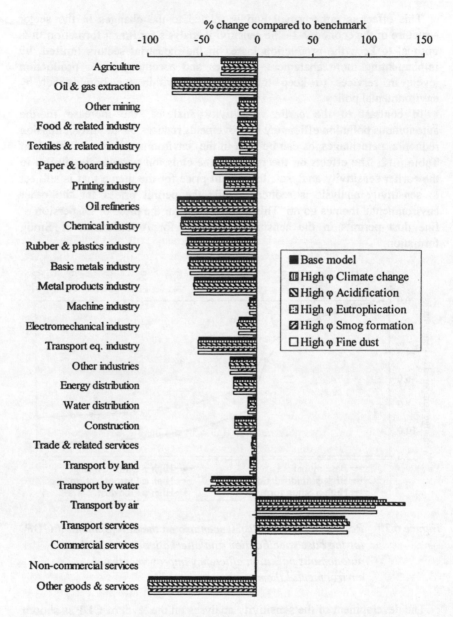

Figure 6.30   Results of the NEPP2030 scenario on sectoral production
volumes in the year 2030 for the base specification and
alternative values of the autonomous pollution efficiency
improvements per environmental theme

The higher autonomous pollution efficiency improvements for Smog formation lead to substantially smaller GDP losses than the base specification or the sensitivity analyses for the other environmental themes. In the long run, GDP stabilises at 9 per cent below the benchmark if the autonomous VOC emission reductions are larger than in the base specification. The difference between the GDP losses in the base specification and the sensitivity analysis for Smog formation rapidly increases until 2030 to 2 percentage points and does not change thereafter. This is caused by the fact that the autonomous pollution efficiency parameter only influences emission levels until 2030, as the assumption is kept for all simulations that emissions after 2030 are stabilised.

Figure 6.30 confirms the observation above that the alternative parameter value for Smog formation in the sensitivity analysis is relatively beneficial for the industrial sectors. Relatively, as the production losses in the industrial sectors compared to the benchmark projection are still substantial. These impacts on the industrial sectors are connected to the ratios of VOC emissions to value added generated in the sector: the sectors with the highest ratios are all industrial. Also remarkable is the impact of the sensitivity analyses on the sectors Transport by air and, to a lesser extent, Transport services. These changes are in line with the interpretations of these sectoral effects in Section 6.5.2.

6.5.5 The Autonomous Abatement Efficiency Improvements

Apart from autonomous efficiency improvements for emissions, the DEAN model also contains autonomous efficiency improvements in the Abatement services sector, φ_A. This parameter is 0.005 in the base specification, and in the sensitivity analysis this value is increased to 0.01 or decreased to 0. The results are presented in Table 6.13. The autonomous abatement efficiency improvements are modelled in DEAN as an increase in the efficiency of the abatement sector, combined with an decrease in the price of abatement (see Section 4.4.3 for more details). This implies that the abatement expenditures are not affected by the parameter φ_A. Consequently, a change in this parameter has no effect on the economy at all. All results in Table 6.13 are identical to the base specification.

The sectoral demand for abatement services is presented in Figure 6.31. As the abatement expenditures are unaffected by the sensitivity analysis, there is no effect on the sectoral composition of abatement demand. The only difference between the different simulations is the scale effect: for higher values of the autonomous abatement efficiency improvement total demand for abatement is higher than in the base specification, while the absence of increases in abatement efficiency leads to lower abatement demand.

*Table 6.13   Results of the NEPP2030 scenario for the year 2030 for
alternative values of the autonomous abatement efficiency
improvements*

	Base spec.	High φ_A	Low φ_A
Macro-economic results (% change in volumes compared to benchmark)			
GDP	-8.45	-8.45	-8.45
NNI	-6.26	-6.26	-6.26
Total private consumption	-6.12	-6.12	-6.12
Total production	-16.00	-16.00	-16.00
Savings/investment	-20.00	-20.00	-20.00
International trade results (% change in volumes compared to benchmark)			
Total imports	-23.19	-23.19	-23.19
Total exports	-22.90	-22.90	-22.90
Trade balance (in % GDP)	1.09	1.09	1.09
Sectoral results (% change in volumes compared to benchmark)			
Private consumption Agriculture	-6.88	-6.88	-6.88
Private consumption Industry	-8.80	-8.80	-8.80
Private consumption Services	-3.23	-3.23	-3.23
Sectoral production Agriculture	-32.64	-32.64	-32.64
Sectoral production Industry	-35.05	-35.05	-35.05
Sectoral production Services	0.49	0.49	0.49
Sectoral production Abatement services	16.59	16.59	16.59
Environmental results (% change in volumes compared to benchmark)			
Emissions Climate change	-45.24	-45.24	-45.24
Emissions Acidification	-65.52	-65.52	-65.52
Emissions Eutrophication	-49.21	-49.21	-49.21
Emissions Smog formation	-51.96	-51.96	-51.96
Emissions Dispersion of fine dust	-62.93	-62.93	-62.93
Prices of main variables (constant 1990 prices)			
Exchange rate index (benchmark = 1)	0.82	0.82	0.82
Price of abatement services(bm. = 1)	0.68	0.68	0.68
Price Climate change (€/ton CO_2-eq.)	17.0	17.0	17.0
Price Acidification (€/acid-eq.)	929.7	929.7	929.7
Price Eutrophication (€/P-eq.)	7.5	7.5	7.5
Price Smog formation (€/kilogram)	1277.0	1277.0	1277.0
Price Fine dust (€/kilogram)	82.4	82.4	82.4

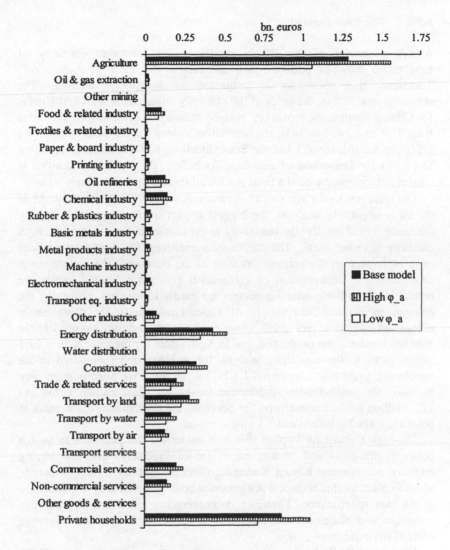

Figure 6.31 Results of the NEPP2030 scenario on the demand for
abatement services in the year 2030 for the base specification
and alternative values of the autonomous abatement efficiency
improvements

6.5.6   The PAS Elasticity

A key parameter of the DEAN model is the estimated elasticity of substitution between pollution and abatement, the PAS elasticity, σ^A. Therefore, this parameter is subjected to sensitivity analysis. Per environmental theme, the value of the elasticity is increased with 0.1. Hence, for Climate change, the sensitivity analysis means that the elasticity increases from 1.24 to 1.34. Similarly, the alternative values for the other themes are 1.516 for Acidification, 1.488 for Eutrophication, 1.286 for Smog formation and 1.364 for Dispersion of fine dust. As before, the sensitivity analysis is carried out for one theme at a time, not for all themes simultaneously.

The main results for this sensitivity analysis are given in Table 6.14. As in the other sensitivity analyses, the biggest impact is caused by the elasticity for Smog formation. But the sensitivity to the change in the value of the PAS elasticity is rather small. The higher PAS elasticity for Acidification does have an impact on the sectoral structure of the economy; the reductions in production and consumption of agricultural goods are limited, while the results for the other production sectors are hardly influenced. Naturally, the changes in demand and supply of agricultural goods are more easily recognised as it is a very small sector compared to industry or services. In absolute numbers, the production loss in Agriculture for the year 2030 is 11.1 billion euros in the sensitivity analysis for Acidification (compared to the benchmark projection), against 12.1 billion in the base specification. For Industry, the corresponding production losses are 125.2 billion euros and 125.3 billion euros, respectively. For Services, the corresponding increases in production are 2.2 billion and 3.1 billion euros.

The higher elasticity implies that it is easier for the polluters to switch between emissions and abatement, or, more precisely, between buying emission permits and buying abatement services. But for Smog formation, virtually all available technical abatement measures are already implemented in the base specification. Therefore, increasing the substitutability between emissions and abatement can only have a minor impact on the economic costs of environmental policy.

The higher PAS elasticity leads to smaller increases in the demand for Abatement services than in the base specification, especially for Smog formation. These changes are concentrated in three polluting sectors: Construction, Trade and related services and Private households. These three sectors are all in the top five of most VOC-emitting sectors in absolute terms. For the Private households, the higher PAS elasticity implies slightly smaller reductions in consumption, including the consumption of Abatement services.

Table 6.14   Results of the NEPP2030 *scenario for the year 2030 for alternative values of the PAS elasticities per environmental theme*

	Base specification	High σ⁴ Climate change	High σ⁴ Acidification	High σ⁴ Eutrophication	High σ⁴ Smog form.	High σ⁴ Fine dust
Macro-economic results (% change in volumes compared to benchmark)						
GDP	-8.45	-8.44	-8.37	-8.44	-8.31	-8.44
NNI	-6.26	-6.25	-6.21	-6.26	-6.15	-6.26
Total private cons.	-6.12	-6.10	-6.09	-6.12	-5.99	-6.12
Total production	-16.00	-15.97	-15.78	-15.99	-15.86	-15.98
Savings/investment	-20.00	-20.02	-19.77	-19.99	-19.75	-19.99
International trade results (%-change in volumes compared to benchmark)						
Total imports	-23.19	-23.15	-22.88	-23.19	-23.06	-23.15
Total exports	-22.90	-22.86	-22.59	-22.91	-22.77	-22.87
Trade bal. (% GDP)	1.09	1.09	1.08	1.09	1.08	1.09
Sectoral results (% change in volumes compared to benchmark)						
Pr. cons. Agriculture	-6.88	-6.86	-6.51	-6.87	-6.78	-6.89
Priv. cons. Industry	-8.80	-8.78	-8.72	-8.80	-8.66	-8.80
Priv. cons. Services	-3.23	-3.20	-3.25	-3.23	-3.10	-3.23
Prod. Agriculture	-32.64	-32.64	-29.85	-32.45	-32.11	-32.73
Prod. Industry	-35.05	-35.09	-35.07	-35.04	-34.73	-35.07
Prod. Services	0.49	0.56	0.68	0.47	0.45	0.55
Prod. Abat. serv.	16.59	16.49	16.32	16.60	15.04	16.59
Environmental results (% change in volumes compared to benchmark)						
Emis. Climate ch.	-45.24	-45.00	-44.73	-45.24	-45.30	-45.24
Emis. Acidification	-65.52	-65.52	-65.52	-65.52	-65.52	-65.52
Emis. Eutrophication	-49.21	-49.21	-49.21	-49.21	-49.21	-49.21
Emis. Smog form.	-51.96	-51.96	-51.96	-51.96	-51.96	-51.96
Emis. Fine dust	-62.93	-62.93	-62.93	-62.93	-62.93	-62.93
Prices of main variables (constant 1990 prices)						
Exchange rate index	0.82	0.82	0.82	0.82	0.82	0.82
Price abat. serv.	0.68	0.68	0.68	0.68	0.68	0.68
Price Climate ch.	17.0	14.8	17.9	17.0	17.3	17.0
Price Acidification	929.7	950.9	748.3	933.3	938.6	945.0
Price Eutrophication	7.5	7.5	9.0	6.7	7.8	7.5
Price Smog form.	1277.0	1279.9	1278.7	1277.5	1268.3	1278.4
Price Fine dust	82.4	83.4	120.8	82.2	85.0	47.2

The prices of emission permits react on the sensitivity analyses in accordance with expectations: a higher PAS elasticity leads to a lower associated permit price. But this impact is rather small. As in the other sensitivity analyses, there are some symmetrical effects on the permit prices for the other themes: the sensitivity analysis on Acidification changes the permit price for Climate change and vice versa. A similar effect holds for Acidification and Dispersion of fine dust.

As can be seen in Figure 6.32, the values of the PAS elasticities do not affect the macro-economic results much. For Smog formation, a higher PAS elasticity leads to a loss in GDP that is in the long run 0.2 percentage points less than in the base specification. For the other environmental themes the effect is even smaller.

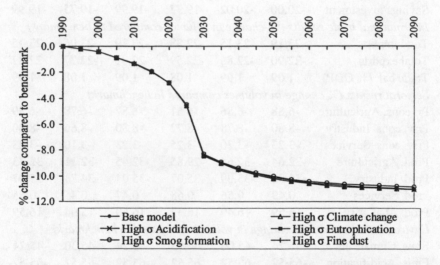

Figure 6.32   Results of the NEPP2030 scenario on the development of GDP for the base specification and alternative values of the PAS elasticities per environmental theme

Finally, Figure 6.33 confirms that the PAS elasticity hardly affects the share of technically abatable emissions that is reduced by the environmental policy. In the year 2050, 97.5 per cent of all technically abatable VOC emissions are abated, while in the sensitivity analysis this percentage increases to 98 per cent.

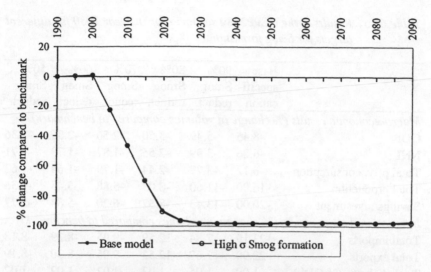

Figure 6.33   Results of the NEPP2030 scenario on the development of technically abatable VOC emissions for the base specification and high PAS elasticity for Smog formation

6.5.7   The Policy Target for Smog Formation

A further sensitivity analysis is carried out to investigate the sensitivity of the model results for the policy target for Smog formation. In the sensitivity analysis, the required emission reductions in 2030 are reduced to 90 per cent, 80 per cent, 70 per cent, 60 per cent and 50 per cent of the original target.

The main results for this sensitivity analysis are given in Table 6.15. The sensitivity analysis reveals that relaxing the emission reduction target for Smog formation to 90 per cent of the *NEPP2030* target can reduce the economic costs of environmental policy substantially (around 3 percentage points of GDP). Relaxing the Smog formation policy even further will still have a positive impact on the economy, but the differences are smaller. When the Smog formation target is relaxed to less than 80 per cent of the base specification target, Smog formation is no longer the dominant environmental theme, and remaining GDP losses are largely due to policy for the other environmental themes.

Relaxing the Smog formation target is not proportionately beneficial for all production sectors. For agriculture, the production losses are hardly influenced by the Smog formation policy. This is due to the low agricultural emissions of VOCs and high emissions for other environmental themes.

Table 6.15 Results of the NEPP2030 scenario for the year 2030 for different targets for Smog formation

	Base specification	90% Smog reduct.	80% Smog reduct.	70% Smog reduct.	60% Smog reduct.	50% Smog reduct.
Macro-economic results (% change in volumes compared to benchmark)						
GDP	-8.45	-5.49	-3.50	-2.56	-2.39	-2.36
NNI	-6.26	-3.99	-2.55	-1.87	-1.73	-1.71
Total priv. consumption	-6.12	-3.77	-2.44	-1.79	-1.64	-1.62
Total production	-16.00	-11.60	-8.03	-5.88	-5.43	-5.36
Savings/investment	-20.00	-13.43	-8.52	-6.20	-5.84	-5.77
International trade results (% change in volumes compared to benchmark)						
Total imports	-23.19	-17.84	-12.59	-9.05	-8.29	-8.18
Total exports	-22.90	-17.67	-12.52	-9.05	-8.30	-8.19
Trade balance (% GDP)	1.09	1.05	1.03	1.02	1.02	1.02
Sectoral results (% change in volumes compared to benchmark)						
Private cons. Agriculture	-6.88	-5.63	-4.98	-4.71	-4.65	-4.64
Private cons. Industry	-8.80	-5.74	-3.78	-2.75	-2.52	-2.48
Private cons. Services	-3.23	-1.61	-0.91	-0.66	-0.60	-0.58
Production Agriculture	-32.64	-29.78	-31.73	-34.50	-35.17	-35.26
Production Industry	-35.05	-23.43	-14.02	-8.33	-7.18	-7.01
Production Services	0.49	-0.73	-1.32	-1.58	-1.59	-1.59
Prod. Abatement services	16.59	17.17	17.24	16.34	15.55	15.27
Environmental results (% change in volumes compared to benchmark)						
Emissions Climate ch.	-45.24	-44.32	-42.63	-40.82	-40.39	-40.34
Emissions Acidification	-65.52	-65.52	-65.52	-65.52	-65.52	-65.52
Emissions Eutrophication	-49.21	-49.21	-49.21	-49.21	-49.21	-49.21
Emissions Smog form.	-51.96	-46.77	-41.57	-36.37	-31.18	-25.98
Emissions Fine dust	-62.93	-62.93	-62.93	-62.93	-62.93	-62.93
Prices of main variables (constant 1990 prices)						
Exchange rate index	0.82	0.92	0.98	1.02	1.02	1.02
Price abatement services	0.68	0.79	0.88	0.94	0.95	0.95
Price Climate change	17.0	24.8	33.0	37.3	38.1	38.3
Price Acidification	929.7	996.8	1014.7	1008.8	1007.7	1007.5
Price Eutrophication	7.5	11.3	12.3	12.0	11.9	11.9
Price Smog formation	1277.0	742.8	316.5	62.2	11.4	4.7
Price Fine dust	82.4	264.1	775.2	1350.3	1499.6	1522.4

For the industrial sectors, the Smog formation policy is very important. A majority of the production losses in the base specification can be attributed to the stringent Smog formation policy. The reduced Smog formation target has a small adverse effect on the services sectors. These sectors can, on average, be labelled as 'winners' from the strict environmental policy, due to the substitution from industrial sectors to services. Therefore, the services are hurt by a less strict Smog formation policy.

The previous sensitivity analyses show that relaxing environmental policy for one theme *grosso modo* leads to higher permit prices for the other themes. Table 6.15 confirms this for all themes; the effect is the strongest for Dispersion of fine dust. Relaxing the Smog formation target implies more action has to be taken to achieve the policy targets for the other themes, and hence higher permit prices, but due to the weak correlation between Smog formation and Acidification and Eutrophication, the relaxed Smog formation policy has only a minor influence on the permit price of Acidification.

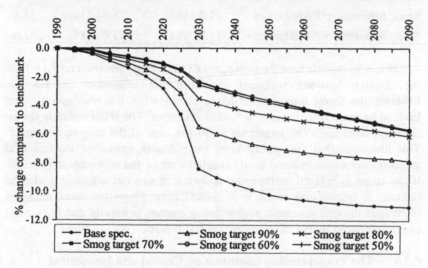

Figure 6.34   Results of the NEPP2030 *scenario on the development of GDP for the base specification and partial target achievement for Smog formation*

Figure 6.34 shows how the path of GDP losses depends on the stringency of the Smog formation target. The figure confirms that a large portion of the economic costs of environmental policy can be avoided by relaxing the VOC emission reduction target. When the Smog formation target is sufficiently relaxed, the path of GDP losses is primarily determined by the policies for the other environmental themes. While a stringent Smog formation target implies more or less constant GDP losses in the long run, a more relaxed target leads to increasing GDP losses over time, due to increasingly high costs for Climate change.

Table 6.16 Contributing parts to VOC emission reductions in the year 2030 for the different policy targets for Smog formation

	Technical measures		Economic restructuring		Total
	m. kg	(%)	m. kg	(%)	m. kg
Base specification	42.4	(50)	43.1	(50)	85.5
Smog formation 90% reduction	46.1	(60)	30.9	(40)	77.0
Smog formation 80% reduction	49.0	(72)	19.4	(28)	68.4
Smog formation 70% reduction	49.3	(82)	10.5	(18)	59.9
Smog formation 60% reduction	43.0	(84)	8.3	(16)	51.3
Smog formation 50% reduction	34.8	(81)	7.9	(19)	42.8

Table 6.16 reveals how the stringency of the Smog formation target affects the division between technical measures and economic restructuring. Relaxing the Smog formation target as compared to the base specification leads to increased emphasis on technical measures. The relationship is almost linear, at least for VOC targets up to 70 per cent of the base specification. This illustrates that the opportunities for reducing emissions via technical measures are exhausted and costly restructuring of the economy is required. If the target is relaxed sufficiently, technical abatement efforts can also be reduced in comparison to the base specification. Note that some emission reductions through economic restructuring remain, primarily due to sectoral changes induced by the other environmental themes.

6.5.8   The Transversality Condition on Capital and Investment

In order to approximate an infinite horizon model with a finite number of periods, a transversality condition on capital has to be adopted. In the literature several transversality conditions have been proposed. The base specification of DEAN uses the assumption that the capital stock in the final period (period T) has to grow with the steady state growth rate:

$$K_T = (1 + g_L) \cdot K_{T-1} \qquad \text{(DEAN-14)}$$

To analyse the influence of this assumption, three alternative assumptions are tested:

(i) following Lau et al. (2002), the final period growth rate of investment is assumed to be identical to the final period growth rate of total consumption of the private households:

$$\frac{I_T}{I_{T-1}} = \frac{W_{T,'priv'}}{W_{T-1,'priv'}}$$

(ii) following Manne and Richels (1992), final period investment is assumed to be in steady state proportion to capital stock:

$$I_T = \left(g_L + \delta\right) \cdot K_T$$

(iii) final period capital stock has to be at least as large as in the benchmark:[11]

$$K_T \geq K_0 \cdot \left(1 + g_L\right)^T$$

The results of the different specifications, as represented in Table 6.17, show that the assumption used in DEAN hardly differs from the proposed assumptions by Lau et al. (2002) and Manne and Richels (1992). This is in line with expectations, as the analysis of the base specification of DEAN revealed that the model converges to a steady state before the time horizon is reached.

Lau et al.'s approach is superior for models with a shorter time horizon, since the growth rate of total consumption may deviate from the steady state. If the time horizon is sufficiently far, total consumption will grow with the steady state growth rate and this alternative specification is identical to the specification in DEAN. The difference between the approach in DEAN and Manne and Richels (1992) is minimal, as both are a variation on the condition that capital and investment have to be on the steady state growth path.

The sensitivity of the model for the transversality condition can best be seen by looking at the development of the main variables in the model. Figure 6.35 shows how GDP is affected by the transversality condition. The development of GDP depends directly on the level of investments as it incorporates depreciation.

Table 6.17   Results of the NEPP2030 scenario for the year 2030 for different transversality conditions

	Base spec.	Lau et al.	Manne& Richels	Minimum K
Macro-economic results (% change in volumes compared to benchmark)				
GDP	-8.45	-8.45	-8.45	-8.35
NNI	-6.26	-6.26	-6.26	-6.26
Total private consumption	-6.12	-6.12	-6.12	-6.26
Total production	-16.00	-16.00	-16.00	-15.91
Savings/investment	-20.00	-20.00	-20.00	-19.37
International trade results (% change in volumes compared to benchmark)				
Total imports	-23.19	-23.19	-23.19	-23.09
Total exports	-22.90	-22.91	-22.91	-22.82
Trade balance (in % GDP)	1.09	1.09	1.09	1.08
Sectoral results (% change in volumes compared to benchmark)				
Private consumption Agriculture	-6.88	-6.88	-6.88	-6.96
Private consumption Industry	-8.80	-8.80	-8.80	-8.94
Private consumption Services	-3.23	-3.22	-3.23	-3.37
Sectoral production Agriculture	-32.64	-32.64	-32.64	-32.53
Sectoral production Industry	-35.05	-35.06	-35.06	-34.92
Sectoral production Services	0.49	0.49	0.49	0.53
Sectoral production Abatement services	16.59	16.59	16.59	16.82
Environmental results (% change in volumes compared to benchmark)				
Emissions Climate change	-45.24	-45.22	-45.24	-46.00
Emissions Acidification	-65.52	-65.52	-65.52	-65.52
Emissions Eutrophication	-49.21	-49.21	-49.21	-49.21
Emissions Smog formation	-51.96	-51.96	-51.96	-51.96
Emissions Dispersion of fine dust	-62.93	-62.93	-62.93	-62.93
Prices of main variables (constant 1990 prices)				
Exchange rate index (benchmark = 1)	0.82	0.82	0.82	0.82
Price of abatement services (bm. = 1)	0.68	0.68	0.68	0.68
Price Climate change (€/ton CO_2-eq.)	17.0	17.0	17.0	18.3
Price Acidification (€/acid-eq.)	929.7	929.8	929.6	922.1
Price Eutrophication (€/P-eq.)	7.5	7.5	7.5	7.6
Price Smog formation (€/kilogram)	1277.0	1277.0	1276.9	1278.9
Price Fine dust (€/kilogram)	82.4	82.4	82.4	82.5

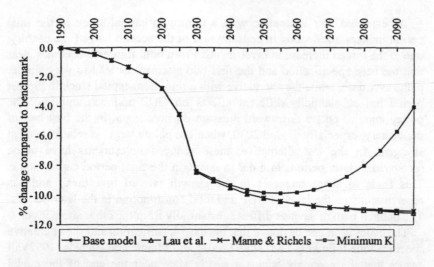

Figure 6.35   Results of the NEPP2030 *scenario on the development of GDP for the base specification and alternative transversality conditions*

The impact of the transversality condition on total consumption of private households is represented in Figure 6.36.

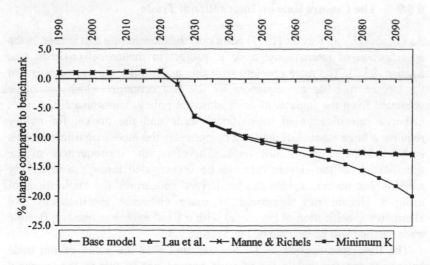

Figure 6.36   Results of the NEPP2030 *scenario on the development of total consumption of private households for the base specification and alternative transversality conditions*

As expected, the alternative with a minimum capital stock in the final period induces a reduction in consumption in the second half of the century, due to the forced increase in investments. From both figures it becomes clear that the base specification and the first two alternatives lead to very similar paths over time, while the alternative with a minimum capital stock in the last period has substantially different effects on GDP and consumption. The policy impulse puts a downward pressure on investment in the first half of the century, especially around 2030, when the policy target is relatively most stringent. In the last alternative, these reduced investments have to be recovered in later periods in order to maintain the final period capital stock. This leads to sharp increases in the growth rate of investment and has repercussions on the level of GDP and total consumption in the later periods. The optimal path of savings differs substantially from the other alternatives.

The conclusion can be drawn that the base specification and the alternative specifications following Lau et al. (2002) and Manne and Richels (1992) all ensure that the economy attains a steady state near the end of the model horizon and erratic near-horizon behaviour is avoided. The last alternative, in contrast, leads to large deviations from the steady state growth path near the model horizon. In the specification with a minimum final capital stock, total consumption is below the level of the other alternatives for all periods; the welfare costs of environmental policy are therefore largest in this alternative.

6.5.9   The Closure Rule on International Trade

As Ginsburgh and Keyzer (1997) point out, the closure rule that is used in the specification of international trade is subject to theoretical criticism (see Section 4.3.2). The main problem with this and similar closure rules is that the closure rule has consequences for the real economy which cannot be separated from the impacts of environmental policy. Unfortunately, a more elaborate specification of international trade and the market for money requires a huge amount of data and complicates the model significantly; this is beyond the scope of this book. Therefore, the consequences of the specification of the closure rule can be investigated through a sensitivity analysis, but no conclusions can be derived concerning the implications of using a closure rule compared to more elaborate specifications. An alternative specification of the model with a fixed exchange rate and flexible trade balance will be investigated in Section 7.3.

The base specification of DEAN assumes that the value of the trade balance is constant, while the price of foreign goods, that is, the '*nominal exchange rate*' in the terminology of de Melo and Robinson (1989), adjusts.

Table 6.18   Results of the NEPP2030 scenario for the year 2030 for alternative values of the international trade closure rule

	Base specification	Fixed in real terms	Fixed share of income
Macro-economic results (% change in volumes compared to benchmark)			
GDP	-8.45	-8.47	-8.47
NNI	-6.26	-6.40	-6.34
Total private consumption	-6.12	-6.50	-6.32
Total production	-16.00	-15.70	-15.86
Savings/investment	-20.00	-19.37	-19.73
International trade results (% change in volumes compared to benchmark)			
Total imports	-23.19	-23.14	-23.17
Total exports	-22.90	-22.31	-22.61
Trade balance (in % GDP)	1.09	1.09	0.96
Sectoral results (% change in volumes compared to benchmark)			
Private consumption Agriculture	-6.88	-7.11	-7.00
Private consumption Industry	-8.80	-9.18	-8.99
Private consumption Services	-3.23	-3.62	-3.43
Sectoral production Agriculture	-32.64	-32.36	-32.51
Sectoral production Industry	-35.05	-34.79	-34.92
Sectoral production Services	0.49	0.81	0.63
Sectoral production Abatement services	16.59	16.89	16.73
Environmental results (% change in volumes compared to benchmark)			
Emissions Climate change	-45.24	-45.36	-45.28
Emissions Acidification	-65.52	-65.52	-65.52
Emissions Eutrophication	-49.21	-49.21	-49.21
Emissions Smog formation	-51.96	-51.96	-51.96
Emissions Dispersion of fine dust	-62.93	-62.93	-62.93
Prices of main variables (constant 1990 prices)			
Exchange rate index (benchmark = 1)	0.82	0.82	0.82
Price of abatement services (bm. = 1)	0.68	0.68	0.68
Price Climate change ($\text{€/ton } CO_2$-eq.)	17.0	17.4	17.2
Price Acidification (€/acid-eq.)	929.7	955.6	942.5
Price Eutrophication (€/P-eq.)	7.5	7.6	7.6
Price Smog formation (€/kilogram)	1277.0	1281.4	1277.9
Price Fine dust (€/kilogram)	82.4	88.6	85.4

Two alternative assumptions are investigated:

(i)   a specification where the trade balance is constant *in real terms*, that is, the real exchange rate adjusts;

(ii) a specification where the trade balance is a fixed share of the income of private households, again with an adjusting real exchange rate.

The first alternative is for instance used by Jensen (2000); the second alternative is used by Gerlagh et al. (2002). The main results for these alternative specifications are given in Table 6.18.

The numerical results indeed confirm that the closure rule influences the real economy, but to a minor extent. Moreover, the effect of the closure rule on relative prices is also minor. In the second alternative, the trade balance decreases with the reduced total consumption of private households.

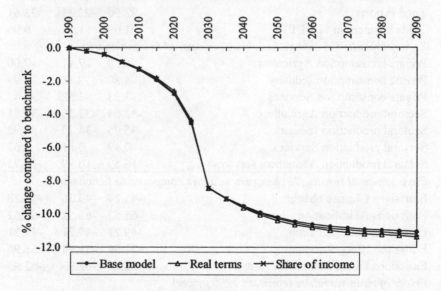

Figure 6.37   Results of the NEPP2030 *scenario on the development of GDP for the base specification and alternative closure rules*

The real exchange rate is hardly affected by the closure rule. This shows that the exchange rate indeed functions as a constraint on international trade, in combination with a scaling of domestic prices. As all prices are presented relative to the consumer price index, this has only a minor impact on domestic results, both for quantities and prices. Figure 6.37 shows that the development of GDP over time is very similar for all three alternative closure rules. This confirms the limited impact of the assumption underlying the closure rule. It can be inferred that alternative variation in the closure rule has only minor impacts on the real economy.

6.6   DISCUSSION AND CONCLUSIONS

This chapter presents an empirical evaluation of the economic costs of environmental policy in The Netherlands, using the dynamic applied general equilibrium model DEAN. The model pays specific attention to empirical options to reduce pollution via abatement. Specific research questions dealt with in this chapter are (see Chapter 1):

3.   What are the impacts of currently proposed environmental policies in The Netherlands on economic growth, sectoral structure, international trade, pollution and abatement in the twenty-first century?
4.   What is the optimal mix of technical abatement measures and economic restructuring that achieves the policy targets at least cost?
5.   How do the economic impacts of environmental policy in The Netherlands depend on the timing of the policy?

To answer these research questions, the DEAN model is used to analyse three scenarios describing current environmental policy in The Netherlands. In the *NEPP2030* scenario, policy targets from the latest National Environmental Policy Plan (VROM, 2001) are imposed from the year 2030 onwards. In the *Delay* scenario, the same targets are implemented with a delay of 10 years, that is, from 2040 onwards. Finally, in the *NEPP2010* scenario, the targets of the *NEPP2030* scenario are supplemented with relatively strict intermediate targets for 2010.

The model as described in Chapter 4 cannot cover all relevant aspects of the economic, environmental and abatement processes involved. Moreover, there is insufficient data to specify all model parameters at the desired level of disaggregation (see Chapter 5). Therefore, the model results should be handled with care, and conclusions are only valid given the precautions as expressed throughout the book. Note that the optimal level of environmental policy cannot be inferred and the analysis has to be confined to an evaluation of the cost-effectiveness of exogenously given scenarios (see Chapters 2 and 3 for more details).

In the following sections, the results described in this chapter are discussed. Firstly, the results of the *NEPP2030* scenario are discussed with respect to the impact on the macro-economy, the sectoral structure of the economy, international trade and the environment, with special attention to the role of abatement. Then, the timing of environmental policy is discussed by comparing the *NEPP2030* scenario with the *Delay* and *NEPP2010* scenarios. The chapter ends with a discussion of the main conclusions to be drawn from the sensitivity analysis.

6.6.1　Macro-economic Results

The enforcement of the environmental policy targets as laid out in the latest National Environmental Policy Plan, implemented in the *NEPP2030* scenario via a system of tradable emission permits, leads to a reduction of economic activity. In the base specification of the model, GDP levels drop in the long run to around 10 to 11 per cent below the benchmark projections. This does not mean that absolute levels of GDP are declining; the annual growth rate of GDP stays well above zero for all periods. Clearly, these numerical results have to be interpreted with care, given the shortcomings in the model specification discussed above. These macro-economic costs of environmental policy cannot be disregarded, but in light of the significant reductions in environmental pressure for several environmental themes simultaneously, they can be characterised as modest. In comparison, current environmental costs in The Netherlands amount to more than 3 per cent of GDP (RIVM, 2002a), though this figure includes the costs of waste management, a theme that is not present in the DEAN model.

In the second half of the twenty-first century, the growth rate of the economy returns to the level of the benchmark projection, implying that environmental policy has only a temporary impact on economic growth. The decline in GDP levels compared to the benchmark projection is, however, lasting. The percentage decline in emissions due to the environmental policy is much larger than the percentage decline in GDP, and absolute economic growth levels are positive. Hence, according to the model it is possible to decouple environmental pressure and economic growth, given the empirical availability of technical abatement measures and substitution possibilities within the economy.

It should be emphasised that the DEAN model cannot be used to assess whether the economic costs of environmental policy are justified, as the benefits of the policy in terms of better environmental quality are not taken into account (see the discussion in earlier chapters). It is up to policy makers to decide whether the environmental benefits outweigh the economic costs or not. The DEAN model can play a role in assessing the economic costs and show relevant mechanisms that influence the interactions between environmental pressure, economic growth and sectoral structure.

Consumers anticipate a stricter future environmental policy by placing more emphasis on current consumption at the expense of future consumption.

The resulting path of total consumption is, however, not completely smooth, as emission targets are imposed for every period and there is a relatively low elasticity of substitution between current and future consumption. This result shows the importance of the forward-looking specification of the model: comparative-static and recursive-dynamic models ignore the impacts of policy on the rate of savings and investment and thereby cannot describe the most likely path from the old to the new equilibrium.

6.6.2   Sectoral Results

The sectoral impacts of environmental policy are much more diverse than the macro-economic results. While some pollution-intensive sectors may be severely affected by environmental policy, this does not hold for all production sectors. In fact, it is very likely that some production sectors can even benefit from stricter environmental targets. These include the sector that provides the abatement technology, but also sectors that produce relatively clean services. Environmental policy will generate both winners and losers. The shift from dirty to clean sectors is relatively important in the DEAN model, as the opportunities for reducing emissions via technical abatement measures are limited.

Some sectors that will have to reduce their production substantially are Oil and gas extraction, Oil refineries, the Rubber and plastics industry and Other goods and services (a heterogeneous set of small subsectors, some of which have high VOC emissions). At the other end, there are the Abatement services and Non-commercial services: the Abatement services sector increases its production value considerably, while the Non-commercial services are hardly affected by environmental policy.

Two other sectors that can benefit from the strict, unilateral environmental targets analysed in the model are Transport by air and Transport services. This result is primarily related to their low VOC emissions, especially in comparison to their closest domestic competitors, that is, the other transport sectors. A low ratio of VOC emissions to total value added for these sectors is also present in the data sets for 1995 (Hofkes et al., 2002) and in other official statistics (Statistics Netherlands, 2002), at least in comparison to the other transport sectors. This suggests that the stringency of the VOC targets is the dominant factor explaining the beneficial impact of environmental policy on Transport by air and Transport services.

6.6.3   International Trade Results

Currently, The Netherlands exports relatively 'dirty' products: there is a strong positive correlation between the sectoral intensities for exports and domestic emissions for all environmental themes, except Eutrophication. If The Netherlands adopts a stringent environmental policy, this will have a relatively strong impact on the exporting sectors. A strong depreciation of the domestic currency is then needed to counter a substantial loss in competitive position. As the domestic price increases are larger than the increase in the price of foreign goods, the depreciation cannot prevent a decrease in the real exchange rate.

In the debate on environmental policy, polluters often claim that a country like The Netherlands cannot 'go it alone'. If a unilateral environmental policy were to be implemented, this would lead to a loss of competitive position with respect to foreign competitors subject to less strict environmental rules. Though this argument is not without merit, there are two qualifications to this reasoning.

Firstly, a unilateral environmental policy allows for a partial transfer of environmental problems to other countries. The domestic economy can specialise in producing, and exporting, relatively clean products, while dirty products can be imported. This so-called 'leakage effect' implies that while the production structure fully adapts to the stricter environmental policy, the changes in consumption patterns can be limited. This has positive impacts on the domestic levels of GDP and welfare. Domestic emissions can be reduced substantially through this leakage effect, but in the case of transboundary environmental problems this may not be desirable from an environmental point of view. For local environmental problems, such as smog formation, such an international transfer of pollution-intensive production processes may not be a problem from an environmental point of view if the pollution causes less harmful effects on the new location.

Secondly, as mentioned above, environmental policy not only creates losers, but also winners. While heavy polluters, including industrial sectors and agriculture, will observe a severe loss in competitive position, the cleaner services sectors can strengthen their position on the international market. Moreover, by taking the lead in producing with clean technologies, domestic producers can create opportunities on international markets. When foreign environmental policies become stricter, they have competition advantages; this is known as the first-mover incentive and is related to the Porter hypothesis that stringent environmental policy can strengthen the competitiveness of domestic producers. For an introduction to the discussion on the Porter hypothesis see Xepapadeas and de Zeeuw (1999).

It may therefore be in the interest of domestic consumers if a unilateral environmental policy with strict policy targets is implemented, without trying to persuade trading partners to adopt similar policies. If, however, the environmental profile of foreign countries differs significantly from the domestic profile, the advantages of multilateral environmental policy become more important.

6.6.4   Environmental Results

The model contains two ways of reducing emissions. Firstly, emissions can be reduced via the implementation of technical abatement measures. These measures describe all available end-of-pipe and process-integrated options and can only reduce a certain amount of emissions. Secondly, economic activity in a polluting sector can be reduced, that is, the economy can be restructured. For most environmental themes included in the model, environmental policy results in the implementation of almost all technical abatement options, except for those that are extremely expensive. The reason for this is that most abatement options are cheaper than the cost of restructuring the economy.

Even though most technical abatement measures are implemented, this does not mean that economic restructuring is of minor importance. On the contrary, given the limited availability of technical abatement measures, substantial emission reductions will have to be realised via economic restructuring. On average, roughly half of all emission reductions stem from the implementation of technical measures and half from economic restructuring. This ratio is more or less stable over time. As the economic costs of economic restructuring are substantial, this implies that a large portion of total economic costs of environmental policy can be attributed to restructuring costs. The significance of both these routes to emission reduction clearly demonstrates the importance of using a methodology that consistently covers both bottom-up and top-down information and mechanisms.

The economic costs of environmental policy can be attributed to the policies for the different environmental themes. Since the model equates the marginal costs of all available options to reduce emissions, the price of the emission permits equals the marginal abatement costs. Moreover, at the margin the polluters will be indifferent between reducing emissions via adoption of a technical measure and reducing emissions via a reduction of the economic activity level.

From 2030 onwards, the economic costs of the policy on Smog formation are very high and this theme dominates the other themes. Given the limited potential to reduce the associated Volatile Organic Compounds (VOC) emissions via technical abatement measures (estimated to be around one-third of emissions), a strict policy target induces large decreases in the production of those sectors emitting VOCs. Moreover, a relatively large part of VOC emissions are attributed to consumers.[12] There are several reasons why it is not likely that the very high price of VOC permits will become reality. The most important is that polluters will react to the high permit price for Smog formation by investigating new technologies to reduce their VOC emissions and thus avoid paying for expensive permits. The base specification of DEAN does not capture such endogenous innovation effects; these will be investigated in the next chapter. The results do, however, show the potential threat for the economy stemming from current Smog formation policy if no additional effort is placed on researching VOC-reducing technologies.

At the other extreme is the Eutrophication policy, which has relatively low costs. Several factors work together to make the emission permits for this theme cheaper than the permits for the other themes, including a high reduction potential for technical abatement measures, a relatively less stringent policy target and a concentration of emissions in one sector (Agriculture). This shows that a sectoral analysis is essential for a proper evaluation of the costs of environmental policy.

In the early periods, by far the largest costs are caused by the environmental theme Soil contamination. Annual costs to clean up polluted soils are estimated to be 8.8 billion euros, based on an everlasting annuity; these costs are assumed to be borne by the government, and cannot be attributed to individual polluters. The public environmental expenditures grow by 2 per cent per year while private expenditures on emission permits increase more rapidly; therefore, the relative importance of Soil contamination decreases over time.

Climate change policy also brings about significant economic costs. The modelling of Climate change differs from the other emission-related themes in the sense that for Climate change, the path of emissions is endogenous and Climate change policy is implemented via tradable permits that allow an addition to the stock of greenhouse gases. For the other emission-related themes, the government auctions annual tradable emission permits. The flexibility in the timing of GHG emission reduction is used by the polluters to place more emphasis on reductions in the later periods, allowing for higher emissions in the early periods. The path of emission reductions that emerges is based on an equalisation of the discounted costs over time.

One mechanism that drives the timing is the positive discount rate, which implies that late emission reductions are relatively cheap in net present value terms. A second mechanism is the increasing marginal costs of technical abatement measures with increasing abatement levels. This leads to a smooth path of emission reductions over time, avoiding peaks in any period. The third mechanism is given by the interaction with other environmental policies. A strong point of the DEAN model is the presence of simultaneous policies for several environmental themes. *Ceteris paribus*, it is efficient to time GHG emission reductions to coincide with the reductions of emissions for the other environmental themes, as these induce changes in the economic structure that also influence GHG emissions. A relatively smooth path of GHG emission reductions emerges, avoiding peaks in any period and with additional emphasis on late reductions. This means that emission reductions can be limited for the first few decades.

The price of emission permits for Climate change are estimated to be around 45 euros per ton in 2050, which is in line with other studies (Weyant, 1999). The cost of Climate change policy in the same year amounts to around 0.9 per cent of GDP, also within the range found in the literature (Weyant, 1999). The price of Climate change permits and hence the costs of Climate change policy increase steadily over time, as abatement efforts increase. The undiscounted price of Climate change permits increases exponentially over time, reflecting an equalisation of discounted costs for Climate change permits. Note that the analysed Climate change policy implicitly assumes that all emission reductions are realised domestically. If flexible mechanisms, as mentioned in the Kyoto Protocol (Joint Implementation and Clean Development Mechanism), are allowed, the economic costs of Climate change policy could be lower.

6.6.5 Timing of Environmental Policy

For all environmental themes except Climate change, the *optimal timing* of environmental policy cannot be assessed in the model, given the absence of environmental benefits.[13] Nonetheless, the strength of the dynamic approach can be exploited by analysing the timing of environmental policy in exogenously given scenarios. Therefore, alternative scenarios are analysed that differ solely in the timing of environmental policy. Delaying environmental policy has the effect that a slower adjustment path towards the new equilibrium is chosen. This leads not only to a more even spread of economic costs over the periods, but also to lower economic costs in total. Though the long-term growth rate of the economy is not affected by the delay, the GDP level is permanently higher than in the base specification. The net present value of consumption losses is also lower in the scenario with a delayed policy. From an environmental point of view, the delay leads to higher emissions for some periods, but long-run emission levels are identical for both scenarios. This means that for pure flow pollutants, the long-term environmental quality is not affected by the delay; for stock pollutants, the higher emissions in the early periods do have a negative effect on long-term environmental quality.

Similarly, implementing relatively strict intermediate targets in addition to the targets of the base scenario leads to a quicker adjustment path with temporarily higher economic costs and temporarily lower emissions. These results depend on the perfect foresight assumption used in the model. The sooner environmental policy is implemented and the stricter it is, the larger the shift from future to current consumption will be.

After the adjustment period, somewhere in the second half of the twenty-first century, the growth rate of the economy returns to its original value. Long-run GDP levels are around 10 to 11 per cent below the benchmark projection, and private consumption is reduced by around 12.5 per cent. This result applies to all three scenarios, and hence the conclusion holds that a temporary difference in environmental policy will only have temporary effects on the economy. The environmental quality is, however, permanently different across the scenarios. The DEAN model cannot give an appraisal as to which of these scenarios is preferred, as they entail a trade-off between a better environmental quality and a larger economy.

6.6.6   Sensitivity Analysis

As not all model parameters could be fully estimated, but had to be calibrated (see Chapter 5), a sensitivity analysis is carried out to analyse the robustness of the model outcomes.

Firstly, the influence of the intertemporal elasticity of substitution in the utility function of the private households is tested. When this elasticity is higher than in the base specification, more emphasis can be placed on current consumption, thereby reducing savings and hence reducing future consumption levels. For a lower intertemporal substitution elasticity, the opposite results apply. These effects are, however, rather small, and the impact of this parameter on the sector structure of the economy and on the environment is limited.

Secondly, a range of sensitivity analyses are carried out with respect to some key parameters describing the individual environmental themes, including the technical potential for emission reduction, the growth rate of this technical potential, the autonomous pollution efficiency improvements and the PAS elasticity. These analyses demonstrate that the model is only sensitive to the specification of the dominant environmental theme, Smog formation. This result is illustrated by the substantial impact of a larger technical potential for emission reductions. In the base specification, the high economic costs of the Smog formation policy can be attributed to a large extent to the absence of technical abatement options. Having a larger technical potential for VOC emission reductions, that is, having more technical abatement options, can therefore reduce the economic costs of environmental policy substantially. Increasing the share of emissions that can be reduced via technical abatement measures with 5 percentage points implies that the decrease in GDP levels is about a quarter of that in the base specification.

The permit price of the environmental theme that is investigated in a sensitivity analysis reacts rather strongly to a change in parameter values. Increasing the ease with which the policy target can be met leads to a reduction in permit price for that environmental theme. In most cases, this leads to higher permit prices for the other environmental themes, as fewer emissions for the other themes are reduced as a side-effect of the required emission reductions for the theme investigated in the sensitivity analysis. This shows how important it is to analyse environmental policy for several environmental themes simultaneously.

Thirdly, the assumptions regarding the transversality condition and the closure rule on international trade are subjected to sensitivity analysis. These show that the assumptions used in the base specification of DEAN influence the model results to a minor extent, and several alternative specifications that are found in the literature give very similar results.

NOTES

1. Remember that a period spans over five years: period 3 starts in 2000, period 4 in 2005.
2. A similar approach would be possible for Acidification and Eutrophication, which also have stock characteristics.
3. Remember that consumers decide on their consumption and savings path based on the maximisation of the net present value of utility, which is a discounted weighted average of consumption.
4. In the benchmark projection, 60 per cent of total investments are used to replace depreciated capital stock.
5. According to Statistics Netherlands (2002), aeroplanes emit on average 5.1 grams VOC per kilogram fuel use; in comparison, passenger cars emit on average 20.7 grams per kilogram fuel use (numbers for 1990).
6. Note that the phenomenon of increasing production, imports and exports of Transport services, is also present in Gerlagh et al. (2002).
7. In AGE models, it makes more sense to interpret activity changes as a reallocation of production factors. Hence, production losses in one sector will create opportunities for production increases in other sectors.
8. Such appraisal of different policies is possible in the current model set-up if the environmental quality is identical across the policies. The construction of such scenarios severely restricts the range of policies that can be analysed.
9. The sensitivity analyses are only carried out for the *NEPP2030* scenario.
10. Note that the low value of the technical potential for Smog formation in the base specification means that the percentage increase in parameter value is larger in this sensitivity analysis than in the sensitivity analyses for the other environmental themes.
11. Though the last alternative, with a lower bound on the absolute value of the capital stock in the final period, is in partial conflict with the property of the model in that the savings rate, and therefore the capital stock, is endogenous to the model, it has been suggested by many authors.
12. In the current version of the model, households cannot reduce their emissions via a substitution from dirty to clean goods, as emissions are coupled to total consumption.

Coupling emissions to consumption of individual goods will lower the estimated economic costs of environmental policy, especially if emissions are more related to luxury goods than to necessary goods.

13. The absence of environmental benefits also means that the optimal stock addition target for Climate change cannot be determined.

7. Alternative specifications of the DEAN model

7.1 INTRODUCTION

The results of the calculations with the base specification of the DEAN model, as discussed in the previous chapter, depend not only on the values of the key parameters, but also on the functional forms of the model equations. The aim of this chapter is to investigate the robustness of the model with respect to some of the most important assumptions underlying the equations. To that end, the *NEPP2030* scenario is simulated with alternative modelling assumptions, most of which are derived directly from the analysis of the base specification of the model in the previous chapter.

Section 7.2 deals with an alternative specification of the world market by assuming multilateral environmental policy. In Section 7.3, this alternative specification is combined with the assumption of a fixed exchange rate. The impact of modelling Climate change as a stock pollutant, as was done in Chapter 6, is investigated in Section 7.4, where Climate change policy is specified in terms of emission permits for each individual period. Next, Section 7.5 deals with an alternative recycling scheme of the revenues of environmental policy, which makes the model more suitable for a so-called double dividend analysis. The last alternative model, discussed in Section 7.6, comprises the possibility for polluters to invest in environmental innovation. This alternative is especially relevant as the base results for Smog formation suggest that there is a shortage of VOC emission reduction measures. Finally, Section 7.7 contains the discussion and conclusions.

7.2 MULTILATERAL ENVIRONMENTAL POLICY

7.2.1 Description of the Alternative Specification

The base specification of the DEAN model shows that unilateral environmental policy tends to induce a partial shift of environmental problems abroad by importing more dirty goods and exporting more clean goods. This is possible, as the model is specified such that domestic and foreign goods (imports and exports) are imperfect substitutes.[1] In this way, production patterns adapt fully to the more stringent environmental policy, while consumption patterns remain relatively stable. Given the position of The Netherlands as a member of the European Union, it is perhaps more appropriate to assume that environmental policy is not unilateral.

The specification of international environmental policy is not possible in the DEAN model, as other countries are not explicitly specified. Moreover, there is insufficient information to enable an understanding of how international environmental policy will affect world market prices. It is, however, possible to run the model with the assumption that relative world market prices change in the same way as relative domestic prices. This alternative resembles multilateral environmental policy if sectoral impacts of environmental policy are similar across countries. A consequence of this alternative assumption is that import and export shares of traded goods do not change in the simulations.

7.2.2 Calibration

This alternative specification is implemented by assuming that the Armington elasticity for substitution between imports and domestic production equals zero. This Armington elasticity governs to what extent domestically produced goods and imported goods are treated as imperfect substitutes (see Section 4.3.2 for more details). A value of zero for this elasticity implies that there is no substitution possible between domestic and foreign goods, and both are demanded in fixed proportions. The absence of this substitution simulates a situation in which there is no difference between domestic and world market prices for the goods.

Similarly, the Armington elasticity of transformation between exports and domestic demand also equals zero. The working of this elasticity is equivalent to the Armington substitution elasticity between imports and domestically produced goods. An elasticity between exports and domestic demand of zero implies fixed proportions of exports and domestic demand, thereby simulating equal relative prices on the domestic and world market.

7.2.3 Results for the Alternative Specification

In this alternative specification, The Netherlands can no longer specialise in environmentally friendly production. Table 7.1 shows how this alternative assumption of the world market affects economic and environmental variables for the *NEPP2030* scenario.

Table 7.1 Results of the NEPP2030 *scenario with a multilateral environmental policy*

	1990	2010	2030	2050
Macro-economic results (% change in volumes compared to benchmark)				
GDP	-0.04	-1.75	-14.56	-15.57
NNI	0.34	-0.34	-11.38	-13.78
Total private consumption	1.04	1.41	-11.50	-17.51
Total production	-0.25	-2.32	-25.49	-23.47
Savings/investment	-2.07	-9.16	-31.30	-25.00
International trade results (% change in volumes compared to benchmark)				
Total imports	-0.40	-3.14	-35.05	-30.71
Total exports	-0.36	-2.92	-32.98	-29.77
Trade balance (in % GDP)	0.99	1.01	1.16	1.18
Sectoral[a] results (% change in volumes compared to benchmark)				
Private consumption Agriculture	0.35	-0.51	-10.82	-14.90
Private consumption Industry	0.98	1.29	-16.01	-19.44
Private consumption Services	1.12	1.61	-6.70	-15.54
Sectoral production Agriculture	-0.28	-2.74	-28.14	-27.33
Sectoral production Industry	-0.57	-3.60	-35.16	-30.58
Sectoral production Services	0.01	-1.28	-17.59	-17.52
Sectoral production Abatement services	-0.01	5.45	19.19	19.46
Environmental results (% change in volumes compared to benchmark)				
Emissions Climate change	-0.32	-16.98	-49.56	-50.23
Emissions Acidification	0.00	-21.84	-65.52	-65.52
Emissions Eutrophication	0.00	-16.40	-49.21	-49.21
Emissions Smog formation	0.00	-17.32	-51.96	-51.96
Emissions Dispersion of fine dust	0.00	-20.98	-62.93	-62.93
Prices of main variables (constant 1990 prices)				
Exchange rate index (benchmark = 1)	0.98	0.93	0.32	0.36
Price of abatement services (bm. = 1)	1.00	1.00	0.47	0.63
Price Climate change[b] (€/ton CO_2-eq.)	3.0	9.8	17.7	42.5
Price Acidification (€/acid-eq.)	4.2	31.7	468.4	1043.3
Price Eutrophication (€/P-eq.)	0.6	3.2	7.3	15.3
Price Smog formation (€/kilogram)	0.1	1.4	2182.2	2279.8
Price Fine dust (€/kilogram)	0.1	1.0	27.9	83.7

Notes:
[a] The 27 production sectors are grouped into three categories.
[b] Expressed in terms of emissions.

The temporary slow-down of the economy is more pronounced in the alternative specification: economic costs in terms of loss of GDP turn out to be around 1.5 times as high as in the base specification (compare Table 6.2). Total production volume and capital investments both decline by more than 25 per cent in 2030. Moreover, the intertemporal shift of consumption is stronger in the alternative specification. These results clearly show that the ability to change import and export patterns can play a big role in keeping the costs of environmental policy small. Note that these results are typical within the AGE framework, as discussed in Section 7.2.1 above.

Another clear difference from the base specification is the decrease in exchange rate. In the base specification, a depreciation of the domestic currency is needed to maintain the trade balance. This depreciation is caused by the relatively large price increases in export-oriented sectors (exporting sectors are relatively 'dirty') and the desire to import more dirty goods (compare Section 6.4). In the alternative specification, such a specialisation of the domestic economy in clean goods is not possible, and there is no depreciation of the domestic currency. This implies that the real exchange rate, that is, the price of foreign goods divided by the domestic consumer price index, decreases more than in the base specification.

The alternative specification also leads to different prices of environmental permits. By 2010, the prices of all environmental theme permits are higher than in the base specification, while in the longer run the results are mixed. The inability to increase the ratio between imports and exports for sectors with high VOC emissions, such as the Chemical industry and the Metal products industry, implies that the demand for Smog formation permits is higher than in the base specification and hence the equilibrium price of the permits is also higher.

Figure 7.1 displays how GDP develops in the base and alternative specifications. The pattern looks very similar for both specifications, and the GDP losses in the alternative specification are roughly 1.5 times as big. The alternative specification does not seem to influence the macro-economic transition path much. Moreover, the conclusion that in the long run the growth rate of GDP is not affected by the environmental policy still holds. In fact, in the alternative specification there seems to be some overshooting in the sense that in the second half of the century, the growth rate is slightly above 2 per cent for at least some decades; this effect is, however, very small. This overshooting is caused by the relatively large emission reductions for Climate change between 2005 and 2040 in the alternative specification as compared to the base specification, allowing higher emissions later in the century.

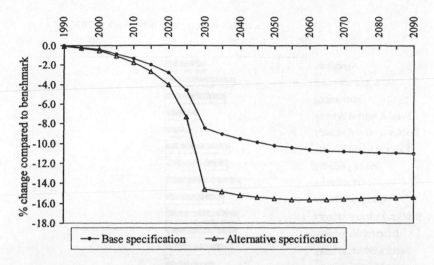

Figure 7.1 Results of the NEPP2030 *scenario on the development of GDP for the base specification and alternative specification with a multilateral environmental policy*

In Figure 7.2 the effects of the *NEPP2030* environmental policy on imports and exports are shown for the alternative specification.[2] It is clear that the alternative assumption on the world market has major impacts on both imports and exports. The implication of the alternative specification is that imports and exports are in proportion to their domestic counterparts, and hence also to each other. From a sectoral perspective, the biggest differences between the base and alternative specifications are for exports: in the alternative specification, exports of the services sectors can no longer be increased, and the exports of industrial goods decline less than in the base specification.

Note that the counter-intuitive results for the sectors Transport by air and Transport services have vanished in the alternative specification, as specialisation in these sectors can no longer occur. Both imports and exports of these sectors decrease substantially, as do their production volumes. The production loss in *NEPP2030* for the year 2030 is 35 per cent for Transport by air and 24 per cent for Transport services (numbers not shown in the figure).

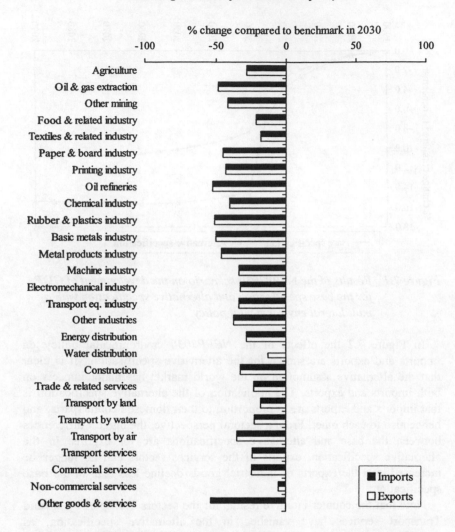

Figure 7.2   Results of the NEPP2030 *scenario on sectoral import and export volumes in the year 2030 for the alternative specification with a multilateral environmental policy*

Figure 7.3 shows how the consumption of private households (in the year 2030, *NEPP2030* scenario) is affected by the alternative assumption on the world market. For all goods, the reduction in consumption is more pronounced in the alternative specification (except for the very small Other mining sector). Especially for the industrial goods the differences are big. This is in line with the idea that industrial goods, which have relatively dirty production processes, cannot be imported in the alternative specification. The result is that in the alternative specification not only production, but also consumption patterns have to fully adjust to the new circumstances.

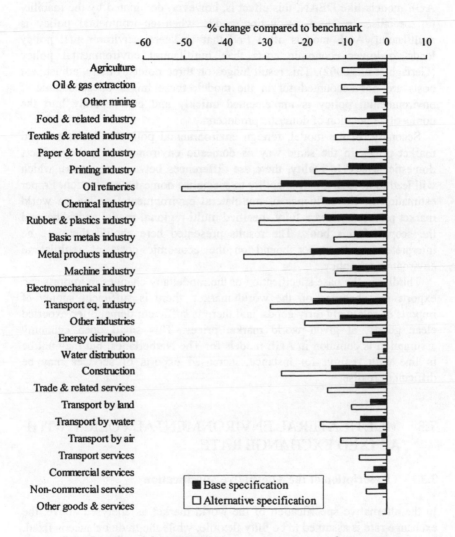

Figure 7.3   Results of the NEPP2030 *scenario on sectoral consumption volumes of private households in the year 2030 for the base specification and the alternative specification with a multilateral environmental policy*

It is often argued that a multilateral environmental policy can prevent a substantial loss in competitive position for domestic producers, and will therefore lead to lower macro-economic costs of environmental policy. In AGE models like DEAN, this effect is, however, dominated by the inability to specialise in clean production goods when environmental policy is multilateral. AGE models often find that unilateral environmental policy leads to lower economic costs than multilateral environmental policy (Gerlagh et al., 2002). This result hinges on three points. Firstly, adjustment costs are not accounted for in the model; these might be substantial if environmental policy is implemented quickly and can severely hurt the competitive position of domestic producers.

Secondly, in the model, foreign environmental policy will affect world market prices in the same way as domestic environmental policy affects domestic prices. In reality, there are differences between countries, which will lead to at least a partial ability to specialise domestic production. Proper estimation of the influence of multilateral environmental policy on world market prices requires a fully specified multi-regional model and is beyond the scope of this book. The results presented here should therefore be interpreted as an upper bound on the economic costs of multilateral environmental policy.

Thirdly, in the base specification of the model any changes in imports and exports are absorbed on the world market: there is sufficient supply of imports of relatively dirty goods, and there is sufficient demand for exported clean goods, at given world market prices. This small open economy assumption is common in AGE models for The Netherlands, but may not be in line with reality: for instance, increased exports of services may be difficult to realise.

7.3   MULTILATERAL ENVIRONMENTAL POLICY WITH A FIXED EXCHANGE RATE

7.3.1   Description of the Alternative Specification

In the alternative specification of the world market as analysed above, the exchange rate is assumed to be fully flexible, while the trade balance is fixed. For some of the major trade partners of The Netherlands it makes, however, more sense to assume a fixed exchange rate and a flexible trade balance. The fixed exchange rate and fixed trade shares together simulate the position of The Netherlands in the European Union. Note that a flexible trade balance implies that the income budget for the private households is endogenous in this alternative.

7.3.2 Calibration

This alternative specification is implemented by assuming that the trade balance adjusts such that the price of foreign goods is unaltered by environmental policy. This implies that the real exchange rate may change over time due to increases in domestic price levels. Moreover, the Armington elasticity for substitution between imports and domestic production and the Armington elasticity of transformation between exports and domestic demand are both zero as in the previous alternative.

7.3.3 Results for the Alternative Specification

The assumption on the trade balance and exchange rate may impact the transition path from the original growth path to the new equilibrium growth path. This is investigated in Figure 7.4 for the development of GDP in the *NEPP2030* scenario. It turns out that while the alternative specification of the world market does influence the GDP levels for all periods, the specification of the fixed exchange rate hardly has an additional effect on GDP levels.

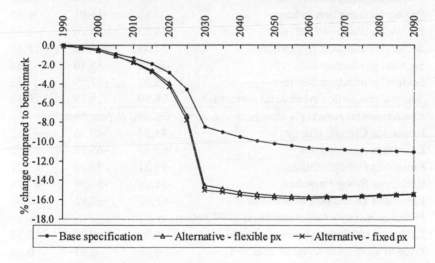

Figure 7.4 Results of the NEPP2030 *scenario on the development of GDP for the base specification and alternative specifications with a multilateral environmental policy*

The main results for the *NEPP2030* scenario for the year 2030 are reproduced in Table 7.2 for the base specification and the two alternative specifications of the world market.

Table 7.2   Results of the NEPP2030 *scenario for the year 2030 for the base
specification and alternative specifications with a multilateral
environmental policy*

	Base spec.	Alternative p_x flexible	Alternative p_x fixed
Macro-economic results (% change in volumes compared to benchmark)			
GDP	-8.45	-14.56	-15.01
NNI	-6.26	-11.38	-11.54
Total private consumption	-6.12	-11.50	-11.45
Total production	-16.00	-25.49	-25.34
Savings/investment	-20.00	-31.30	-33.29
International trade results (% change in volumes compared to benchmark)			
Total imports	-23.19	-35.05	-35.73
Total exports	-22.90	-32.98	-32.76
Trade balance (in % GDP)	1.09	1.16	2.65
Sectoral results (% change in volumes compared to benchmark)			
Private consumption Agriculture	-6.88	-10.82	-10.23
Private consumption Industry	-8.80	-16.01	-16.45
Private consumption Services	-3.23	-6.70	-6.15
Sectoral production Agriculture	-32.64	-28.14	-26.49
Sectoral production Industry	-35.05	-35.16	-35.34
Sectoral production Services	0.49	-17.59	-17.32
Sectoral production Abatement services	16.59	19.19	20.14
Environmental results (% change in volumes compared to benchmark)			
Emissions Climate change	-45.24	-49.56	-49.13
Emissions Acidification	-65.52	-65.52	-65.52
Emissions Eutrophication	-49.21	-49.21	-49.21
Emissions Smog formation	-51.96	-51.96	-51.96
Emissions Dispersion of fine dust	-62.93	-62.93	-62.93
Prices of main variables (constant 1990 prices)			
Exchange rate index (benchmark = 1)	0.82	0.32	0.58
Price of abatement services (bm. = 1)	0.68	0.47	0.48
Price Climate change (€/ton CO_2-eq.)	17.0	17.7	18.7
Price Acidification (€/acid-eq.)	929.7	468.4	565.8
Price Eutrophication (€/P-eq.)	7.5	7.3	8.4
Price Smog formation (€/kilogram)	1277.0	2182.2	2148.4
Price Fine dust (€/kilogram)	82.4	27.9	35.3

The most important observation from Table 7.2 is that the specification of the exchange rate has far less influence on model outcomes than the assumption on the world market. The macro-economic results are very similar for both alternatives; the main differences are in savings (slightly higher in the first decades and slightly lower in later decades), the sectoral composition of consumption and, as expected, in the trade balance. The fixed exchange rate leads to a substantial increase in budget surplus. The same mechanisms that caused the decrease in the exchange rate now induce an increase in trade surplus. Note that sectoral changes in imports and exports are determined in this specification by changes in domestic production.

Prices are also influenced by the alternative specification of the fixed exchange rate: the real exchange rate decreases, which implies an increase in domestic price levels. For most environmental themes, the permit price is higher than in the alternative specification with a flexible exchange rate. The exception is Smog formation. These differences stemming from the changes in sectoral developments are rather small.

Figure 7.5 shows how the exchange rate assumption impacts the sectoral composition of the economy. The figure shows the impact of the *NEPP2030* scenario on production volumes for the year 2030 for the alternative specifications. For most industrial sectors, a fixed exchange rate leads to larger production losses than a fixed trade balance, at least for the year 2030. For the transport-related sectors, the opposite is true. For Commercial services and Non-commercial services, the differences are negligible and for all other sectors, the differences are relatively small.

The conclusion may be drawn that the specification with a fixed exchange rate and adjusting trade balance leads to similar results as the specification with an adjusting exchange rate and fixed trade balance. The only important difference between the specifications is the channel through which the changes in the relation between The Netherlands and its trading partners are accommodated: via an adjustment of the exchange rate or trade balance.

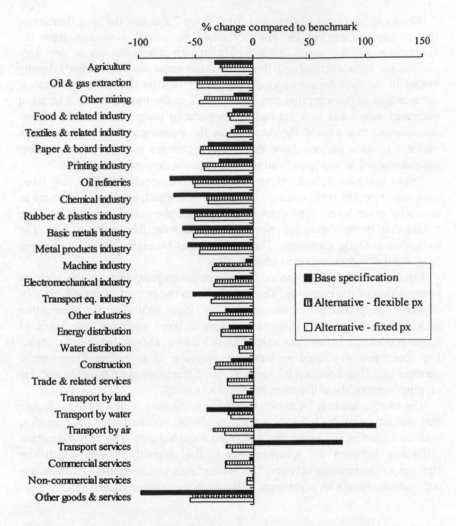

Figure 7.5   Results of the NEPP2030 *scenario on sectoral production
              volumes in the year 2030 for the alternative specifications with a
              multilateral environmental policy*

7.4   A MODEL WITH GREENHOUSE GASES AS FLOW POLLUTANTS

7.4.1   Description of the Alternative Specification

In the base specification of the DEAN model, greenhouse gases are treated as stock pollutants. Policy aims at reducing the total addition to the stock, not at restricting emissions for individual periods. As a consequence, the path of greenhouse gas emissions is flexible. To gain insight into the importance of this flexibility, an alternative model is specified in which Climate change is specified as a flow pollutant, just as the other environmental themes. That is, the *proposed path* of emission reductions from the base specification is now imposed (see Section 6.2.2), and the government issues emission permits instead of stock addition permits. Note that environmental pressure, as measured by total addition to the stock of GHGs, is identical for both specifications.

7.4.2   Calibration

No new information is needed to calibrate the alternative model with greenhouse gases as flow pollutants. The policy target in terms of emissions is already available in the base specification, though it was not enforced as such. Replacing the stock-oriented target with the flow-oriented path of emission targets is sufficient.

7.4.3   Results for the Alternative Specification

Table 7.3 presents the main results of the *NEPP2030* scenario with the alternative specification of Climate change. As there is less flexibility on the market for Climate change permits, it is not surprising that the economic costs of the *NEPP2030* scenario are higher in the alternative specification. In 2050, the GDP loss equals 11.7 per cent, against 10.2 per cent in the base specification. The other macro-economic results are in line with this observation.

The abatement expenditures are higher in the alternative specification than in the base specification. The production volume of the Abatement services sector increases in the year 2030 by almost 25 per cent compared to the benchmark, while in the base specification, it increases by less than 17 per cent. This shows that the imposed emission path of greenhouse gases is not optimised and that it induces additional abatement costs for Climate change. The positive effect on GDP of the higher value added generated in the

Abatement services sector does not fully mitigate the negative impact of higher abatement costs for the other production sectors.

Table 7.3   Results of the NEPP2030 *scenario with the alternative specification of Climate change*

	1990	2010	2030	2050
Macro-economic results (% change in volumes compared to benchmark)				
GDP	-0.01	-1.26	-9.60	-11.71
NNI	0.31	-0.23	-7.29	-9.90
Total private consumption	0.89	1.05	-7.39	-12.10
Total production	-0.10	-2.15	-17.96	-18.55
Savings/investment	-1.71	-6.71	-21.89	-21.33
International trade results (% change in volumes compared to benchmark)				
Total imports	-0.18	-3.27	-25.51	-25.19
Total exports	-0.18	-3.21	-25.32	-25.37
Trade balance (in % GDP)	0.99	1.01	1.10	1.13
Sectoral results (% change in volumes compared to benchmark)				
Private consumption Agriculture	0.52	-0.33	-9.25	-11.69
Private consumption Industry	0.86	0.81	-10.34	-13.92
Private consumption Services	0.93	1.36	-4.17	-10.18
Sectoral production Agriculture	-0.08	-9.34	-45.87	-48.14
Sectoral production Industry	-0.35	-3.36	-35.67	-31.69
Sectoral production Services	0.09	-0.62	-1.71	-5.77
Sectoral production Abatement services	0.01	2.94	24.27	20.54
Environmental results (% change in volumes compared to benchmark)				
Emissions Climate change	0.00	-17.64	-52.91	-52.91
Emissions Acidification	0.00	-21.84	-65.52	-65.52
Emissions Eutrophication	0.00	-16.40	-49.21	-49.21
Emissions Smog formation	0.00	-17.32	-51.96	-51.96
Emissions Dispersion of fine dust	0.00	-20.98	-62.93	-62.93
Prices of main variables (constant 1990 prices)				
Exchange rate index (benchmark = 1)	1.00	1.01	0.85	0.91
Price of abatement services (bm. = 1)	1.00	1.00	0.69	0.79
Price Climate change ($€$/ton CO_2-eq.)	2.8	17.0	127.6	194.9
Price Acidification ($€$/acid-eq.)	3.7	33.6	698.6	1028.4
Price Eutrophication ($€$/P-eq.)	0.5	2.6	4.0	5.7
Price Smog formation ($€$/kilogram)	0.1	2.4	1170.8	1190.5
Price Fine dust ($€$/kilogram)	0.1	1.2	63.7	98.5

The development of GDP for the base and alternative specification are shown in Figure 7.6. As with the alternative specification of the world market, the pattern is similar to the base specification, while the absolute GDP losses are higher in the alternative specification. Again, the conclusion holds that the growth rate of GDP is unaffected by the environmental policy in the long run; the level of GDP in this alternative specification is around 12.5 per cent below the benchmark.

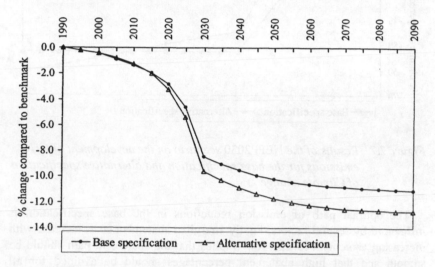

Figure 7.6   Results of the NEPP2030 *scenario on the development of GDP for the base specification and alternative specification of Climate change*

The alternative specification of the Climate change policy allows an analysis of the optimal versus imposed paths of GHG emissions. Figure 7.7 shows the path of GHG emission reductions in the base specification, with full intertemporal flexibility, and the alternative specification, with an imposed path.

The main difference between both curves is that in the base specification, emission reductions continue to increase from the first period, 1990, to the very last, 2090. In this way, emission reductions are more evenly spread over the full model horizon. Moreover, relatively large emission reductions are achieved in the later periods. In other words, after some initial emission reductions that are only possible in the base specification, emission reductions are delayed relative to the imposed path, though the effect is not very big.

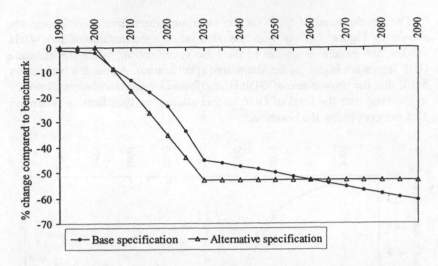

Figure 7.7   Results of the NEPP2030 *scenario on the development of GHG*
emissions for the base specification and alternative specification
of Climate change

The optimal path of emission reductions in the base specification is
influenced by several factors. Firstly, marginal abatement costs increase with
increasing abatement levels. This implies that the abatement path should be
smooth and that high abatement percentages should be avoided for all
periods. Secondly, the autonomous decrease of marginal abatement costs
over time implies that, *ceteris paribus*, it is better to reduce emissions as late
as possible. Thirdly, the net present value of a reduction in consumption in
later periods is relatively small, due to the positive discount rate. This effect
also favours late reductions of GHG emissions. Fourthly, there is a positive
decay rate of the stock of GHGs. This means that early emissions will decay
more until the end of the century than late emissions. Again, this favours late
emission reductions. Fifthly, the economic restructuring that is induced by
the policies for other environmental themes influences the reduction in GHG
emissions. This implies that the path of GHG emissions should adapt to the
imposed path for the other themes.

All in all, the optimal path of GHG emission reductions is governed by
minimising the net present value of all abatement costs associated with the
environmental theme Climate change. A relatively smooth path emerges, that
tends to follow the path of the other environmental themes, with an additional
emphasis on emission reductions in the later periods. The path is not entirely
smooth though, as the sudden change in the slope of the reduction curve in
the year 2030 shows. This kink in the curve mirrors the economic impacts of

the environmental policy for the other themes, and is also present in the curve for GDP. Figure 7.8 shows how these emission reductions affect GHG emissions.

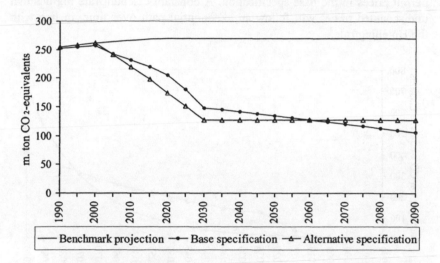

Figure 7.8   Results of the NEPP2030 *scenario on the development of GHG emissions for the benchmark projection, base specification and alternative specification of Climate change*

The emission path of GHGs is not related in DEAN to climate impacts. Early emission reductions will lead to less radiative forcing, less temperature rise and hence less damages. These effects are not covered in DEAN. Using the DICE model (Nordhaus, 1994), the differences in radiative forcing from both emission paths can be calculated. Between 2020 and 2070, the imposed emission path leads to less radiative forcing than the flexible path; the size of the effect is never more than 0.1 per cent of global radiative forcing. Using a simplified version of DICE, based on Germain and van Steenberghe (2001) and reported in Dellink et al. (2003), the net present value of global reduction in climate damages from earlier emission reductions in The Netherlands is estimated to be roughly between 1 and 2 million euros.

The difference in the emission path of GHGs also has its impact on the price of Climate change permits. The permit prices for the base and alternative specifications are represented in Figure 7.9. The prices for the base specification are expressed in terms of costs of emissions. This emission price is calculated as the cost of acquiring stock addition permits that allow one additional ton of CO_2-equivalent emissions. As some emissions are taken up by sinks, one ton of emissions leads to less then one ton of additional stock of greenhouse gases (the difference is captured by the marginal atmospheric retention rate; see Section 4.4.1 for more details). The principle of equalisation of abatement costs is also reflected in the development of the permit prices in the base specification. A constant discount rate implies that undiscounted prices will follow an exponential path over time, in line with the Hotelling rule.

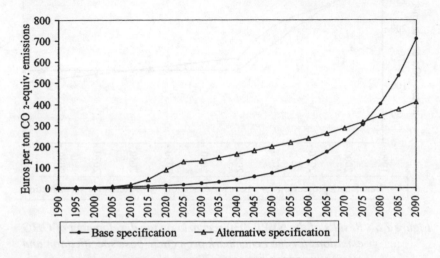

Figure 7.9   Results of the NEPP2030 *scenario on the development of Climate change permit prices (undiscounted) for the base specification and alternative specification of Climate change*

For the periods between 2000 and 2070, the price of Climate change permits is higher in the alternative specification, in line with the imposed bigger emission reductions for these periods in the base specification. The slope of the curve in the alternative specification implies a more or less constant growth rate of the permit prices of around 2 per cent per year. This outcome is also observed for other environmental themes, at least roughly. At this time, the required emission reductions are constant (both in absolute terms and in percentages), while the economy returns to its original growth rate of 2 per cent.

Summarising, the analysis above shows that if the government implements emission permits for stock pollutants, it is likely that this will induce excessive costs, as policy makers have insufficient information to determine the optimal path of emission reductions. Adopting a stock-oriented policy can lead to considerable cost savings as polluters are flexible in the timing of their emission reduction efforts.

7.5 ALTERNATIVE RECYCLING OF ENVIRONMENTAL PERMIT REVENUES

7.5.1 Description of the Alternative Specification

The revenues for the government from the sale of environmental permits are substantial. In the base specification, they are recycled to households in a lump sum manner. The main reason for this is that this recycling scheme is not distortionary. The government may also choose to recycle the environmental permit revenues by reducing existing distortionary taxes. One may regard this alternative specification as a greening of the tax system.

A specification where revenues from environmental policy are used to reduce existing distortionary taxes lends itself to an analysis of the possibilities for a so-called double dividend; that is, where the environmental tax reform can increase environmental quality as well as achieving other objectives. In the literature, there is no consensus whether an environmental tax reform may lead to an increase in employment and/or (economic) welfare or neither (Bosello et al., 2001). Given the assumptions of a clearing labour market and a fixed supply of labour in the AGE framework, the DEAN model is not suitable for investigating whether the environmental tax reform will lead to increases in employment or not, but the possibilities for a double dividend in terms of welfare can be analysed.

7.5.2 Calibration

The distortionary taxes are present in the base specification. The only issue for calibrating the alternative is how much to reduce which taxes. Given the fact that revenues are large, the assumption is made that all existing taxes are reduced proportionately to offset increases in government income from the sale of environmental permits. If the revenues of the sale of environmental permits are larger than the revenues from existing taxes, the remainder will be redistributed as a lump sum to the private households.

7.5.3 Results for the Alternative Specification

Table 7.4 shows the results of the model calculations with the alternative recycling scheme for environmental permit revenues. As can be seen in Table 7.4, the economic costs of the policy are lower if the revenues from the sale of the environmental permits are used to reduce existing taxes. This reduction of existing market distortions is, however, by no means large enough to mitigate the negative impact of the environmental policy on economic welfare. Therefore, according to these simulations, there is no double dividend to be reaped from the environmental tax reform.

Table 7.4   Results of the NEPP2030 scenario with the alternative recycling scheme for environmental permit revenues

	1990	2010	2030	2050
Macro-economic results (% change in volumes compared to benchmark)				
GDP	-0.01	-0.79	-7.57	-9.49
NNI	0.17	-0.24	-5.40	-7.91
Total private consumption	0.50	0.38	-4.80	-9.49
Total production	-0.22	-1.38	-15.50	-16.05
Savings/investment	-0.96	-3.69	-19.05	-17.83
International trade results (% change in volumes compared to benchmark)				
Total imports	-0.46	-2.18	-22.72	-22.73
Total exports	-0.45	-2.16	-22.51	-22.91
Trade balance (in % GDP)	0.99	1.00	1.08	1.10
Sectoral results (% change in volumes compared to benchmark)				
Private consumption Agriculture	0.16	-0.42	-6.44	-9.03
Private consumption Industry	0.44	0.23	-7.89	-11.47
Private consumption Services	0.58	0.58	-1.44	-7.39
Sectoral production Agriculture	-1.18	-6.47	-35.40	-36.30
Sectoral production Industry	-0.45	-2.08	-36.52	-31.61
Sectoral production Services	0.05	-0.40	2.81	-2.04
Sectoral production Abatement services	-0.04	4.59	17.34	16.37
Environmental results (% change in volumes compared to benchmark)				
Emissions Climate change	-1.16	-14.77	-44.87	-49.62
Emissions Acidification	0.00	-21.84	-65.52	-65.52
Emissions Eutrophication	0.00	-16.40	-49.21	-49.21
Emissions Smog formation	0.00	-17.32	-51.96	-51.96
Emissions Dispersion of fine dust	0.00	-20.98	-62.93	-62.93
Prices of main variables (constant 1990 prices)				
Exchange rate index (benchmark = 1)	1.00	1.01	0.92	1.00
Price of abatement services (bm. = 1)	1.00	1.00	0.77	0.90
Price Climate change (€/ton CO_2-eq.)	2.5	8.0	20.5	53.6
Price Acidification (€/acid-eq.)	3.9	26.6	1222.8	1397.5
Price Eutrophication (€/P-eq.)	0.6	2.6	7.4	11.9
Price Smog formation (€/kilogram)	0.1	1.5	1573.8	1677.9
Price Fine dust (€/kilogram)	0.1	1.0	88.5	115.6

Given the increasing marginal abatement costs for increasingly strict environmental policy targets, a small (strong) double dividend cannot be ruled out for less ambitious policy targets. Such an analysis is, however, beyond the scope of the current study.

In its weakest form, a double dividend may be present if a model specification with recycling via reduction of distortionary taxes leads to higher welfare levels than a specification with lump sum redistribution (Babiker et al., 2003). This is indeed the case in the simulations with DEAN; hence, the alternative specification brings the economy closer to the efficient, first-best situation.

Figure 7.10 displays the impact of the alternative specification on the development of GDP in the *NEPP2030* scenario. As expected, the reduction of existing market distortions leads to smaller reductions in GDP throughout the model horizon. The alternative recycling scheme has, however, no major impact on the timing of environmental costs: the differences between both specifications are rather stable over time. In the long run, the level of GDP is around 10.5 per cent below the benchmark projection, against 11 per cent in the base specification.

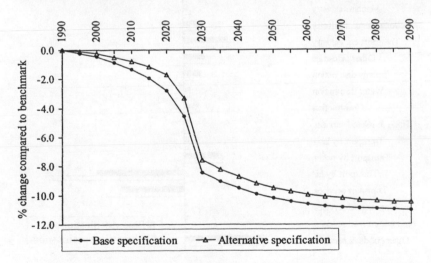

Figure 7.10   Results of the NEPP2030 *scenario on the development of GDP for the base specification and alternative recycling scheme for environmental permit revenues*

As the different production sectors have different characteristics with respect to labour and capital taxes, the expectation is that the alternative recycling scheme will lead to different sectoral results. Figure 7.11 shows the production losses in the year 2030 for the *NEPP2030* scenario.

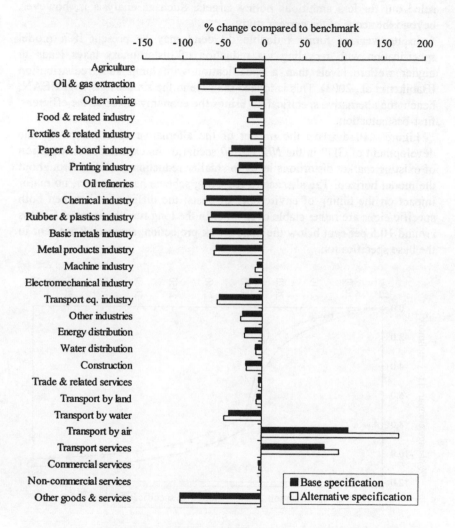

Figure 7.11   Results of the NEPP2030 *scenario on sectoral production volumes in the year 2030 for the alternative recycling scheme for environmental permit revenues*

It turns out that, for most sectors, the production changes are hardly affected by the alternative recycling scheme. One reason for this is that the tax rates do not differ much between the different sectors, especially for labour taxes. Moreover, the consumption taxes are related to total consumption and have identical rates across consumption categories; hence, changes in consumption taxes will not influence the sectoral structure.

The main differences are the production changes for Transport by air and Transport services. As discussed in Chapter 6, these changes are caused by the high price of emission permits for Smog formation. As the alternative recycling scheme leads to VOC emission permit prices that are even higher than in the base specification, it is not surprising that the specialisation in these two sectors is also amplified. The only sector that has relatively low tax rates for both labour and capital taxes is Transport by water. The alternative recycling scheme does not help this sector as much as the other production sectors, and therefore production losses in this sector are larger than in the base specification. At the other extreme are the Oil refineries and Non-commercial services that both have relatively high tax rates. Both sectors are indeed slightly better off with the alternative recycling scheme. Figure 7.12 shows the development of the value of the environmental permits over time for the model specification with an alternative recycling scheme. The prices of the various themes relative to each other are similar to the relative permit prices in the base specification. Moreover, the developments over time are in line with the base specification. The major difference is the scale of the permit prices: the permit prices are roughly 10 to 30 per cent higher in the alternative specification.

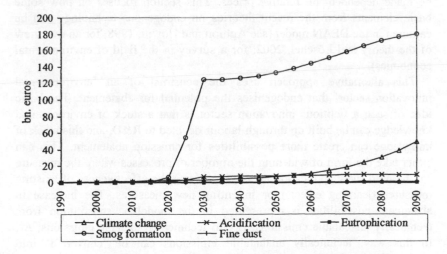

Figure 7.12   Results of the NEPP2030 *scenario on the development of environmental permit values for the alternative recycling scheme for environmental permit revenues*

The introduction of the environmental permit system for various environmental themes leads to a complete greening of the tax system. When the environmental policy is fully implemented (in the *NEPP2030* scenario in the year 2030), the government revenues from the sale of the permits are higher than the tax revenues from existing taxes. In this alternative specification, this implies that all existing taxes (on labour, capital and consumption) are abolished and still the lump sum transfer to the private households is increased. This result is primarily driven by the huge revenues from the sale of Smog formation permits.

7.6 A MODEL WITH ENDOGENOUS ENVIRONMENTAL INNOVATION

7.6.1 Description of the Alternative Specification

The base version of the DEAN model contains endogenous *diffusion* of abatement technology, but *innovation* in abatement technology is exogenous. It is, however, likely that increasingly stringent environmental policies and a large increase in demand for abatement will have an impact on environmental technological change via innovation. This holds especially for Smog formation. In model terms, the growth rate of the technical potential should be made dependent on relative prices. This section focuses on how some basic elements from the recent theories on endogenous technology can be captured in the DEAN model (see Aghion and Howitt, 1998, for an overview of the theory and Löschel, 2002, for a survey in the field of environmental economics).

This alternative approach uses the construct of an 'environmental innovation sector' that endogenises the potential for abatement. The basic idea of such a fictitious innovation sector is that a stock of environmental knowledge can be built up through labour devoted to R&D, and this stock of knowledge can create more possibilities for emission abatement. This can either take the form of widening the number of processes where the measure can be used (new application areas), increasing the effectiveness of existing measures (learning effects) or inventing new measures. The increase in abatement possibilities is represented in the model as substitution from technically unabatable emissions, E^U, to technically abatable emissions, E^A. In this way, technically unabatable emissions can be 'converted' into technically abatable emissions, but this is costly.

The environmental innovation sector, EI, can provide equivalent services as E^U and is specified by environmental theme (e), production sector (j) and time period (t). It needs both environmental knowledge, H, and a combination of technically abatable emissions E^A and abatement A to provide this service. The specification is such that at the initial ratio between emissions and abatement in the lower level of the function, one unit of technically unabatable emissions can be substituted by one unit of abatable emissions:[3]

$$EI_{e,j,t} = Min \left\{ H_{e,j,t}, CES \left(E^A_{e,j,t}, \frac{A_{e,j,t}}{\beta_{EI}}; \sigma^A_{e,j} \right) \right\} \qquad (7.1)$$

There are separate sectors for each environmental theme and for each production sector. In other words, environmental knowledge and environmental innovation are completely immobile. For households, no environmental innovation sector is specified. The starting point for substitution between emissions and abatement through innovation does not have to be identical to the starting point for the calibrated substitution curve, but should be calibrated separately. This factor β_{EI} equals unity for the calibrated PAS curves that are present in the base specification of the DEAN model. Typically, the factor is larger than unity for the innovation sector to reflect that new innovations are not as productive (yet) as the most productive existing abatement techniques.

The knowledge sector is modelled relatively simply: a part of existing knowledge survives to the next period (that is, there is some knowledge destruction) and next period stock can be increased through the input of labour.

$$H_{e,j,t+1} = (1 - \delta_H) \cdot H_{e,j,t} + LH_{e,j,t} \qquad (7.2)$$

with δ_H the 'destruction' rate of existing environmental knowledge and $LH_{e,j,t}$ the labour devoted to R&D. The amount of environmental services that can offset the technically unabatable emissions is calibrated such that the *ex ante* increase in technically abatable emissions exactly matches the decrease in technically unabatable emissions. The additional technically abatable emissions can be substituted by increases in abatement. In this way, the innovation does interact with the original substitution curve, even though it is modelled as additional to this original curve.

The innovation sector will not be active in the benchmark, since at benchmark prices the costs of the innovation are by definition higher than the costs of permits for E^U (the emission permit costs are the same, while the innovation sector also requires labour). The innovation sector will become active if the price of the emission permits becomes so high that it is cheaper to accept the extra labour and abatement costs to reduce the pressure on the emissions permit market. Consequently, it serves as an upper bound on the permit price and in this way it is similar to the backstop technologies often modelled in energy models (Manne and Richels, 1992). A key difference from the backstop technology is that in the DEAN model the environmental innovation has to be explicitly produced, using scarce economic resources.

The alternative specification with endogenous environmental innovation, shown in Table 7.5, involves replacing equation (DEAN-27) in the full model description as reported in Chapter 4 with (DEAN-36) and equation (DEAN-25) with (DEAN-39). Moreover, equations (DEAN-37) and (DEAN-38) are added to the model. Equations (DEAN-34) and (DEAN-35) are removed from the model, that is, $\varphi_A = 0$.

Table 7.5 The alternative model with endogenous environmental innovation

$$ES_{e,j,t} = CES\left\{(E^U_{e,j,t} + EI_{e,j,t}), CES(E^A_{e,j,t}, A_{e,j,t}; \sigma^A_{e,j}); \sigma^{ES}_{e,j}\right\}$$
$$\forall(e,j,t) \tag{DEAN-36}$$

$$EI_{e,j,t} = CES\left\{H_{e,j,t}, CES(E^A_{e,j,t}, \frac{A_{e,j,t}}{\beta_{EI}}; \sigma^A_{e,j}); \sigma^{EI}_{e,j}\right\} \quad \forall(e,j,t),$$
with $\sigma^{EI}_{e,j} = 0 \tag{DEAN-37}$

$$H_{e,j,t+1} = (1 - \delta_H) \cdot H_{e,j,t} + LH_{e,j,t} \quad \forall(e,j,t) \tag{DEAN-38}$$

$$\sum_{j=1}^{J} L_{j,t} + L_{A,t} + \sum_{e=1}^{E}\sum_{j=1}^{J} LH_{e,j,t} = \overline{L}_t \quad \forall t; \text{ determines } p_{L,t} \tag{DEAN-39}$$

Parameters and variables

β_{EI} Efficiency parameter of new environmental innovation emission reduction measures compared to existing measures

δ_H Destruction rate of existing knowledge

$\sigma^{EI}_{e,j}$ Substitution elasticity between environmental knowledge and technically abatable emissions/abatement aggregate for environmental theme e for sector j (always equal to zero)

$EI_{e,j,t}$ Annual production of environmental innovation sector for environmental theme e by sector j in period t

$H_{e,j,t}$ Annual environmental knowledge for environmental theme e by sector j in period t

$LH_{e,j,t}$ Annual labour input for environmental knowledge for environmental theme e by sector j in period t (R&D activity)

7.6.2   Calibration

The alternative model with endogenous environmental innovation contains some new parameters that have to be calibrated; see the list of new parameters and variables above. Since the endogenous environmental innovation sector is not active in the benchmark projection, the production of the environmental innovation sector, $EI_{e,j,t}$, the environmental knowledge, $H_{e,j,t}$, and the associated labour demand, $LH_{e,j,t}$, are calibrated to zero.

The destruction rate of environmental knowledge is assumed to be 3 per cent per year, though no empirical basis could be found to validate this number.

The substitution elasticity between environmental knowledge and the aggregate of technically abatable emissions and abatement, $\sigma_{e,j}^{EI}$, has to equal zero to reflect the Leontief function as discussed above.

Hence, the key parameter to be calibrated is the parameter that governs the relative efficiency of new environmental innovation emission reduction measures compared to existing measures. There is no empirical data available for this parameter and therefore the model results are calculated for different values. A high value of $\beta_{EI} = 500$ implies that environmental innovation will only occur if the price of emission permits becomes very high. A lower value, such as $\beta_{EI} = 100$ or $\beta_{EI} = 50$, will lead to cheaper and therefore more widespread environmental innovation.

7.6.3   Results for the Alternative Specification

The main results of the different model calculations are given in Table 7.6. Only the results for the *NEPP2030* scenario are presented for the year 2030. It is clear from Table 7.6 that the possibility of increasing the scope for technical abatement measures via endogenous environmental innovation leads to lower costs of environmental policy. The loss in GDP, which equals almost 8.5 per cent in the base specification, is much smaller in the alternative model with endogenous environmental innovation. The cost-decreasing effect of the environmental innovation sector is reflected throughout the economy. Net national income, total private consumption, total production and capital investments are all substantially less affected than in the base specification. And the cheaper the environmental innovation, that is, the lower the value of β, the smaller the macro-economic costs of environmental policy.

Table 7.6   *Results of the* NEPP2030 *scenario for the year 2030 for different*
values of β_{EI} *in the alternative model with endogenous*
environmental innovation

	High β	Middle β	Low β
Macro-economic results (% change in volumes compared to benchmark)			
GDP	-4.52	-2.61	-2.10
NNI	-3.46	-2.02	-1.66
Total private consumption	-3.67	-2.18	-1.86
Total production	-8.49	-5.10	-4.08
Savings/investment	-10.08	-5.72	-4.43
International trade results (% change in volumes compared to benchmark)			
Total imports	-13.08	-7.49	-6.01
Total exports	-13.06	-7.53	-6.06
Trade balance (in % GDP)	1.04	1.02	1.02
Sectoral results (% change in volumes compared to benchmark)			
Private consumption Agriculture	-5.61	-5.00	-4.30
Private consumption Industry	-4.93	-2.91	-2.42
Private consumption Services	-2.26	-1.31	-1.16
Sectoral production Agriculture	-31.44	-34.52	-30.40
Sectoral production Industry	-14.77	-6.63	-4.92
Sectoral production Services	-1.62	-1.46	-1.25
Sectoral production Abatement services	49.53	28.41	24.64
Environmental results (% change in volumes compared to benchmark)			
Emissions Climate change	-40.92	-39.44	-37.30
Emissions Acidification	-65.52	-65.52	-65.52
Emissions Eutrophication	-49.21	-49.21	-49.21
Emissions Smog formation	-51.96	-51.96	-51.96
Emissions Dispersion of fine dust	-62.93	-62.93	-62.93
Prices of main variables (constant 1990 prices)			
Exchange rate index (benchmark = 1)	0.98	1.01	1.01
Price of abatement services (bm. = 1)	0.88	0.95	0.96
Price Climate change (€/ton CO_2-eq.)	27.7	37.7	36.6
Price Acidification (€/acid-eq.)	1115.7	1315.8	921.8
Price Eutrophication (€/P-eq.)	12.4	12.5	16.5
Price Smog formation (€/kilogram)	365.0	80.7	42.0
Price Fine dust (€/kilogram)	347.0	76.7	39.8

The sectoral economic effects are not so uniform, though. The environmental innovation leads to smaller production losses in the industrial sectors, but this comes at the expense of larger production losses in services. For some levels of β, agricultural production is worse off than in the base specification, while for other values the opposite is true. These sectoral impacts will be analysed in more detail below. Obviously, the introduction of an environmental innovation sector benefits the Abatement services sector. For a high value of β, the increase is large: almost 50 per cent above the benchmark projection. For lower values of β, the increase is smaller, but still above the increase that is realised in the base specification. A lower value of β implies a broader scope for emission reduction via technical abatement measures, but this is more than mitigated by the lower costs of the newly invented abatement measures. Therefore, total demand for Abatement services is highest for higher values of β.

The impact of the alternative specification on the prices of environmental permits is ambiguous. Firstly, a direct effect occurs: if there is environmental innovation for a certain environmental theme, the price of the permits for that theme will be lower. This reflects the idea that via environmental innovation, technically unabatable emissions can be transformed into technically abatable emissions and then substituted by abatement services. Given the relatively low cost of abatement compared to the costs of economic restructuring, this leads to a lower price of the environmental permit for the theme where the environmental innovation sector is active.

The second effect on the prices of environmental permits is indirect: because the environmental innovation sector takes away some pressure for one environmental theme, the relative pressure on the permit markets for the other environmental themes is increased. If less economic restructuring is induced by one environmental theme, this leads *ceteris paribus* to lower emission reductions for the other environmental themes as well.[4] Therefore, the prices of the emission permits for which the environmental innovation sector is not active increase compared to the base specification.

Figure 7.13 displays the development of GDP in the NEPP2030 scenario for the different values of β. The results for the base specification can be interpreted as an upper bound on the economic costs of environmental policy, that is it represents the case that innovation of new abatement techniques is prohibitively costly.

For the low value of β, there is a sudden decrease in GDP in the year 2085. This is caused by a crowding-out of capital investment by the emergence of environmental innovation for Climate change. Until 2080, the costs of Climate change permits do not induce any environmental innovation, but by 2085, the threshold value is exceeded and the endogenous environmental innovation sector for Climate change abatement becomes active. This draws resources away from other activities, thereby reducing GDP. The loss in GDP is, however, still smaller than for higher values of β. As this effect is only envisaged for the end of the twenty-first century, the empirical relevance of this effect is small.

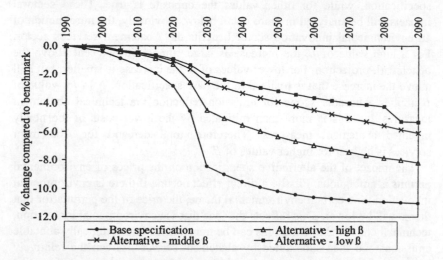

Figure 7.13 Results of the NEPP2030 *scenario on the development of GDP for the base specification and the alternative model with endogenous environmental innovation*

The effects of the alternative specification on the production of the different sectors in the year 2030 for the *NEPP2030* scenario are shown in Figure 7.14. For most sectors, production losses are smaller if environmental innovation is cheaper. This is not true for every sector, though. Since the permit price goes up for some environmental themes, while for others it goes down, the alternative specification has varying degrees of impact on the production sectors. For example, the agricultural sector, which is characterised by relatively high emission intensities for Climate change, is, in 2030, worst off for the middle value of β, as in this specification the price of Climate change permits is highest.

If environmental innovation is available, the industrial sectors are much better off than in the base specification. Instead of having to buy extremely expensive emission permits, they can devote labour to environmental R&D and so reduce their emissions. This result holds especially for sectors that have high VOC emissions, but relatively low emissions for the other environmental themes; these include the Printing industry, the Construction sector and Trade and related services. In the base specification, the services sectors can profit from the forced reductions in industrial production. If these forced reductions are less prominent or even absent, this implies lower production volumes in services compared to the base specification.

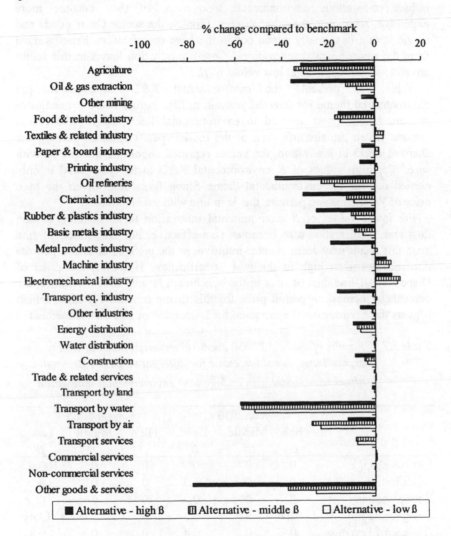

Figure 7.14   Results of the NEPP2030 *scenario on sectoral production volumes in the year 2030 for the alternative model with endogenous environmental innovation*

Transport by water is the sector that is most severely affected by environmental policy if low-cost environmental innovation is available. This sector is characterised by high emission intensities for Acidification, Eutrophication and Dispersion of fine dust, primarily caused by the low value added that is generated in this sector. These environmental themes do not induce endogenous environmental innovation, so they become more expensive, relative to the other themes. Finally, the sector Other goods and services, that is virtually wiped out in the base specification, benefits most from the environmental innovations, though production losses in this sector are still substantial, even at low values of β.

Table 7.7 presents the environmental R&D expenditures per environmental theme for selected years in million euros. These expenditures concern labour costs devoted to environmental R&D, aggregated across sectors. Given the simplification of the model specification concerning the share of R&D in innovation, the values reported should be interpreted with care.[5] For high values of β, environmental R&D in the year 2030 is only carried out for the environmental theme Smog formation. Given the high price of VOC emission permits, this is in line with expectations.

For lower values of β, environmental innovation for Dispersion of fine dust and Acidification also becomes cost-effective. For Dispersion of fine dust, this result may seem counter-intuitive, as the price of emission permits does not seem so high in the base specification. However, the price of Dispersion of fine dust permits in the benchmark is very low. Therefore, the percentage increase in permit price for this theme is relatively high, which triggers the environmental innovation for Dispersion of fine dust abatement.

Table 7.7 *Results of the* NEPP2030 *scenario on environmental R&D expenditures in million euros for different values of* β_{EI} *in the alternative model with endogenous environmental innovation*

| | year 2030 | | | year 2085 | | |
	High β	Middle β	Low β	High β	Middle β	Low β
Climate change	0	0	0	0	0	100.0
Acidification	0	0	1.9	0	0	0
Eutrophication	0	0	0	0	0	0
Smog formation	2.7	5.3	6.3	3	7.4	13.4
Dispers. of fine dust	0	0.2	0.4	0	0	0.8

In Table 7.7 the environmental R&D expenditures are also shown for 2085, to show that the increase in the price of Climate change permits over time triggers the activation of the environmental innovation sector for Climate change by 2085. This only occurs for low values of β, as for higher values it is too expensive to invest in environmental R&D for Climate change. For Dispersion of fine dust, the need for environmental R&D is reduced in the later periods for the intermediate value of β, as enough environmental knowledge for this theme has been built up to sustain the required level of environmental innovation.

The impact of environmental innovation can also be seen in the development of technically unabatable emissions. If environmental innovation takes place in the sector, technically unabatable emissions are substituted by technically abatable emissions. Figure 7.15 shows this for the environmental theme Smog formation: the lower the costs of environmental innovation, the larger the reductions in technically unabatable VOC emissions.

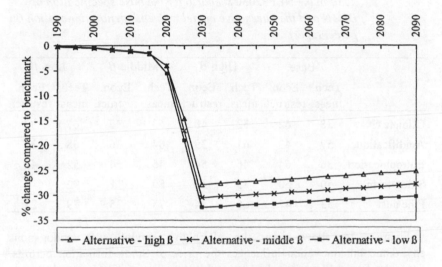

Figure 7.15   Results of the NEPP2030 scenario on the development of technically unabatable VOC emissions for the alternative model with endogenous environmental innovation

The possibility of increasing the potential for technical abatement measures via endogenous innovation leads to different shares of technical measures and economic restructuring in total emission reductions, as shown in Table 7.8. Note that total emission reduction is identical for all alternatives, except for Climate change, where endogenous timing influences total emission reductions.

For all environmental themes, the share of economic restructuring declines when endogenous innovation becomes cheaper (lower β). As expected, this effect is most pronounced for Smog formation. In the base specification, half of all emission reductions have to be realised through economic restructuring, while in the alternative specification with a low value of β, this share is reduced to 8 per cent. For some other environmental themes, such as Eutrophication, the innovation sector is not active in the year 2030. Still the share of economic restructuring decreases when endogenous innovation is available. This switch from economic restructuring to technical abatement measures is an indirect effect of the innovation of new measures for Smog formation, as this implies less economic restructuring. As explained above, this increases the relative pressure for the other environmental themes and leads to the implementation of more technical measures.

Table 7.8   Shares of contributing parts to emission reductions in the year 2030 in the NEPP2030 scenario for the base specification of DEAN and the alternative model with endogenous innovation (in percentages)

	Base		High β		Middle β		Low β	
	Tech. meas.	Econ. restruct.	Tech. meas.	Econ. restruct.	Tech. meas.	Econ. restruct.	Tech. meas.	Econ. restruct.
Climate ch.	38	62	52	48	63	37	67	33
Acidification	57	43	61	39	64	36	68	32
Eutrophication	36	64	46	54	46	54	52	48
Smog form.	50	50	75	25	89	11	92	8
Fine dust	53	47	66	34	75	25	79	21

Figure 7.16 shows how the alternative model with endogenous environmental innovation influences the price of Smog formation permits. From the figure it is clear that the endogenous innovation sector becomes active as soon as the permit price exceeds a certain threshold, which is directly related to the value of β. The alternative specification does not impose an absolute bound on the undiscounted permit price. The sharp increase in the Smog formation permit price in the year 2030, as it occurs in the base specification, is prevented by investing in environmental R&D, but the undiscounted permit price does increase over time. Given the simplicity of the specification of the environmental knowledge sector, no hard empirical conclusions should be drawn from this effect.

The influence of environmental innovation on the permit prices can also be illustrated for Climate change, as is done in Figure 7.17. For high and middle values of β, there is no environmental innovation for Climate change abatement, and the price of the permits is above the level of the base specification. The introduction of low-cost environmental innovation in 2085 levels off the permit price in the low β case by reducing the pressure on the market for Climate change permits.

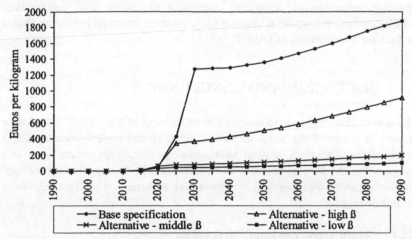

Figure 7.16 *Results of the NEPP2030 scenario on the development of Smog formation permit prices for the base specification and the alternative model with endogenous environmental innovation*

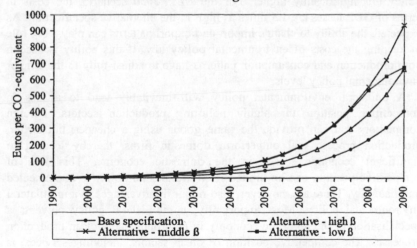

Figure 7.17 *Results of the NEPP2030 scenario on the development of Climate change permit prices for the base specification and the alternative model with endogenous environmental innovation*

In conclusion, the simulations of the alternative specification with endogenous environmental innovation show that polluters will react to high prices for pollution permits by investing in R&D to increase the potential for emission reduction via technical abatement measures. This mechanism, which can limit the macro-economic costs of environmental policy, is absent in the base specification of DEAN.

7.7   DISCUSSION AND CONCLUSIONS

The aim of this chapter is to analyse the robustness of the DEAN model with respect to some of the most important assumptions underlying the model specification. Therefore, several alternative specifications are analysed and compared to the base specification of the model. In this concluding section, these alternative specifications are discussed with respect to their relevance for policy makers.

7.7.1   Multilateral Environmental Policy

If the specification of the model is changed such that environmental problems can no longer be transferred abroad, the economic costs of the environmental policy are significantly higher. For the *NEPP2030* scenario, the costs in terms of GDP losses are 1.5 times as high in the alternative specification. As expected, the ability to change import and export patterns can play a big role in keeping the costs of environmental policy low. If this ability is absent, both production and consumption patterns have to adjust fully to the stricter environmental policy levels.

A unilateral environmental policy will inevitably lead to a loss in competitive position for highly polluting production sectors. Foreign competitors that can provide the same goods using a cheaper, but dirtier, production process will outperform domestic firms, thereby leading to significant economic losses in the domestic economy. This loss of competitive position can be limited if environmental policy is implemented multilaterally. There are, however, also major disadvantages to a multilateral environmental policy. Most importantly, a multilateral policy prevents a specialisation of the domestic economy in environmentally clean production processes. The competitive position of clean sectors, including services, is threatened by the foreign environmental policy. This argument links to the argument put forward in the previous chapter that environmental policy not only generates 'losers', but also 'winners'. A multilateral environmental policy will lead to a more even spread of production losses across the economy.

From an environmental perspective a multilateral policy has clear advantages for transboundary pollutants, including greenhouse gases. For local environmental problems, a lax foreign environmental policy is not detrimental to domestic environmental quality, while the impact on foreign environmental quality depends on the local circumstances of the place which economic activity shifts to. Essentially, the relocation of economic activity that generates local pollution is good for the domestic environment but bad for the domestic economy, while the opposite holds for the new location of this activity. As the DEAN model cannot assess the trade-off between economic activity and environmental quality, it is not possible to say whether this is an improvement or not. Consequently, it is also impossible to assess from the analysis whether a unilateral or multilateral environmental policy should be preferred.

7.7.2   Multilateral Environmental Policy with a Fixed Exchange Rate

One can combine the alternative specification of the world market with the assumption that the exchange rate is fixed and the trade balance flexible (the other specifications assume a flexible exchange rate with a fixed trade balance). The multilateral environmental policy in combination with a fixed exchange rate reflects the position of The Netherlands in the European Union. Note that the real exchange rate is endogenous, as domestic price levels may change over time. It turns out that the macro-economic, sectoral and environmental results of the model are quite robust to the assumption regarding the exchange rate. The main difference caused by the fixed exchange rate is the channel through which the changes in the relation between The Netherlands and its trading partners are accommodated. For the economic impacts of environmental policy, it is of much more importance whether the policy is implemented unilaterally or multilaterally.

7.7.3   The Model with Greenhouse Gases as Flow Pollutants

The Climate change policy can be implemented as an emission policy, instead of being stock-oriented, while keeping the target identical in terms of environmental quality, that is, the same total stock addition over the full model horizon. The emission policy leads to substantially higher economic costs of Climate change policy as well as a higher price of Climate change permits, except for the last few periods; long-run GDP levels are more than 1 percentage point lower than in the base specification with a stock policy. Hence, removing the flexibility to time the reduction of GHG emissions is costly although it does not improve environmental pressure in the long run.

It is not likely that policy makers will be able to predict the optimal path of emissions in the highly complex surroundings of simultaneous policies for different environmental themes, since they don't have all the information that individual polluters have. Fixing a path of emission reductions by government by implementing a system of emission permits may then lead to substantially higher economic costs than implementing a system of stock addition permits. The emission policy may lead to a somewhat higher environmental quality, as polluters have an incentive to delay their reduction efforts when timing is flexible, but this environmental difference is very small. Therefore, if policy makers have reasons for preferring an emission-oriented policy to a stock-oriented policy, for example, more certainty that the target will be met, they have to weigh these arguments against the additional economic costs of an emission policy.

7.7.4   The Alternative Recycling Scheme for Environmental Permit Revenues

The recycling scheme for revenues from the sale of environmental permits can influence the economic costs of environmental policy. In some cases, the positive economic impact of a reduction of existing distortionary taxes may be larger than the negative impact of the environmental policy, and hence the policy reform may stimulate the economy, a so-called double dividend. In the simulations with DEAN, a recycling scheme via a reduction of existing distortionary taxes instead of via a lump sum transfer indeed has a positive impact on the economy, but this effect is small.

This positive effect of the reduction of existing tax distortions on the economy is substantially smaller than the negative effect of environmental policy as reported by the base specification. Therefore, no double dividend can be reaped. This implies that there are positive economic costs associated with environmental policy, at least within the boundaries of the analysis performed here, and that policy makers can only justify these costs if the positive impact of a higher environmental quality outweighs these economic costs. This is principally a political decision that can be substantiated by detailed analysis of the benefits of emission reductions. Such an analysis is beyond the scope of this book.

Given the limited availability of technical abatement measures and other specification details of the DEAN model, the revenues from the sale of environmental permits are projected to be large. This implies that existing tax rates can be reduced substantially. In fact, in the *NEPP2030* scenario a complete greening of the tax system is envisaged from 2030 onwards. Policy makers have to be aware of the huge financial flows involved and have to implement sufficient mechanisms to accommodate these transactions.

Moreover, clear rules are needed on how to spend additional revenues that might be collected by the government.

7.7.5 The Model with Endogenous Environmental Innovation

The possibility of increasing the technical potential for emission reduction via endogenous environmental innovation can prevent excessive economic costs of environmental policy. Once the price of an emission permit exceeds some threshold value, R&D is devoted to increasing the scope for technical abatement measures. The opportunity to avoid paying for extremely expensive emission permits is especially relevant for those sectors that emit relatively greater amounts of VOCs, but have relatively low emissions for the other environmental themes. If environmental innovation is relatively costly, only environmental R&D devoted to reducing VOC emissions is cost-effective. At lower costs of environmental innovation, environmental R&D is more widespread.

A side-effect of the endogenous innovation for some environmental themes is an additional emphasis on the implementation of technical abatement measures for other environmental themes, as less economic restructuring is induced. These linkages between the different environmental themes are important for the assessment of the economic costs of environmental policy and show how important it is to address multiple environmental problems simultaneously.

The alternative specification with endogenous environmental innovation, regardless of how coarsely it is specified, contains an important reaction strategy of polluters to the stringent environmental targets. The base specification does not cover this mechanism and is less likely to become reality. Given the substantial impact of this mechanism on the outcomes of the model, even in qualitative terms, it is important that empirical models be developed that can describe this mechanism in more detail.

If policy makers want to avoid the excessive costs of Smog formation policy, they can either relax the policy targets, or stimulate research and development on technologies that can reduce VOC emissions. A less stringent policy has the obvious disadvantage that it leads to a worse environmental quality.

NOTES

1. This approach is explained in Section 4.3.2.
2. As there are no imports for Water distribution and no exports of Other goods and services, these results are absent in the figure.

3. The absence of a scale parameter for environmental knowledge in this function ensures that efficiency in the environmental innovation sector is purely determined by coefficient β_{EI}. This simplification may not be in line with empirical observations.
4. Note that this mechanism depends on a positive correlation between the emissions for the various themes.
5. Though the absolute numbers presented in Table 7.7 cannot be interpreted straightforwardly, the numbers for different years and different environmental themes can be compared.

8. Final discussion and conclusions

8.1 INTRODUCTION

In order to make good estimations of the economic impacts of environmental policy, both the direct and indirect economic effects have to be assessed. In this book, the DEAN model is presented and applied to environmental policies in The Netherlands. The model is a multi-sectoral dynamic applied general equilibrium model with special attention to the specification of pollution and abatement for several major environmental themes simultaneously.

The main methodological contribution lies in the consistent integration of a dynamic applied general equilibrium model with pollution and abatement for several environmental themes. In particular, the methodology which adds essential bottom-up information on abatement measures into a top-down framework can improve the analysis of the direct and indirect costs of environmental policy. Key information included in the model is (i) abatement costs at different levels of abatement (the abatement cost curves), (ii) the technical potential of emission reduction that can be achieved by implementing technical abatement measures and (iii) the cost components of these technical abatement measures. These cost components describe the inputs used in the abatement process and include labour costs, capital costs and energy costs. All these elements are specified in a dynamic manner, for each period specifically.

The model that is built using this methodology can contribute to an improved empirical analysis of the direct and indirect costs of simultaneous environmental policies in The Netherlands. The empirical application is essential as it demonstrates that the methodology is applicable.

Before the book comes to final conclusions, this chapter considers some important aspects of the model specification. These include the implicit assumptions on the neo-classical framework, particularly about the flexibility of markets and the dynamic behaviour of agents (the extent of forward-looking behaviour); the consequences of the assumed implementation of environmental policies via a system of tradable permits; and investigations of methodological caveats and data problems in the DEAN simulations, including the imperfect link between economic and environmental processes and the desire for improved abatement cost data. After comparing the results of the dynamic DEAN model with the comparative-static SNI-AGE model, the research questions will be recalled in order to discuss the most important methodological and policy conclusions drawn.

This chapter is organised as follows. Section 8.2 puts the analysis in perspective by considering the influence of some of the most important model assumptions, beginning with a discussion of the impact of the neo-classical framework adopted (Section 8.2.1). Next, the influence of the perfect-foresight assumption is analysed in Section 8.2.2; this discussion incorporates the conclusions drawn in Chapter 3. Then, in Section 8.2.3, the choice of the policy instrument and its implications are discussed, while Section 8.2.4 deals with the caveats that remain in methodology and data; these largely reflect the conclusions of Chapters 4 and 5. In Section 8.2.5 the analysis using the DEAN model is compared to the outcomes of the comparative-static SNI-AGE model on which DEAN is based. Section 8.3 answers the methodological research questions 1 and 2 by formulating essential recommendations for the scientific community. Similarly, Section 8.3.2 presents the recommendations for policy makers, thereby answering the empirical research questions 3-5. These two sections build on the conclusions from Chapters 6 and 7, while also taking the literature review from Chapter 2 into account. Finally, Section 8.4 concludes the discussion.

8.2   PUTTING THE ANALYSIS INTO PERSPECTIVE

8.2.1   The Neo-classical Framework

The methodology used here builds on the theory of neo-classical economics. As any theory, the neo-classical framework uses restrictive assumptions that may not be in line with reality. These include perfectly flexible markets, rational behaviour of the economic agents, substitutability between different resources, convex production and utility functions, non-satiation and the absence of adjustment costs. For a discussion of these points see Blanchard and Fischer (1989). Two elements are worth a closer look here.

Firstly, a crucial assumption in the neo-classical framework is that markets are assumed to work perfectly. This implies that all markets are in equilibrium, including the labour market. Wages and other prices are assumed to be fully flexible in order to accommodate any differences between supply and demand. Empirical analysis has shown that this may not be an unreasonable assumption when the markets exhibit excess demand for labour (wages can go up), but a reduction in wages in times of unemployment (excess supply) is much more difficult to realise. As mentioned in Section

7.5, labour market equilibrium without price rigidity implies that the DEAN model cannot be used for the analysis of the employment effects of environmental policies.

Secondly, adjustment costs are absent. A worker moving from one sector to another does not have to be retrained, machines can be sold without having to bear costs of premature write-off, and so on. This assumption is important, as the model simulations show substantial changes in economic activity for various sectors. Such reallocations can be made without any adjustment costs and can be implemented instantaneously. In reality, changes in the structure of the economy are cheaper if agents have sufficient time to adapt their behaviour. Therefore, it is recommended that policy makers impose stringent environmental targets gradually (as is done in the policy scenarios investigated in Chapters 6 and 7).

These restrictive assumptions can and have been relaxed in other studies (Blanchard and Fischer, 1989). However, an undisputed macro-economic theory encompassing all these extensions does not exist. Applying a widely used methodology with known strong and weak points has the advantage that it allows a focus on the mechanisms that are at the core of this study. Therefore, these extensions can be used in further analysis when focusing on specific elements in the environment-economy interactions, but are beyond the scope of this book.

8.2.2 The Dynamic Behaviour of the Economic Agents

In the specification of the dynamic behaviour of the agents in DEAN, a *forward-looking specification*, based on the Cass-Koopmans-Ramsey model with perfect foresight, is used as the basis. The forward-looking specification is chosen since it best reflects the optimising behaviour of consumers. The perfect foresight assumption is perhaps debatable from an empirical viewpoint, but it seems unlikely that none of the agents takes a long-term perspective towards decisions.[1] The endogenous savings rate is an important advantage of this specification over the Solow-Swan based recursive-dynamic specification as it allows for the specification of a more flexible and realistic transition path towards the new equilibrium.

Chapter 3 compares the forward-looking specification with two alternatives, a comparative-static and a recursive-dynamic specification, in a simplified setting. The *comparative-static specification* has the major disadvantage that it cannot show the transition path towards the new equilibrium, as individual periods are not specified. This specification is, however, useful to illustrate that the economic costs of environmental policy increase more than proportionately with the increasing strictness of environmental policy. Moreover, the direction and order of magnitude are for most macro-economic variables in line with the long-term results for the forward-looking specification. The comparative-static specification neither covers the labour-augmenting technological progress that governs economic growth over time, nor the autonomous pollution efficiency improvements that imply lower growth rates for emissions than for economic activity. Consequently, this specification overestimates the total economic costs of environmental policy as compared to the dynamic analysis. The analysis for the comparative-static specification does not show any qualitative results that are opposite to the results from the forward-looking specification, though this conclusion may depend on the simplicity of the model.

The second alternative, the *recursive-dynamic specification*, does provide a transition path towards the new equilibrium, but this is based on a naïve assumption about consumer behaviour. The recursive-dynamic specification does not show the reduced savings induced by the stricter environmental policy, due to a lack of foresight about the future state of the economy and environment (the information conveyed in future prices), combined with the assumption of a fixed savings share. The consequence of this naïve assumption is that the recursive-dynamic specification does not cover the intertemporal shift in consumption and hence leads to substantially different results for both the short and long run; the middle to long-run results are similar, though. In the long run, the recursive-dynamic specification underestimates reductions in GDP caused by the environmental policy, as the economy is on a higher growth path than is optimal for domestic consumers.

The alternative specifications of the dynamic behaviour of the agents also have an impact on the sectoral composition of the economy. In the forward-looking specification, the reduced savings and investments lead to a reduced demand for goods from the industrial sector, the largest supplier of investment goods. Therefore, the alternative specifications underestimate the production loss in industry, and consequently overestimate pollution in industry. In the 3-sector setting, this means that more pollution has to be abated in agriculture, which puts a downward pressure on agricultural production.

Each model specification has its own merits. The strength of the comparative-static specification is its simplicity and transparency. Some readers may regard the recursive-dynamic specification as the most realistic specification, as it does not assume perfect foresight. The forward-looking specification has the advantage that the savings decision is based on consumer optimisation. For the research questions dealt with in this book, a long-term view, and therefore the forward-looking specification, seems to be most appropriate.

8.2.3   The Choice of the Policy Instrument

Tradable permits are chosen in this book as the instrument to implement policy targets. This instrument has two major strong points from a theoretical perspective (see Perman et al., 2003, for a discussion on environmental policy instruments):

(i)   tradable permits are cost-effective;
(ii)   tradable permits are effective.

The criterion of *cost-effectiveness* is important in economic analysis, since it ensures that policy targets are reached at minimum cost. Policy instruments that lack the criterion of cost-effectiveness lead to higher costs, while attaining the same environmental targets, and therefore induce additional, excessive costs. For example, command-and-control instruments such as absolute or relative standards, commonly used in environmental policy in the past decades, are highly unlikely to achieve a cost-effective outcome, since abatement efforts are not optimally distributed over the polluters. Some polluters will be burdened by high abatement costs, while other sectors leave relatively cheap abatement options unused. From a societal point of view, this implies excessive costs, which can be avoided by choosing a cost-effective policy instrument. Implementing a cost-effective instrument means that only the economic costs of the policy targets are assessed in the model and not any additional costs associated with the choice of the policy instrument. This provides the appropriate reference point for policy makers. If policy makers decide to use a different mix of policy instruments, they have to offset the advantages of this mix with the excess costs involved.

It should be noted that cost-effectiveness is not guaranteed in the DEAN model, as the permits interact with existing distortionary taxes, that is, the analysis is carried out in a second-best setting (Atkinson and Stiglitz, 1980). The influence of existing distortionary taxes on market-based environmental policies is analysed in detail in, for instance, Bovenberg and de Mooij (1994), Bovenberg and Goulder (1996), Ligthart and van der Ploeg (1999), de Mooij (1999) and Babiker et al. (2003). The tax rates used in DEAN, as described in Chapter 5, are not very discriminatory: the use of capital and labour by production sectors is taxed, and there is a uniform tax on consumption.[2] Consequently, the distortionary effect of these taxes in the model simulations is likely to be limited. The relatively low sensitivity of the model to the way in which the environmental permit revenues are recycled (compare Section 7.5) confirms this.

The *effectiveness* or dependability of a policy instrument describes to what extent the government can be sure that a certain environmental quality is achieved. Emission taxes, for instance, are less effective than tradable permits as the amount of emission reduction is left to the polluters to decide. With tradable permits, the government directly controls total emission reduction by adjusting the amount of permits it auctions.

Related to these two strong points, tradable permits have the advantage over command-and-control instruments that the regulator (the government) does not require detailed information on the abatement costs of all polluters. The government only determines the total pollution that is allowed, leaving the distribution of abatement efforts to the market.

Furthermore, the concept of tradable permits fits with the general equilibrium approach: the permits essentially comprise another market that has to be in equilibrium and for which an equilibrium price has to be found, in interaction with other markets.

Clearly, there are also drawbacks to tradable permits. For instance, setting up a permit market for large groups of heterogeneous polluters may be practically impossible or prohibitively expensive due to the monitoring and control costs involved. Secondly, auctioning the permits may influence the distribution of income and wealth between polluters in a direction that is judged as unfair. Thirdly, the policy maker cannot control the location of the emissions. Therefore, so-called pollution havens, where emissions are concentrated, may arise in undesirable places.

The analysis abstracts from transaction costs. This implies that the working of the tradable permit market is frictionless and polluters can buy and sell permits without transaction costs. This assumption fits with the assumption of perfect foresight. Since polluters have foresight over future prices, policy targets and so on, they can decide *ex ante* exactly how many permits to buy to match their *ex post* pollution level. Therefore, there is no need for trading of permits between the polluters.

The choice of tradable pollution permits in the DEAN model does not imply a policy recommendation. This instrument is chosen because it provides the best reference point and because it fits naturally with the general equilibrium framework. Policy makers need to assess the full consequences of the implications of the different instruments, including their cost-effectiveness, effectiveness, practical implementability and the transaction costs involved when they decide upon the mix of policy instruments used to enforce the policy targets. Jensen and Rasmussen (2000) analyse different ways to allocate tradable emission permits and their impact on the economy. A comparison of policy instruments is beyond the scope of this book; for an introduction see Jung et al. (1996) and Parry and Williams (1999).

Using a different mix of policy instruments, and considering transaction costs, implies that the economic costs of environmental policy in reality are most likely larger than assessed in this book. These additional costs are, however, not proportional with the strictness of the policy target, as there are fixed costs involved in setting up a system. Using different policy instruments also has consequences for the sectoral structure of the economy. If the government decides to restrict pollution for specific sectors, it may induce or prohibit changes in sectoral composition of the economy and thereby prevent a cost-effective outcome.

8.2.4 Caveats in Methodology and Data

Several improvements can be made to the methodology used in the DEAN model. Firstly, the endogenous specification of technological change is important not only for the estimation of future abatement costs, but also for the direction of technological progress. It is likely that stricter environmental policy will induce a shift in the direction of technological progress towards environment-saving technologies, that is, the invention of new technical abatement measures. This may lead to a partial crowding-out of investments in labour-saving technologies, with negative impacts on the economy. The alternative specification of DEAN with endogenous innovation in abatement technology suggests that the inclusion of endogenous technological change can significantly influence the model results. Given the increasing literature in this field (see Löschel, 2002), this is a promising field of further study.

Secondly, the absence of uncertainty in the model will affect the optimal path of emission reductions. Agents behave differently in risky situations; uncertainty about future costs and benefits from pollution control, including uncertainty about model parameters, affects the behaviour of the economic agents, has implications for environmental policymaking (for example, using a precautionary principle will lead to relatively stringent policy targets) and influences the model results. The impacts of the various uncertainties and attitudes to risk with all their interactions are too complex to enable a judgement a priori as to how robust the model results are. The effort needed to incorporate risk and uncertainty in complex models such as DEAN is, however, very large.

A third methodological improvement concerns the specification of pollution. Emissions should be linked to specific inputs in the production and utility functions instead of to output, to account for the indirect effects of changes in demand for these specific inputs. The methodology used in DEAN captures the *direct* cost aspects of the changes in inputs, but not the *indirect* effects of the reduced demand on other markets. As discussed in Chapter 2, such a link may be conceivable for energy-related emissions, but for other pollutants, the polluting processes cannot be directly coupled to specific inputs. This may be ameliorated by defining the economic sectors in the model in terms of homogeneous processes, based on a detailed accounting matrix. Such an accounting matrix does not exist yet and requires a high level of disaggregation.

Next, improvements can be made to the methodology to include abatement costs in the model. The most important ones are the proper modelling of interactions between measures, and the use of economic scenarios behind the cost estimates of the measures. A proper modelling of interactions between measures should include the effects that some abatement measures have on emissions of pollutants for another environmental theme. The current methodology identifies the total potential for emission reduction correctly, but overestimates the costs involved, because some direct abatement costs are double counted. Further analysis is needed to capture all interactions consistently; this can build on Brink et al. (2001). The fact that the cost estimates of abatement measures depend on some economic scenario is unavoidable, as these costs are future costs that cannot be observed but have to be estimated.

There are also caveats with respect to the data. Unfortunately, the DEAN model cannot deal with all available data. For example, the benchmark projection describes a balanced growth path in which all economic sectors grow at the same pace, which denies the differences in sectoral growth rates observed in reality. Furthermore, a further disaggregation of the available data, be it economic or environmental, would increase the accuracy of the numerical results.

Important environmental themes that are not captured in DEAN include dispersion of pollutants (for example, heavy metals) to water and soil, land use and space requirements, waste disposal and biodiversity. There are several reasons why these themes are not included in the analysis, including missing policy targets, missing emission data, missing abatement (cost) data or a missing methodology to properly specify the environmental theme in a multi-sectoral economic model.

Another important caveat is the lack of a feedback mechanism from the environment to the economy. The benefits of environmental policy in the form of lower environmental damages or a higher amenity value of environmental quality are not taken into account. This means that no evaluation can be made as to whether the costs of environmental policy are justified. The optimal level of environmental policy cannot be assessed. Rather, the analysis has to be confined to the cost-effectiveness of an exogenously given policy level. The main reason why these feedbacks are not included in DEAN is the lack of data on the benefits of environmental policy for all themes except Climate change.

As the policy target has to be specified exogenously, a full path of emission targets for each period has to be specified. The data for these are lacking, as environmental policy plans only provide emission targets for certain target years. This issue can be resolved in two ways. Firstly, environmental policy makers may provide better intermediate targets than currently used in the model. Secondly, the emission path may be made endogenous, analogous to the modelling of the environmental theme Climate change. This alternative has the advantage that the optimal timing of emissions can be calculated for stock pollutants, but has the disadvantage that it is not applicable to flow pollutants.

The last, but certainly not least important caveat in the model concerns the data used to specify the abatement cost curves. The sectoral basis for these curves is insufficient to specify them for each sector individually. Moreover, the manner in which inventories of technical abatement measures are currently compiled leaves room for improvement. For example, hardly any attention is given to specification of technical abatement measures that go beyond current policy targets, or that entail a radical break with the existing economic structure. Clearly, improved estimates of abatement costs and the technical potential for emission reduction will improve the quality of the model simulations.

8.2.5   The Relation with the SNI-AGE Model Revisited

As discussed in Chapter 1, the DEAN model is based on previous research and especially on the comparative-static AGE-SNI model (Gerlagh et al., 2002). There are several reasons why the models produce different results. These differences are visible in the assessment of the economic costs: the SNI-AGE model depicts a reduction in national income of roughly 50 per cent, depending on the variant chosen, while national income losses in the base specification of the DEAN model are restricted to around 10 per cent.

The relative importance of the various environmental themes is different in both models. In line with the differences in environmental targets (see below), the theme Climate change is more important in SNI-AGE, while the theme Smog formation is a bigger problem in DEAN. Both models show that in practice one environmental theme is likely to be dominant and the targets for the other themes can be reached at relatively low costs, given the economic restructuring of the economy that is needed to achieve the target for the dominant theme.

The first reason for differences in model results is that the outcomes crucially depend on the environmental targets imposed. The empirical results for both models cannot be directly compared as DEAN entails actual policy targets while SNI-AGE incorporates sustainability standards. For most environmental themes, the policy targets used in DEAN are actually stricter than the sustainability standards used in SNI-AGE. For instance, the policy target for the theme Smog formation as used in the DEAN model entails a reduction of 85 per cent in 2030, compared to 1990 emission levels, while the Smog formation sustainability standard equals less than 50 per cent reduction compared to 1990. The notable exception is the theme Climate change, where the sustainability standard (-79 per cent) is stricter than the actual policy target for 2030 (-50 per cent). The working of these environmental targets is also different, as DEAN is a dynamic model with a transition path towards the targets, while AGE-SNI is a comparative-static model where the jump towards the new level of pollution is instantaneous. In DEAN, agents have several decades to adjust to the increasingly strict environmental policy, and have time to change their behaviour.

A second reason for differences in results is that government income is independent of the scenario in DEAN, while in SNI-AGE government income varies with changes in the income of private households. Thirdly, the inputs in the abatement sector differ between the models; for instance, capital forms an important input for the abatement sector in DEAN (40 per cent in the benchmark), while the abatement sector in the SNI-AGE model uses no capital at all.

Fourthly, there are autonomous pollution efficiency improvements in DEAN that for all environmental themes except Climate change lead to a decrease of emissions over time in the benchmark. This implies that for these environmental themes, the relative strictness of the policy target decreases. Fifthly, DEAN is calibrated to represent a steady state in the benchmark, which involves adjusting consumption and investment levels.

Finally, there are some differences that are likely to only have a minor impact on the results. These include the two additional environmental themes included in the SNI-AGE model (depletion of the ozone layer and dispersion of heavy metals to water) and the specification that public abatement expenditures are regarded as economic activity in the DEAN model, and thus contribute to national income, while in the SNI-AGE model public abatement expenditures are excluded from national income.[3]

To enable further comparison, additional simulations of the DEAN model were carried out in which specific differences between both models are removed.[4] The specification with climate change as a flow pollutant (see Section 7.4) is used as the basis for this decomposition analysis. This model version has a long run loss in national income of 11 per cent.

Firstly, the policy targets for 2030 are set in the DEAN model to the sustainability standards used in SNI-AGE. The economic structure of the economy is substantially different when using the alternative targets; Agriculture and the transport sectors are much more severely affected, while industrial sectors such as the Printing, Machine and Electromechanical industries are less negatively affected. The reduction in Net National Income in this alternative specification of DEAN (rising steadily to 26 per cent at the end of the twenty-first century) is still much smaller than in the SNI-AGE model, confirming that the differences in outcomes between the models cannot be fully attributed to the differences in targets.

Secondly, the model was adapted to incorporate the SNI-AGE assumption on the development of government income, in combination with the alternative policy targets. This simulation leads to a reduction in national income of almost 30 per cent at the end of the twenty-first century and even more pronounced changes in the structure of the economy. A third step in this decomposition analysis consists of changing the production inputs of the abatement sector (the so-called spending effects). This step turns out to have a substantial impact on national income: in the long run, national income decreases by more than 40 per cent. Reducing the autonomous pollution efficiency improvements in the revised DEAN model to 1.5 per cent per annum[5] as a fourth step leads to a long-run national income level that is almost 42 per cent below the benchmark. The results of the additional simulations are summarised in Table 8.1.

Table 8.1   Effects of model assumptions on long-run national income losses in the NEPP2030 *scenario (percentage change compared to the benchmark)*

(a):	DEAN; GHGs as flow pollutants	-11
(b):	(a) + changed targets	-26
(c):	(b) + changed government income condition	-30
(d):	(c) + changed spending effects	-40
(e):	(d) + changed autonomous pollution efficiency improvements	-42

The remaining difference in national income between the revised DEAN and SNI-AGE model can be attributed to other differences between the models, including the speed of implementation of the policy and the calibration of DEAN to a steady state (see above). Note that the importance of the various differences between the models cannot be directly inferred from the analysis above. If the additional simulations were carried out in a different order, their impact on the long-run level of national income may be different.

These simulations reveal that under these alternative assumptions, that is, revision (e), Climate change is indeed the dominant environmental theme, with a permit price in 2030 of almost 2500 euros per ton CO_2-equivalents (23 euros/ton in the base specification of DEAN and around 1500 euros/ton in the SNI-AGE model). These permit prices may seem unrealistically high, but one should bear in mind that the policy target requires a reduction of emissions of almost 80 per cent compared to the benchmark, much more than analysed in most other studies. For example, Metz et al. (2001) report GDP losses for OECD Europe between 0.3 and 2.1 per cent for compliance with the Kyoto Protocol, and an associated carbon tax of 20-1000 US$/tC (roughly 5-300 euros/ton CO_2-equivalents). The high permit prices indicate the large economic impact of the strict target for Climate change.

It should be noted that AGE models such as DEAN are not very suitable to carry out such drastic policies. For example, the assumption of a constant elasticity of substitution may not hold when the policy impulse is so large. Moreover, the assumption of exogenous technological progress is crucial and unrealistic when permit prices rise to extreme levels.

Despite these differences between the working of the models, there are also some similarities in the results. Firstly, both models show that as environmental targets become increasingly strict, the economic costs increase more than proportionately. This is most easily seen in the comparative-static model as reported in Chapter 3. Secondly, the government revenues from the sale of the environmental permits can be huge. Both the SNI-AGE model and the specification of DEAN with revenue recycling via reduction of existing taxes show that a complete greening of the tax system is possible. Thirdly, the changes in production volume differ substantially between the various sectors. Most industrial sectors observe severe production losses, while the services sectors have much smaller losses or can even increase production. The sectoral differences are to a large extent related to the relative strictness of the different environmental themes: different environmental policies induce different changes in sectoral activity.

In conclusion, there are similarities between the model simulations with DEAN and the SNI-AGE analyses, including the huge value of the environmental permits and widely varying sectoral impacts. There are, however, also some striking differences between the studies, particularly in the impact on national income and the dominant environmental theme. These can be largely attributed to differences in assumptions underlying the models.

8.3   CONCLUSIONS AND RECOMMENDATIONS

8.3.1   Methodology Conclusions

This book shows how empirical information on technical abatement measures can be used in evaluating the long-term economic costs of multi-pollutant environmental policy. The multi-sectoral dynamic applied general equilibrium model DEAN is presented, with special attention to pollution and abatement. In this way, detailed empirical data is used to estimate the direct and indirect costs of environmental policy. This section deals with the answers to the methodological research questions formulated in Chapter 1:

1. How can the main bottom-up information on abatement options be integrated into a top-down dynamic applied general equilibrium model?
2. How can policies for various environmental problems be simultaneously analysed in a dynamic applied general equilibrium model?

The essential bottom-up elements of the technical abatement options can be represented in the economic model by specifying a separate 'abatement production sector' (research question 1). Firstly, for each environmental problem, the emission reductions and associated costs of all measures (both process-integrated as well as end-of-pipe) are summarised in abatement cost curves. Secondly, a CES function is estimated to best fit the abatement cost curve, again for each environmental problem separately. These CES functions state that different combinations of emissions and abatement can deliver the same 'environmental services', that is, they allow the same level of economic activity. The elasticity for this CES function, labelled the 'PAS elasticity', describes for each environmental problem the possibilities for substituting between pollution and abatement and reflects marginal abatement costs.

Technical abatement measures can only reduce emissions to a limited extent. The abatement cost curves can be used to calculate this technical potential for emission reduction. For all environmental problems analysed here, the technical potential for abatement via technical measures is well below actual and projected emission levels. This feature is captured in DEAN by distinguishing between 'technically abatable emissions' and 'technically unabatable emissions'. The latter can only be reduced by changing the volume of economic activity, that is, production or consumption quantities. The technically abatable emissions are combined with the output of the abatement production sector, using the PAS elasticity to describe the substitution possibilities. This combination, 'environmental services', is connected to the output of production sectors or consumption of households. The inputs in the production function for the abatement production sector reflect the cost components of the technical measures (including labour, energy and capital costs).

The abatement cost curves do not include the possibilities for reducing emissions via changes in the volume of economic activity, that is, economic restructuring. These are fully covered by the multi-sectoral top-down model. The general equilibrium framework ensures that emission reductions will be realised where they are cheapest. Therefore, the environmental policy targets are reached at least cost, and the optimal mixture of emission reductions via technical abatement measures and via economic restructuring is determined endogenously in the model.

By aggregating different pollutants into environmental themes, the interactions between these related pollutants are properly taken into account (research question 2). This also simplifies the construction of abatement cost functions as these can be constructed at the level of environmental themes instead of at the level of individual pollutants. The methodology to cover all interactions between the different environmental themes, for instance in technical abatement measures, still needs further research.

For environmental themes consisting of stock pollutants, such as greenhouse gases, the policy target can be specified for the addition to the stock, thus leaving the path of emissions flexible. For flow-pollutants, a full path of emission targets is imposed. Analysing several environmental problems simultaneously is highly important from an empirical point of view, even if the research question is not new from a methodological viewpoint. The relevance of the simultaneous analysis lies not only in the environmental interactions between the pollutants, but also in their economic interactions. The optimal mix of technical measures and economic restructuring as the source of emission reductions for a certain environmental theme is affected by the strictness of all environmental policy targets.

The dynamic approach has proven to be essential. Many of the relevant economic and environmental aspects have a dynamic character. These include capital accumulation and efficiency improvements in production, emissions and abatement; moreover, a dynamic approach is necessary to model stock pollutants properly. The influence of the dynamic features can be assessed by comparing the comparative-static, recursive-dynamic and forward-looking specifications. The differences between the results for DEAN and the comparable but static SNI-AGE model also show how important the dynamic specification can be in qualitative terms.

8.3.2   Policy Conclusions

Apart from methodological conclusions and recommendations, the analysis in this book is also used to answer the empirical research questions (see Chapter 1):

3. What are the impacts of currently proposed environmental policies in The Netherlands on economic growth, sectoral structure, international trade, pollution and abatement in the twenty-first century?
4. What is the optimal mix of technical abatement measures and economic restructuring that achieves the policy targets at least cost?

5. How do the economic impacts of environmental policy in The Netherlands depend on the timing of the policy?

The simulations with the DEAN model can answer these research questions, within the boundaries of the analysis as discussed in Section 8.2. Implementation of the policy targets as laid down in the fourth National Environmental Policy Plan (NEPP4) for The Netherlands (VROM, 2001) leads to a temporary slowdown of the economy. During the transition phase towards the new equilibrium, costly adjustments have to be made to the domestic economy to ensure compliance with the long-term policy targets. This transition phase lasts several decades, but in the second half of the twenty-first century, the original growth rate is restored and a lasting decoupling of economic growth and environmental pressure is established. The level of economic activity is smaller than without the policy: long-run GDP levels are roughly 10 per cent below the benchmark projection.[6]

The strict environmental policy targets can only be reached if domestic producers switch from producing relatively 'dirty' products to cleaner goods and services. These changes in the sectoral structure of the economy are substantial and production losses in some sectors are large; these include the energy supply sectors and heavy industry. There are, however, also relatively clean services sectors that can benefit from the new environmental policy. The impact on consumption patterns depends crucially on the assumption with respect to environmental policy in other countries: if dirty goods can be imported and clean goods exported, then changes in consumption patterns are limited. If the environmental policy is internationally co-ordinated, consumption patterns are also forced to become more environmentally friendly.

The Netherlands currently specialises in producing and exporting industrial products that require high emissions. Consequently, the effect of stringent environmental policy is that the international competitive position of these sectors is severely affected. This leads to sharp reductions in exports of industrial goods. To keep the trade balance unchanged (the assumption in the base specification), the domestic currency is depreciated. This provides new opportunities for exporting relatively clean services. When the trading partners also adopt stringent environmental policy targets (that is, an internationally co-ordinated policy), such changes in the specialisation of the domestic economy are no longer possible.

The environmental policy targets lead to long-run emission levels that are more than 50 per cent below the benchmark projection. Thus, environmental quality increases substantially. Smog formation appears to be the dominant environmental theme, as the options to reduce the VOC emissions that contribute critically to smog formation are limited. Tradable permit prices for

VOC emissions become very expensive if there is no innovation in new VOC-reducing technical abatement measures. For Climate change, it is optimal to time emission reductions to coincide with emission reductions for the other themes, with some additional emphasis on emission reductions in the later decades. Long-run costs of Climate change policy are estimated to be slightly less than 1.5 per cent of GDP, in line with other studies.

Concerning research question 4, the answer is that both parts are essential. In the base specification of the DEAN model, the share of technical abatement measures is between 35 and 60 per cent for all themes. For some environmental themes, including Smog formation, this implies that the technical options are exhausted and economic restructuring is necessary to meet the policy target. For other themes, such as Eutrophication, the most expensive technical options are more costly than changes in the volume of economic activity. Therefore, the optimal mix is to implement only the cheapest technical measures and complement this with economic restructuring. Note that this economic restructuring is partially induced by stringent policy targets for other environmental themes, with emission reductions for other environmental themes as a side effect. The share of economic restructuring in total emission reductions is related to the stringency of the policy targets: for less stringent targets, the share of economic restructuring declines.

The timing of environmental policy (research question 5) is important for the producers and consumers to make their decisions. This is especially the case for stock pollutants, where the timing of emissions has a long-term influence on environmental quality. This in turn has consequences for the decisions concerning the adoption of technical measures or changes in economic activity to meet the policy targets for other environmental problems. Perhaps even more importantly, consumers will anticipate on stringent future environmental policy by switching in the short run from savings to consumption. This has a positive impact on current utility and slows economic growth. Lower economic growth leads to lower emissions in the future, and hence less effort has to be put into future abatement. Since marginal abatement costs increase with increasing strictness of the policy target, the least-cost combination of a slowdown of economic growth, technical measures and economic restructuring is thus realised.

8.3.3 Recommendations

The relatively simple prototype model specifications presented in Chapter 3 already show many of the important mechanisms that play a role in the DEAN model. These include a sharp increase in abatement expenditures as a direct effect of environmental policy, combined with some economic restructuring, mainly from agriculture and industry to the relatively clean services. Most available technical abatement measures are implemented, but not all, as the costs of economic restructuring are high, but still lower than the costs of the most expensive measures. Nonetheless, the detailed specification of DEAN as used in Chapters 6 and 7 is needed to draw empirical conclusions and policy recommendations.

The first recommendation is that policy makers should pay more attention to the economic opportunities induced by a stringent environmental policy. Analysis of environmental policy mostly focuses on the economic threats of these policies, that is, on sectors that are affected by the policy. The opportunities that environmental policy creates for other production sectors, including the abatement sector and potentially also some services sectors, are often ignored. The implementation of environmental policy boils down to a reallocation of resources in the economy, not just a shrinking of economic activity. Consequently, the macro-economic impact of stringent environmental policies is relatively modest, though certainly not negligible, and the growth rate of the economy is only temporarily affected. According to calculations with the DEAN model, the costs of environmental policies (excluding the costs of waste management) will rise to slightly more than 10 per cent of GDP. Currently, environmental costs amount to roughly 2 per cent of GDP (RIVM, 2002a). Note that this and the other policy recommendations are only valid given the qualifications discussed above, including the implementation of environmental policy in a cost-effective manner and without transaction costs.

Secondly, changes in sectoral structure of the economy (economic restructuring) are as important for reaching the environmental policy targets at minimum costs as the implementation of technical abatement measures. Both sources of emission reductions are vital in terms of their contribution to achieving the policy targets as well as in terms of the associated costs. More stringent environmental policies imply more emphasis on economic restructuring as a means to achieve the targets. If policy makers impose restrictions on the changes in sectoral structure, for example, by providing additional support to specific sectors or exempting some economic activities from the policy, they have to realise that the macro-economic costs of the policy will increase substantially and/or that the policy target may not be reached.

Thirdly, strict long-term environmental policy may lead to an *increase* in consumption in the short run. This increase is caused by an intertemporal shift in consumption. In the short run, private households consume more and save less. This slows down economic growth and contributes to reducing environmental pressure in the long run. This is beneficial for the current generation, while it has a mixed effect on future generations: less economic welfare, but better environmental quality.

Fourthly, there are advantages (opportunities) as well as disadvantages (threats) to an internationally co-ordinated environmental policy. Polluters and their interest groups mostly stress the severe loss in competitive position of domestic producers in case of unilateral environmental policy. According to the calculations with DEAN, however, the domestic economic costs of environmental targets, based on internationally co-ordinated environmental policy, are substantially higher than the costs of a unilateral policy. The main reason for this is that a multilateral policy prevents a specialisation of the domestic economy in environmentally friendly production processes. Currently, The Netherlands specialises to some extent in producing emission-intensive ('dirty') products; in case of a unilateral environmental policy, this will change to a specialisation in cleaner production processes. While internationally co-ordinated policies are necessary to reduce environmental damages caused by transboundary pollutants, for local and regional pollutants a unilateral policy can be used to improve domestic environmental quality. The environmental impact at the new location of the dirty producer depends on the local characteristics and may be harmful, but not necessarily. Hence, less strict foreign environmental policy concerning local and regional pollutants may, from a narrow perspective, be in the interest of domestic consumers, as it implies that dirty goods can be imported at relatively low prices.

Fifthly, the simultaneous analysis of environmental policy for several environmental themes leads to a lower estimate of the economic costs involved, because of the many interactions between the different themes. These interactions are both environmental and economic. The correlation between the emission intensities for the different themes are almost all positive; the biggest correlation is between Acidification and Dispersion of fine dust. Hence, the economic restructuring that is induced by one environmental theme has important consequences for emission patterns for other environmental themes. The cost-effective outcome is to co-ordinate the timing of the different environmental policies. It is therefore recommended that policy makers keep these interactions in mind when interpreting the numerical outcomes of sector- or theme-specific studies.

Sixth, according to the simulations with the DEAN model Smog formation will become the dominant environmental theme in the coming decades, mainly due to a lack of technical abatement options to reduce VOC emissions, which critically contribute to the process. An alternative specification of DEAN shows that environmental innovation, that is, the availability of new technical abatement measures, can prevent the high costs of environmental policy. It is therefore of utmost importance that the government does not hamper research and development on technologies that can reduce VOC emissions. If new technological options for the theme Smog formation are not invented, the costs of this part of environmental policy may be so high, and specific sectors may be so severely affected, that policy makers will have to adjust the policy target under pressure from threatened groups of polluters.

Seventh, clear rules are necessary on the redistribution of the potentially huge revenues of pollution permits. Reducing existing taxes can play a major role, but might not be sufficient: a complete greening of the tax system is envisaged in the DEAN model. Policy makers will have to be aware of the huge financial flows involved and implement adequate mechanisms to accommodate these transactions.

Eighth, the government can choose to implement policy for the theme Climate change in the form of annual greenhouse gas (GHG) emission targets, but policy makers should realise that this implies substantially higher costs than a more flexible system where only the stock of greenhouse gases is controlled. There is a trade-off between enforcing emission reductions to make sure that polluters take timely action to reduce emissions, thereby accepting high economic costs, and relying on polluters to implement emission reductions when these are cost-effective.

Ninth, postponing GHG emission reductions and co-ordinating these reductions with other environmental policies can significantly reduce the costs of Climate change policy, while environmental quality is hardly affected. Policy makers should not immediately panic when GHG emission reductions are smaller than the intermediate targets. The cost-effective path of GHG emission reductions incorporates low emission reductions in the first few decades. This does not imply inaction on behalf of the government. There are important time lags, especially in the build-up of capital; and slow adaptation to a less carbon-intensive economy can lower costs.

Tenth, though the DEAN model cannot calculate the optimal timing of environmental policy, the model simulations show that delaying the policy targets will lead to a slower adjustment path towards a more environmentally friendly economy and lower economic costs, but at the expense of temporarily higher emissions and hence lower environmental quality. It is up to politicians to make the trade-off between economic costs and environmental quality as this involves an implicit valuation of the benefits of an increased environmental quality. Unfortunately, empirical research that estimates these benefits is not readily available, except perhaps for Climate change.

8.4   FINAL REMARKS

This book contributes to the understanding of the dynamic feedback mechanisms between environmental activity and abatement in the context of multi-pollutant environmental policy. The consistent integration of essential bottom-up information on abatement measures in a top-down framework has been shown to be both implementable and applicable. In this way, a better assessment can be made of both the direct and indirect economic effects of environmental policy for several major environmental themes. The empirical application to The Netherlands shows that if environmental policies can be implemented simultaneously and in a cost-effective manner, the economic costs of these policies can be limited via a mixture of adoption of technical abatement measures, economic restructuring and a temporary slowdown of economic growth.

Several caveats remain with respect to methodology and data. These hopefully provide a stimulus for further research in this field, as an improved comprehension of the interactions between economic growth, sectoral structure, pollution and abatement can lead to better environmental policies. It is evident that such improved understanding is essential; there are significant direct and indirect economic costs of environmental policies, which undoubtedly await us in the coming decades, as illustrated here.

NOTES

1. Though the perfect foresight assumption is an extreme case of forward-looking behaviour.
2. Note that in reality the tax system is much more complex and contains several exemption and other discriminatory elements that make the taxes more distorting.
3. Hueting claims that these so-called defensive expenditures should not be added to national income, since they restore an environmental welfare loss that was not subtracted from national income (Gerlagh et al., 2002).
4. Available from the author upon request.
5. A model version calibrated with zero efficiency improvements in emissions could not be solved by GAMS due to numerical problems.
6. These results are in the absence of endogenous innovation of new abatement technologies. Such innovations will reduce the macro-economic costs of environmental policy and may provide a stimulus to the economy.

References

Adriaanse, A. (1993), *Environmental Policy Indicators*, The Hague: Sdu.

Aghion, P. and P. Howitt (1998), *Endogenous Growth Theory*, Cambridge, MA: MIT Press.

Aiken, D.V. and C.A. Pasurka (2002), 'Least-cost air pollution control: a CGE joint production framework', mimeo, U.S. Environmental Protection Agency, Washington.

Alcamo, J. (ed.) (1994), *IMAGE 2.0: Integrated Modeling of Global Climate Change*, Dordrecht: Kluwer.

Alcamo, J., R.W. Shaw and L. Hordijk (1990), *The RAINS Model of Acidification: Science and Strategies in Europe*, Dordrecht: Kluwer.

Anderson, D. (2001), 'Technical progress and pollution abatement: an economic view of selected technologies and practices', *Environment and Development Economics,* **6**, 283-311.

Armington, P. (1969), 'A theory of demand for products distinguished by place of production', IMF Staff Papers 16, 159-78.

Atkinson, A.B. and J.E. Stiglitz (1980), *Lectures on Public Economics*, London: McGraw-Hill.

Auerbach, A.J. and L.J. Kotlikoff (19870, *Dynamic Fiscal Policy*, Cambridge: Cambridge University Press.

Ayres, R.U. (1999), 'Materials, economics and the environment', in J.C.J.M. van den Bergh (ed.), *Handbook of Environmental and Resource Economics*, Cheltenham, UK and Northampton, USA: Edward Elgar, pp. 867-94.

Babiker, M.H., G.E. Metcalf and J.M. Reilly (2003), 'Tax distortions and global climate policy', *Journal of Environmental Economics and Management*, **46**, 269-87.

Babiker, M.H., J.M. Reilly, M. Mayer, R.S. Eckaus, I.S. Wing and R.C. Hyman (2001), 'The MIT emissions prediction and policy analysis (EPPA) model: revisions, sensitivities and comparison of results', Joint program on the science and policy of global change report 71, MIT, Cambridge.

Ballard, C.L. and L.H. Goulder (1985), 'Consumption taxes, foresight, and welfare: a computable general equilibrium analysis', in J. Piggott and J.

Whalley (eds), *New Developments in Applied Equilibrium Analysis*, Cambridge: Cambridge University Press, pp. 253-82.

Barker, T., S. Baylis and P. Madsen (1993), 'A UK carbon/energy tax: the macroeconomic effects', *Energy Policy*, **21**, 296-308.

Barro, R.J. and X. Sala-i-Martin (1995), *Economic Growth*, New York: McGraw-Hill.

Bartelings, H., R.B. Dellink and E.C. van Ierland (2004), 'Modelling market distortions in an applied general equilibrium framework: the case of flat fee pricing in the waste market', in J.C.J.M. van den Bergh and M. Janssen (eds), *Industrial Ecology: Materials Use and Spatial Scales*, forthcoming.

Baudry, M. (2000), 'Joint management of emission abatement and technological innovation for stock externalities', *Environmental and Resource Economics*, **16**, 161-83.

Baumol, W.J. (1977), *Economic Theory and Operations Analysis*, London: Prentice Hall.

Berg, P.J.C.M. van den, G.M.M. Gelauff and V.R. Okker (1988), 'The Freia-Kompas model for The Netherlands: a quarterly macroeconomic model for the short and medium term', *Economic Modelling*, **5**, 170-236.

Bergh, J.C.J.M. van den (ed.) (1999), *Handbook of Environmental Economics*, Cheltenham, UK and Northampton, USA: Edward Elgar.

Bergman, L. (1988), 'Energy policy modeling: a survey of general equilibrium approaches', *Journal of Policy Modeling*, **10**, 377-99.

Bergman, L. (1990), 'Energy and environmental constraints on growth: a CGE modeling approach', *Journal of Policy Modeling*, **12**, 671-91.

Bergman, L. (1991), 'General equilibrium effects of environmental policy: a CGE-modeling approach', *Environmental and Resource Economics*, **1**, 43-61.

Blanchard, O.J. and S. Fischer (1989), *Lectures on Macroeconomics*, Cambridge, MA: MIT Press.

Blitzer, C.R., R.S. Eckaus, S. Lahiri and A. Meeraus (1994), 'A general equilibrium analysis of the effects of carbon emission restrictions on economic growth in a developing country: Egypt', in J. Mercenier and T.N. Srinivasan (eds), *Applied General Equilibrium and Economic Development*, Ann Arbor: University of Michigan Press, pp. 255-78.

Blok, K. (1991), 'On the reduction of carbon dioxide emissions', thesis, Utrecht University, Utrecht.

Blok, K., E. Worrell, R.A.W. Albers and R.F.A. Culenaere (1991), 'Data on energy conservation techniques for The Netherlands', Report W-90008, Utrecht University, Utrecht.

Boer, B. de (2000a), 'Assessment of sustainability standards', in H. Verbruggen, 'Final report on calculations of a sustainable national income according to Hueting's methodology', report O-00/10, Institute for Environmental Studies, Vrije Universiteit, Amsterdam.

Boer, B. de (2000b), 'The greenhouse effect', mimeo, Statistics Netherlands, Voorburg.

Boer, B. de (2002), 'Provisional accounting matrix for 2000', mimeo, Statistics Netherlands, Voorburg.

Boer, B. de and P. Bosch (1995), 'The greenhouse effect: an example of the prevention cost approach', paper prepared for the second meeting of the London group on national accounts and the environment, Washington, March 15-17.

Böhringer, C. (1998), 'The synthesis of bottom-up and top-down in energy policy modeling', *Energy Economics*, **20**, 233-48.

Böhringer, C., K. Conrad and A. Löschel (2000), 'Carbon taxes and joint implementation: an applied general equilibrium analysis for Germany and India', ZEW report, Mannheim.

Böhringer, C. and T.F. Rutherford (2002), 'Carbon abatement and international spillovers: a decomposition of general equilibrium effects', *Environmental and Resource Economics*, **22**, 391-417.

Böhringer, C., T.F. Rutherford and A. Voss (1999), 'Global CO_2 emissions and unilateral action: policy implications of induced trade effects', *International Journal of Global Energy Issues*, **11**, 18-22.

Booij, J.T. and J.W. Velthuijsen (1992), 'Economic and environmental effects of the EC proposed energy tax for The Netherlands', in F. Laroui and J.W. Velthuijsen (eds), *The Economic Consequences of an Energy Tax in Europe: An Application with HERMES*, Amsterdam: SEO.

Bosello, F., C. Carraro and M. Galeotti (2001), 'The double dividend issue: modeling strategies and empirical findings', *Environment and Development Economics*, **6**, 9-45.

Bovenberg, A.L. and L.H. Goulder (1996), 'Optimal environmental taxation in the presence of other taxes: general-equilibrium analysis', *American Economic Review*, **86**, 985-1000.

Bovenberg, A.L. and B.J. Heijdra (2002), 'Environmental abatement and intergenerational distribution', *Environmental and Resource Economics*, **23**, 45-84.

Bovenberg, A.L. and R.A. de Mooij (1994), 'Environmental levies and distortionary taxation', *American Economic Review*, **84**, 1085-89.

Brink, J.C. (2003), personal communication, Rijksinstituut voor Volksgezondheid en Milieu, Bilthoven.

Brink, C., E.C. van Ierland, L. Hordijk and C. Kroeze (2001), 'Cost-effective emission abatement in Europe considering interrelations in agriculture', *The Scientific World*, **1**.

Burniaux, J.-M., J.P. Martin, G. Nicoletti and J. Oliveira Martins (1992a), 'GREEN: a multi-sector, multi-region general equilibrium model for quantifying the costs of curbing CO_2 emissions: a technical manual', Economics Department Working Papers 116, OECD, Paris.

Burniaux, J.-M., J.P. Martin, G. Nicoletti and J. Oliveira Martins (1992b), 'The costs of reducing CO_2 emissions: evidence from GREEN', Economics Department Working Papers 115, OECD, Paris.

Butter, F.A.G. den, R.B. Dellink and M.W. Hofkes (1995), 'Energy levies and endogenous technology in an empirical simulation model for The Netherlands', in A.L. Bovenberg and S. Cnossen (eds), *Public Economics and the Environment in an Imperfect World*, Boston: Kluwer Academic Publishers, pp. 315-36.

Bye, B. (2000), 'Environmental tax reform and producer foresight: an intertemporal computable general equilibrium analysis', *Journal of Policy Modeling*, **22**, 719-52.

Capros, P., T. Georgakopoulos, A. Filippoupolitis, S. Kotsomiti, G. Atsaves, S. Proost, D. van Regemorter, K. Conrad and T.F.N. Schmidt (1998), 'The GEM-E3 model reference manual', Report, National Technical University, Athens.

Cass, D. (1965), 'Optimum growth in an aggregative model of capital accumulation', *Review of Economic Studies*, **32**, 233-40.

Chaudhuri, P. (1989), *The Economic Theory of Growth*, New York: Harvester Wheatsheaf.

Chiang, A.C. (1984), *Fundamental Methods of Mathematical Economics*, 3rd edition, London: McGraw-Hill.

Conrad, K. (1992), 'Applied general equilibrium modeling for environmental policy analysis', Discussion paper 475-92, Mannheim University, Mannheim.

Conrad, K. (1999), 'Computable general equilibrium models for environmental economics and policy analysis', in J.C.J.M. van den Bergh (ed.), *Handbook of Environmental and Resource Economics*, Cheltenham, UK and Northampton, USA: Edward Elgar, pp. 1060-88.

Conrad, K. (2001), 'Computable general equilibrium models in environmental and resource economics', Beiträge zur angewandten Wirtschaftsforschung 601-01, Institut für Volkswirtschaftslehre und Statistik, Mannheim.

Conrad, K. and M. Schröder (1991), 'Economic impact: an AGE model for a German state', *Environmental and Resource Economics*, **1**, 289-312.

Conrad, K. and M. Schröder (1993), 'Choosing environmental policy instruments using general equilibrium models', *Journal of Policy Modeling*, **15**, 521-44.

CPB/RIVM (2002), 'Economie, energie en milieu: een verkenning tot 2010', Centraal Planbureau en Rijksinstituut voor Volksgezondheid en Milieu, Den Haag/Bilthoven.

CPB (2000), 'Naar een efficiënter milieubeleid: een maatschappelijk-economische analyse van vier hardnekkige milieuproblemen', Centraal Planbureau, Den Haag.

Dellink, R.B. (2002), 'Testing the predication abilities of the DEAN model', mimeo, Wageningen University, Wageningen.

Dellink, R.B., M. Finus, E.C. van Ierland and J.C. Altamirano-Cabrera (2003), 'Empirical background paper of the STACO model', mimeo, Wageningen University, Wageningen.

Dellink, R.B., R. Gerlagh, M.W. Hofkes and L. Brander (2001), 'Calibration of an applied general equilibrium model for The Netherlands in 1990', report W01-17, Institute for Environmental Studies, Vrije Universiteit, Amsterdam.

R.B. Dellink, M.W. Hofkes, E.C. van Ierland and H. Verbruggen (2004), 'Dynamic modelling of pollution abatement in a CGE framework', *Economic Modelling*, 21, 965-89.

Dellink, R.B. and H.M.A. Jansen (1995), 'Socio-economic aspects of the greenhouse effect: applied general equilibrium model', Report 410 100 113, NRP Programme Office, Bilthoven.

Dellink, R.B. and K.F. van der Woerd (1997), 'Kosteneffectiviteit van milieuthema's', report R-97/10, Institute for Environmental Studies, Vrije Universiteit, Amsterdam.

De Nederlandsche Bank (2002), *Annual Report 2001*, Dordrecht: Kluwer.

Destais, G. (1996), 'Economic effects of environmental policies and constraints: what can we learn from computable general equilibrium models?', in S. Faucheux, D. Pearce and J. Proops (eds), *Models of Sustainable Development*, Cheltenham, UK and Northampton, USA: Edward Elgar, pp. 87-102.

Diewert, W.E. (1974), 'Applications of duality theory', in M.D. Intriligator and D.A. Kendrick (eds), *Frontiers of Quantitative Economics*, Amsterdam: North-Holland, pp. 106-206.

Dissou, Y., C. MacLeod and M. Souissi (2002), 'Compliance costs of the Kyoto Protocol and market structure in Canada: a dynamic general equilibrium analysis', *Journal of Policy Modeling*, 24, 751-79.

Ellerman, A.D. and A. Decaux (1998), 'Analysis of post-Kyoto CO_2 emissions trading using marginal abatement curves', Joint program on the science and policy of global change Report 40, MIT, Cambridge.

Elzenga, H.E., V. Herzberg, H.J.B.M. Mannaerts, M. Mulder, R. Thomas and L.G. Wesselink (2001), 'Fysieke productieontikkelingen in de industrie:

het gebruik van STREAM bij verkenningen', report 778001004, Rijksinstituut voor Volksgezondheid en Milieu, Bilthoven.

Espinosa, J.A. and V.K. Smith (1995), 'Measuring the environmental consequences of trade policy: a nonmarket CGE analysis', *American Journal of Agricultural Economics*, **77**, 772-77.

European Environmental Agency (1998), *Europe's Environment: the Second Assessment*, Copenhagen: European Environmental Agency.

Eyckmans, J., D. van Regemorter and V. van Steenberghe (2001), 'Is Kyoto fatally flawed? An analysis with MacGEM', Working Paper 2001-18, Center for Economic Studies, KU Leuven, Leuven.

Färe, R., S. Grosskopf and D. Tyteca (1996), 'An activity-analysis model of the environmental performance of firms: application to fossil-fuel-fired electric utilities', *Ecological Economics*, **18**, 161-75.

Felder, S. and R. Schleiniger (2002), 'National CO_2 policy and externalities: some general equilibrium results for Switzerland', *Energy Economics*, **24**, 509-22.

Fischer, G., Y. Ermoliev, M.A. Keyzer and C. Rosenzweig (1996), 'Simulating the socio-economic and biogeophysical driving forces of land-use and land-cover change: the IIASA land-use change model', IIASA Working Paper WP-96-010, International Institute for Applied Systems Analysis, Laxenburg.

Gerlagh, R. (1998), 'The efficient and sustainable use of environmental resource systems, thesis', Vrije Universtiteit, Amsterdam.

Gerlagh, R., R.B. Dellink, M.W. Hofkes and H. Verbruggen (2001), 'An applied general equilibrium model to calculate a Sustainable National Income for The Netherlands', Report W01-16, Institute for Environmental Studies, Vrije Universiteit, Amsterdam.

Gerlagh, R., R.B. Dellink, M.W. Hofkes and H. Verbruggen (2002), 'A measure of Sustainable National Income for The Netherlands', *Ecological Economics*, **41**, 157-74.

Gerlagh, R. and M.A. Keyzer (2001), 'Sustainability and the intergenerational distribution of natural resource entitlements', *Journal of Public Economics*, **79**, 315-41.

Gerlagh, R. and B.C.C. van der Zwaan (2003), 'Gross World Product and consumption in a global warming model with endogenous technological change', *Resource and Energy Economics*, **25**, 35-57.

Germain, M. and V. van Steenberghe (2001), 'Constraining equitable allocations of tradable greenhouse gases emission quotas by acceptability', Discussion paper 2001/5, CORE-Université Catholique de Louvain, Louvain-la-Neuve.

Ginsburgh, V. and M.A. Keyzer (1997), *The Structure of Applied General Equilibrium Models*, Cambridge, MA: MIT Press.

Goulder, L.H. (1995), 'Effects of carbon taxes in an economy with prior tax distortions: an intertemporal general equilibrium analysis', *Journal of Environmental Economics and Management*, **29**, 271-97.

Goulder, L.H. and S.H. Schneider (1999), 'Induced technological change and the attractiveness of CO_2 abatement policies', *Resource and Energy Economics*, **21**, 211-53.

Gradus, R. and J.A. Smulders (1993), 'The trade-off between environmental care and long-term growth: pollution in three prototype growth models', *Journal of Economics*, **58**, 25-51.

Groot, H.L.F. de (1998), 'Economic growth, sectoral structure and unemployment', thesis, Tilburg University, Tilburg.

Grubler, A. and S. Messner (1998), 'Technological change and the timing of mitigation measures', *Energy Economics*, **20**, 495-512.

Haan, M. de and S.J. Keuning (1996), 'Taking the environment into account: the NAMEA approach', *Review of Income and Wealth*, **42**, 131-48.

Hall, R.E. (1988), 'Intertemporal substitution in consumption', *Journal of Political Economy*, **96**, 339-57.

Hanemaaijer, A. (2000), personal communication, Rijksinstituut voor Volksgezondheid en Milieu, Bilthoven.

Harrison, G.W., S.E. Hougaard Jensen, L. Haagen Pedersen and T.F. Rutherford (eds) (2000), *Using Dynamic General Equilibrium Models for Policy Analysis*, Amsterdam: North-Holland.

Hayashi, F. (1982), 'Tobin's q, rational expectations and optimal investment rule', *Econometrica*, **50**, 213-24.

Hazilla, M. and R.J. Kopp (1990), 'Social cost of environmental quality regulations: a general equilibrium analysis', *Journal of Political Economy*, **98**, 853-73.

Hettich, F. (2000), *Economic Growth and Environmental Policy: a Theoretical Approach*, Cheltenham, UK and Northampton, USA: Edward Elgar.

Hofkes, M.W. (1996), 'Modelling sustainable development: an economy-ecology intergrated model', *Economic Modelling*, **13**, 333-53.

Hofkes, M.W. (2001), 'Environmental policies: short term versus long term effects', *Environmental and Resource Economics*, **20**, 1-26.

Hofkes, M.W., R. Gerlagh, W. Lise and H. Verbruggen (2002), 'Sustainable National Income: a trend analysis for The Netherlands for 1990-1995', report R-02/02, Institute for Environmental Studies, Vrije Universiteit, Amsterdam.

Honig, E., A.H. Hanemaaijer, R. Engelen, A. Dekkers and R. Thomas (2000), 'Techno 2000: modellering van de daling van eenheidskosten van technologieen in de tijd', RIVM report 773008003, Rijksinstituut voor Volksgezondheid en Milieu, Bilthoven.

Houghton, J.D., B.A. Callander and S.K. Varney (eds.) (1992), *The Enhanced Greenhouse Effect 1992. The Supplementary Reports to the IPCC Scientific Assessment*, Cambridge: Cambridge University Press.

Howarth, R.B. and R.B. Norgaard (1992), 'Environmental valuation under sustainable development', *American Economic Review*, **82**, 473-77.

Hueting, R. (1980), *New Scarcity and Economic Growth*, Amsterdam: North-Holland.

Hueting, R. (1996), 'Three persistent myths in the environmental debate', *Ecological Economics*, **18**, 81-8.

Hueting, R. and B. de Boer (2001), 'Environmental valuation and sustainable national income according to Hueting', in E.C. van Ierland, J. van der Straaten and H.R.J. Vollebergh (eds), *Economic Growth and Valuation of the Environment: A Debate*, Cheltenham, UK and Northampton: Edward Elgar, pp. 17-77.

Hyman, R.C., J.M. Reilly, M.H. Babiker, A. DeMasin and H.D. Jacoby (2002), 'Modeling non-CO_2 greenhouse gas abatement', Joint program on the science and policy of global change Report 94, MIT, Cambridge.

Ierland, E.C. van (1993), 'Macroeconomic analysis of environmental policy', thesis, University of Amsterdam, Amsterdam.

Ignaciuk, A., C. Kroeze and E.C. van Ierland (2002), 'Models and databases to analyze interactions between emissions of air pollutants in Europe', *World Resource Review*, **14**, 25-53.

IPCC (1996), *Revised Guidelines for National Greenhouse Gas Inventories*, Bracknell: Intergovernmental Panel on Climate Change.

Isoard, S. and A. Soria (2001), 'Technical change dynamics: evidence from the emerging renewable energy technologies', *Energy Economics*, **23**, 619-36.

Jacobsen, H.K. (1998), 'Intergrating the bottom-up and top-down approach to energy-economy modelling: the case of Denmark', *Energy Economics*, **20**, 443-61.

Jacobsen, H.K. (2001), 'Technological progress and long-term energy demand - a survey of recent approaches and a Danish case', *Energy Policy*, **29**, 147-57.

Jaffe, A.B., R.G. Newell and R.N. Stavins (2002), 'Environmental policy and technological change', *Environmental and Resource Economics*, **22**, 41-69.

Jensen, J. (2000), 'How valuable are delayed cutbacks in Danish carbon emissions?', in G.W. Harrison, S.E. Hougaard Jensen, L. Haagen Pedersen and T.F. Rutherford (eds), *Using Dynamic General Equilibrium Models for Policy Analysis*, Amsterdam: North-Holland, pp. 53-77.

Jensen, J. and T.N. Rasmussen (2000), 'Allocation of CO_2 emissions permits: a general equilibrium analysis of policy instruments', *Journal of Environmental Economics and Management*, **40**, 111-36.

Jones, C.I. (1995), 'Time series tests of endogenous growth models', *Quarterly Journal of Economics*, **110**, 495-525.

Jorgenson, D.W. and P.J. Wilcoxen (1990), 'Intertemporal general equilibrium modeling of U.S. environmental regulation', *Journal of Policy Modeling*, **12**, 715-44.

Jorgenson, D.W. and P.J. Wilcoxen (1993a), 'Reducing US carbon emissions: an econometric general equilibrium assessment', *Resource and Energy Economics*, **15**, 7-25.

Jorgenson, D.W. and P.J. Wilcoxen (1993b), 'Reducing U.S. carbon dioxide emissions: an assessment of different instruments', *Journal of Policy Modeling*, **15**, 491-520.

Jung, C., K. Krutilla and R. Boyd (1996), 'Incentives for advanced pollution abatement technology at the industry level: an evaluation of policy alternatives', *Journal of Environmental Economics and Management*, **30**, 95-111.

Kandelaars, P.P.A.A.H. (1998), 'Material-product chains: economic models and applications', thesis, Vrije Universiteit, Amsterdam.

Keller, W.J. (1980), *Tax Incidence: A General Equilibrium Approach*, Amsterdam: North-Holland.

Keuning, S.J. (1993), 'An information system for environmental indicators in relation to the national accounts', in W.F.M. de Vries, G.P. den Bakker, M.B.G. Gircour, S.J. Keuning and A. Lensen (eds), *The Value Added of National Accounting*, Statistics Netherlands, The Hague: SDU Publishers, pp. 287-305.

Klaassen, M.A.W., D. Vos, A.J. Seebregts, T. Kram, S. Kruitwagen, R.G.J. Huiberts and E.C. van Ierland (1999), 'MARKAL-IO: Linking an input-output model with MARKAL', Global Change NRP-report 410 200 015, Energie Centrum Nederland, Petten.

Komen, M.H.C. (2000), 'Agriculture and the environment: applied general equilibrium policy analyses for The Netherlands', thesis, Wageningen University, Wageningen.

Komen, M.H.C. and J.H.M. Peerlings (2001), 'Endogenous technological switches in Dutch dairy farming under environmental restrictions', *European Review of Agricultural Economics*, **28**, 117-42.

Koopmans, C. and D.W. te Velde (2001), 'Bridging the energy efficiency gap: using bottom-up information in a top-down energy demand model', *Energy Economics*, **23**, 57-75.

Koopmans, C., D.W. te Velde, W. Groot and J.A. Hendriks (1999), 'NEMO:Netherlands Energy demand MOdel: a top-down model based on bottom-up information', Research Memorandum 155, Centraal Planbureau, The Hague.

Koopmans, T.C. (1965), 'On the concept of optimal economic growth', in *The Econometric Approach to Development Planning*, Amsterdam: North-Holland.

Kooten, G.C. van and E.H. Bulte (2000), *The Economics of Nature: Managing Biological Assets*, Oxford: Blackwell.

Lau, M.I., A. Pahlke and T.F. Rutherford (2002), 'Approximating infinite-horizon models in a complementarity format: a primer in dynamic general equilibrium analysis', *Journal of Economic Dynamics and Control*, **26**, 577-609.

Leontief, W. (1970), 'Environmental repercussions and the economic structure: an input-output approach', *Review of Economics and Statistics*, **52**, 262-70.

Ligthart, J.E. and F. van der Ploeg (1999), 'Environmental policy, tax incidence and the cost of public funds', *Environmental and Resource Economics*, **13**, 187-207.

Löschel, A. (2002), 'Technological change in economic models of environmental policy: a survey', *Ecological Economics*, **43**, 105-26.

Magat, W.A. (1978), 'Pollution control and technological advance: a dynamic model of the firm', *Journal of Environmental Economics and Management*, **5**, 1-25.

Mankiw, N.G., D. Romer and D.N. Weil (1992), 'A contribution to the empirics of economic growth', *Quarterly Journal of Economics*, **107**, 407-38.

Mannaerts, H.J.B.M. (2000), 'STREAM: Substance Throughput Related to Economic Activity Model: a partial equilibrium model for material flows in the economy', Research Memorandum 165, Centraal Planbureau, Den Haag.

Manne, A.S., R. Mendelsohn and R.G. Richels (1995), 'Merge: a model for evaluating regional and global effects of GHG reduction policies', *Energy Policy*, **23**, 17-34.

Manne, A.S. and R.G. Richels (1992), *Buying Greenhouse Insurance*, Cambridge, MA: MIT Press.

Manne, A.S. and R.G. Richels (1995), 'The greenhouse debate: economic efficiency, burden sharing and hedging strategies', *Energy Journal*, **16**, 1-37.

Manne, A.S. and R.G. Richels (1999), 'The Kyoto protocol: a cost-effective strategy for meeting environmental objectives', *Energy Journal*, **20**, 1-24.

Melo, J. de and S. Robinson (1989), 'Product differentiation and the treatment of foreign trade in computable general equilibrium models of small economies', *Journal of International Economics*, **27**, 47-67.

Metz, B., O. Davidson, R. Swart and J. Pan (eds) (2001), 'Climate change 2001: Mitigation', Contribution of working group III to the Third assessment report of the Intergovernmental Panel on Climate Change, Cambridge: Cambridge University Press.

Milliman, S.R. and R. Prince (1989), 'Firm incentives to promote technological change in pollution control', *Journal of Environmental Economics and Management*, **17**, 247-65.

Mooij, R.A. de (1999), 'Environmental taxation and the double dividend', thesis, Voorburg.

Mot, E.S., P.J. van den Noord, D.D. van der Stelt-Scheele and M.A. Koning (1989), 'HERMES, The Netherlands', SEO report, University of Amsterdam, Amsterdam.

Naqvi, F. (1998), 'A computable general equilibrium model of energy, economy and equity interactions in Pakistan', *Energy Economics*, **20**, 347-73.

Nestor, D.V. and C.A. Pasurka (1995a), 'CGE model of pollution abatement processes for assessing the economic effects of environmental policy', *Economic Modelling*, **12**, 53-9.

Nestor, D.V. and C.A. Pasurka (1995b), 'Alternative specifications for environmental control costs in a general equilibrium framework', *Economics Letters*, **48**, 273-80.

Nordhaus, W.D. (1991), 'To slow or not to slow: the economics of the greenhouse effect', *The Economic Journal*, **101**, 920-37.

Nordhaus, W.D. (1994), *Managing the Global Commons*, Cambridge, MA: MIT Press.

Nordhaus, W.D. and Z. Yang (1996), 'RICE: a regional dynamic general equilibrium model of optimal climate change policy', *American Economic Review*, **86**, 741-65.

Nugent, J.B. and C.V.S.K. Sarma (2002), 'The three Es - efficiency, equity, and environmental protection - in search of "win-win-win" policies: a CGE analysis of India', *Journal of Policy Modeling*, **24**, 19-50.

Okken, P.A. (1991), 'CO_2 reduction consensus? A conceptual framework for global CO_2 reduction targets, the importance of energy technology development', report ECN-RX-91-093, Energie Centrum Nederland, Petten.

Okken, P.A., P. Lako, D. Gerbers, T. Kram and J. Ybema (1992), 'CO_2 removal in competition with other options for reducing CO_2 remissions', *Energy Conversion and Management*, **33**, 6-10.

Otto, V.M., T. Kuosmanen and E.C. van Ierland (2002), 'Does diffusion trigger new innovations: a frontier approach', paper presented at the Annual Meeting of the Institute for Operations Research and the Management Sciences, San Jose, USA.

Parry, I.W.H. and R.C. Williams III (1999), 'A second-best evaluation of eight policy instruments to reduce carbon emissions', *Resource and Energy Economics*, **21**, 347-73.

Pasurka, C.A. (2001), 'Technical change and measuring pollution abatement costs: an activity analysis framework', *Environmental and Resource Economics*, **18**, 61-85.

Peck, S.C. and T.J. Teisberg (1992), 'CETA: a model for carbon emissions trajectory assessment', *The Energy Journal*, **13**, 55-75.

Perman, R., Y. Ma, J. McGilvray and M. Common (2003), *Natural Resource and Environmental Economics*, 3rd edition, Harlow: Pearson Education.

Phaneuf, D.J. and T. Requate (2002), 'Incentives for investment in advanced pollution abatement technology in emission permit markets with banking', *Environmental and Resource Economics*, **22**, 369-90.

Phlips, L. (1974), *Applied Consumption Analysis*, Amsterdam: North-Holland.

Pigou, A. (1938), *The Economics of Welfare*, London: Macmillan.

Ramsey, F. (1928), 'A mathematical theory of saving', *Economic Journal*, **38**, 543-59.

Rasmussen, T.N. (2001), 'CO_2 abatement policy with learning-by-doing in renewable energy', *Resource and Energy Economics*, **23**, 297-325.

RIVM (2000), *Nationale Milieuverkenning 5: 2000-2030*, Rijksinstituut voor Volksgezondheid en Milieu, Bilthoven.

RIVM (2002a), *Milieubalans 2002*, Rijksinstituut voor Volksgezondheid en Milieu, Bilthoven.

RIVM (2002b), *Milieucompendium 2002*, Rijksinstituut voor Volksgezondheid en Milieu, Bilthoven.

RIZA (1996), *Watersysteem Verkenningen*, Rijksinstituut voor Integraal Zoetwaterbeheer en Afvalwaterbehandeling, Lelystad.

Robinson, S., S. Subramanian and J. Geoghegan (1994), 'Modeling air pollution abatement in a market-based incentive framework for the Los Angeles basin', in G. Klaassen and F.R. Foersund (eds), *Economic Instruments for Air Pollution Control*, Dordrecht: Kluwer Academic Publishers, pp. 46-72.

Rutherford, T.F. (2000), 'Carbon abatement, technical change and intergenerational burden sharing', in G.W. Harrison, S.E. Hougaard Jensen, L. Haagen Pedersen and T.F. Rutherford (eds), *Using Dynamic General Equilibrium Models for Policy Analysis*, Amsterdam: North-Holland, pp. 79-117.

Rutherford, T.F. (2001), 'Calibration of models with multi-year periods', mimeo, University of Colorado, Boulder.

Schmieman, E.C. (2001), 'Acidification and tropospheric ozone in Europe: towards a dynamic economic analysis', thesis, Wageningen University, Wageningen.

Schumpeter, J.A. (1934), *The Theory of Economic Development*, Oxford: Oxford University Press.

Seebregts, A.J., G.A. Goldstein and K. Smekens (2001), 'Energy/environmental modeling with the MARKAL family of models', ETSAP Report ECN Policy Studies, Petten.

Shoven, J.B. and J. Whalley (1992), *Applying General Equilibrium*, Cambridge: Cambridge University Press.

Smajgl, A. (2002), 'The scarcity of fossil fuels and GHG mitigation: an AGE modeling technique', Discussion Paper 334, University of Münster, Münster.

Smulders, J.A. (1994), 'Growth, market structure and the environment: essays on the theory of endogenous economic growth', thesis, Tilburg University, Tilburg.

Smulders, J.A. (2000), 'Economic growth and environmental quality', in H. Folmer and H.L. Gabel (eds), *Principles of Environmental and Resource Economics*, Cheltenham, UK and Northampton, USA: Edward Elgar, pp. 602-64.

Smulders, J.A. and R. Gradus (1996), 'Pollution abatement and long-term growth', *European Journal of Political Economy*, 12, 505-32.

Solow, R.M. (1956), 'A contribution to the theory of economic growth', *Quarterly Journal of Economics*, 70, 65-90.

Solow, R.M. (1974), 'The economics of resources or the resources of economics', *American Economic Review*, 64, 1-14.

Srinivasan, T.N. (1982), 'General equilibrium theory, project evaluation and economic development', in M. Gersovitz, C.F. Diaz-Alejandro, G. Ranis and M.R. Rosenzweig (eds), *The Theory and Experience of Economic Development*, London: George Allen and Unwin, pp. 229-51.

Statistics Netherlands (1991), *Tax Incidence in The Netherlands: Accounting and Simulations*, Statistische onderzoekingen M42, Voorburg: Statistics Netherlands.

Statistics Netherlands (1996), *National Accounts*, Voorburg: Statistics Netherlands.

Statistics Netherlands (2000), 'Data for the SNI-AGE model: 1990', mimeo, Voorburg: Statistics Netherlands.

Statistics Netherlands (2002), 'Statline', statline.cbs.nl.

Stone, R. (1954), 'Linear expenditure systems and demand analysis: an application to the pattern of British demand', *The Economic Journal*, 64, 522-7.

Sunman, H. (1991), 'A modelling approach to the estimation of pollution abatement costs: the development of PACE', Discussion Paper, Environmental Resources, London.

Swan, T.W. (1956), 'Economic growth and capital accumulation', *Economic Record*, **32**, 334-61.

Tol, R.S.J. (2002a), 'Estimates of the damage costs of climate change: part 1: benchmark estimates', *Environmental and Resource Economics*, **21**, 47-73.

Tol, R.S.J. (2002b), 'Estimates of the damage costs of climate change: part 2: dynamic estimates', *Environmental and Resource Economics*, **21**, 135-60.

Tsakok, I. (1990), *Agricultural Price Policy: A Practitioner's Guide to Partial-Equilibrium Analysis*, London: Cornell Univeristy Press.

United Nations (1993), *Integrated Environmental and Economic Accounting*, New York: United Nations.

Varian, H.R. (1984), 'The nonparametric approach to production analysis', *Econometrica*, **52**, 579-97.

Velthuijsen, J.W. (1995), 'Determinants of investment in energy conservation', SEO-report 357, Amsterdam.

Vennemo, H. (1997), 'A dynamic applied general equilibrium model with environmental feedbacks', *Economic Modelling*, **14**, 99-154.

Verbruggen, H. (2000), 'Final report on calculations of a sustainable national income according to Hueting's methodology', report O-00/10, Institute for Environmental Studies, Vrije Universiteit, Amsterdam.

Verbruggen, H., R.B. Dellink, R. Gerlagh, M.W. Hofkes and H.M.A. Jansen (2001), 'Alternative calculations of a sustainable national income for The Netherlands according to Hueting', in E.C. van Ierland, J. van der Straaten and H.R.J. Vollebergh (eds), *Economic Growth and Valuation of the Environment: A Debate*, Cheltenham, UK and Northampton, USA: Edward Elgar, pp. 275-312.

VROM (1994), 'Methodiek Milieukosten', Publicatiereeks Milieubeheer 1994/1, Dutch Ministry of Housing, Spatial Planning and the Environment.

VROM (1998a), 'Kosten en baten in het milieubeleid, definities en berekeningsmethoden', Publicatiereeks Milieustrategie 1998/6, Dutch Ministry of Housing, Spatial Planning and the Environment.

VROM (1998b), 'National Environmental Policy Plan 3', Dutch Ministry of Housing, Spatial Planning and the Environment, The Hague.

VROM (2001), 'National Environmental Policy Plan 4', Dutch Ministry of Housing, Spatial Planning and the Environment, The Hague.

Welsch, H. (1996), 'Recycling of carbon/energy taxes and the labor market', *Environmental and Resource Economics*, **8**, 141-55.

Wendner, R. (2001), 'An applied dynamic general equlibrium model of environmental tax reforms and pension policy', *Journal of Policy Modeling*, **23**, 25-50.

Weyant, J. (ed.) (1999), 'The cost of the Kyoto Protocol: a multi-model evaluation', special issue of the *Energy Journal*.

Whalley, J. and R. Wigle (1991), 'The international incidence of carbon taxes', in R. Dornbusch and J.M. Poterba (eds), *Global Warming: Economic Policy Responses*, Cambridge, MA: MIT Press, pp. 233-74.

Wolfgang, O. (1999), 'Reflections on abatement modelling', Memorandum 34/99, University of Oslo, Oslo.

Xepapadeas, A. and A.J. de Zeeuw (1999), 'Environmental policy and competitiveness: the Porter hypothesis and the composition of capital', *Journal of Environmental Economics and Management*, **37**, 165-82.

Xie, J. (1996), *Environmental Policy Analysis: A General Equilibrium Approach*, Aldershot: Avebury.

Xie, J. and S. Saltzman (2000), 'Environmental policy analysis: an environmental computable general-equilibrium approach for developing countries', *Journal of Policy Modeling*, **22**, 453-89.

Zwaan, B.C.C. van der, R. Gerlagh, G. Klaassen and L. Schrattenholzer (2002), 'Endogenous technological change in climate change modelling', *Energy Economics*, **24**, 1-19.

Index

abatement, 1, 27-31, 38, 49
  economic restructuring, 27,
    110, 225
  technical measures, 259
  end-of-pipe measures, 27,
    110, 225
  process-integrated measures,
    27, 110, 225
abatement cost curves, 49-52, 81-
  3, 110-24
  acidification, 117-18
  climate change, 115-17
  dispersion of fine dust, 120-21
  eutrophication, 118-19
  smog formation, 119-20
Acidification, 34, 41, 54, 117,
  149, 165
Allow growth scenario, 56-8, 64
Applied General Equilibrium
  (AGE) models, 5, 13, 16-20,
  37, 45
Armington specification, 78, 105,
  232, 239

balanced growth path, 22, 45
bottom-up models, 3, 11, 28

calibration, 15, 19, 54, 101
  abatement sector, 109-10
  depreciation rate, 124
  greenhouse gas accumulation,
    135
  income elasticities, 128
  interest rate, 125

international trade, 105, 232,
  239
labour supply growth, 124
PAS elasticities, 131
policy target, 135
pollution, 106-9
pollution permit prices, 132
production function, 129
social accounting matrix, 102-
  5
stock mutations, 79
trade elasticities, 131
trade margins, 79
utility function, 125
Cass-Koopmans-Ramsey model,
  8, 23, 47, 273
Climate change, 34, 41, 54, 80,
  115, 152, 165, 169, 226, 243
comparative-static model, 42, 43,
  45, 55, 273
Constant Elasticity of Substitution
  (CES) function, 46, 47, 72

DEAN model, 6, 73-4, 86-8, 147,
  222, 231
Delay scenario, 148-53, 170
Desiccation, 36, 121-3, 169
DICE model, 26, 80, 135, 247
Dispersion of fine dust, 36, 41,
  120, 136, 149, 165

emission reduction, *see*
  abatement
endogenous growth models, 14

Environmental policy, *see*
National Environmental Policy
Plan
environmental-economic models,
12, 24
Eutrophication, 35, 41, 118, 149,
165, 169, 226
exchange rate, 238

fine particles, *see* dispersion of
fine dust
forward-looking model, 42, 44,
45, 56, 74, 273

golden rule of capital
accumulation, 22
greenhouse gases, *see* climate
change
Gross Domestic Product (GDP),
103

Immediate action scenario, 56-8
input-output models, 13

Late action scenario, 56-8, 64
Linear Expenditure System
(LES), 75-7, 93

macro-econometric models, *see*
neo-Keynesian models

NAMEA, 102-3
National Environmental Policy
Plan, 1, 5, 135, 136, 149, 304
neo-classical growth models, 14,
20-24, 272
neo-Keynesian models, 14
NEPP2010 scenario, 148-53, 170
NEPP2030 scenario, 148-53, 231

overlapping generations models,
15

partial equilibrium models, 13
perfect foresight, *see* forward-
looking model
photochemical smog, *see* smog
formation
pollution, 5, 24-5, 27, 33, 38,
48
Pollution – Abatement
Substitution (PAS) curves, 49-
52
Pollution – Abatement
Substitution (PAS) elasticities,
131, 208-11

Ramsey model, *see* Cass-
Koopmans-Ramsey model
recursive-dynamic model, 42, 43,
45, 56, 273

Smog formation, 35, 41, 119, 149,
165, 168, 211, 225
SNI-AGE model, 6-8, 279-82
Social Accounting Matrix (SAM),
102, 138-41, 144
Soil contamination, 36, 121-3,
169, 226
Solow-Swan model, 8, 22, 47
Stone-Geary utility function, 77
summer smog, *see* smog
formation
Sustainable National Income
(SNI), 6-8

technological progress, 46, 132,
134, 254-7
top-down models, 3, 11, 27
tradable pollution permits, 48, 98-
100, 249, 275-7
transversality condition, 217

volatile organic compounds, *see*
smog formation